THE ANTIRACIST SCHOOL LEADER

What to

KNOW, SAY, & DO

DAMAN HARRIS

Solution Tree | Press

Copyright © 2024 by Solution Tree Press

Materials appearing here are copyrighted. With one exception, all rights are reserved. Readers may reproduce only those pages marked "Reproducible." Otherwise, no part of this book may be reproduced or transmitted in any form or by any means (electronic, photocopying, recording, or otherwise) without prior written permission of the publisher.

555 North Morton Street
Bloomington, IN 47404
800.733.6786 (toll free) / 812.336.7700
FAX: 812.336.7790

email: info@SolutionTree.com
SolutionTree.com

Visit **go.SolutionTree.com/diversityandequity** to download the free reproducibles in this book.

Printed in the United States of America

Library of Congress Cataloging-in-Publication Data

Names: Harris, Daman, author.

Title: The antiracist school leader : what to know, say, and do / Daman Harris.

Description: Bloomington, IN : Solution Tree Press, [2024] | Includes bibliographical references and index.

Identifiers: LCCN 2023027915 (print) | LCCN 2023027916 (ebook) | ISBN 9781954631311 (paperback) | ISBN 9781954631328 (ebook)

Subjects: LCSH: Educational leadership--Social aspects--United States. | Anti-racism--United States. | Racism in education--United States. | Discrimination in education--United States.

Classification: LCC LB2805 .H3285 2024 (print) | LCC LB2805 (ebook) | DDC 371.2/0110973--dc23/eng/20230824

LC record available at https://lccn.loc.gov/2023027915

LC ebook record available at https://lccn.loc.gov/2023027916

Solution Tree
Jeffrey C. Jones, CEO
Edmund M. Ackerman, President

Solution Tree Press
President and Publisher: Douglas M. Rife
Associate Publishers: Todd Brakke and Kendra Slayton
Editorial Director: Laurel Hecker
Art Director: Rian Anderson
Copy Chief: Jessi Finn
Production Editor: Gabriella Jones-Monserrate
Proofreader: Mark Hain
Text and Cover Designer: Kelsey Hoover
Acquisitions Editors: Carol Collins and Hilary Goff
Assistant Acquisitions Editor: Elijah Oates
Content Development Specialist: Amy Rubenstein
Associate Editor: Sarah Ludwig
Editorial Assistant: Anne Marie Watkins

THIS BOOK IS DEDICATED TO

JACQUELINE HARRIS
the woman who anchored my past;

KARON DUNCAN
the woman who guided me to the present;

&

TRACIE HARRIS
the woman who walks with me toward the future.

ACKNOWLEDGMENTS

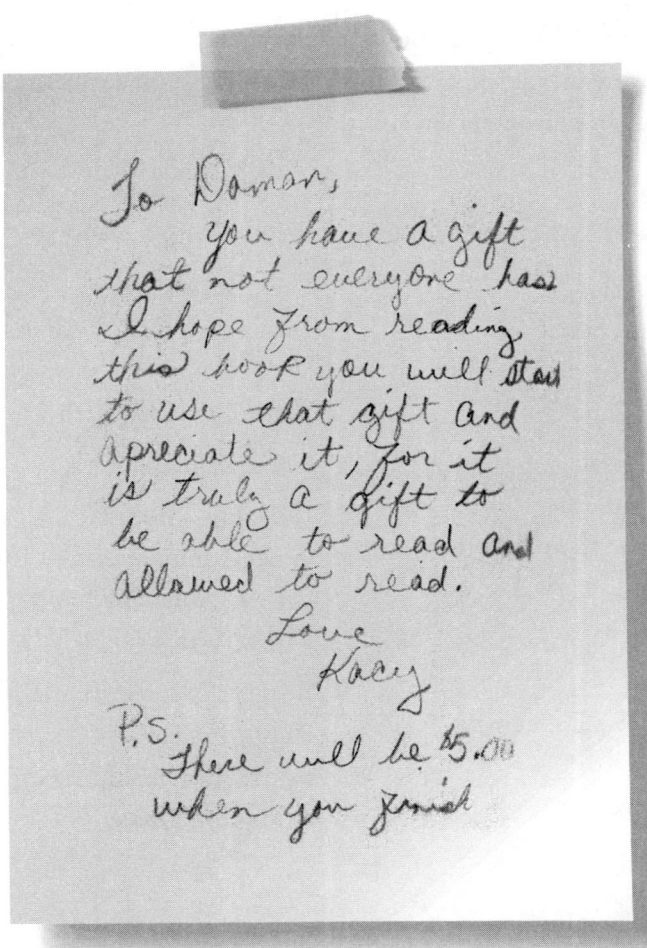

To Daman,

You have a gift that not everyone has. I hope from reading this book you will start to use that gift and appreciate it, for it is truly a gift to be able to read and allowed to read.

Love,

Kacy

P.S. There will be $5.00 when you finish.

The seeds of this book were planted by the network of love that has always surrounded me. The preceding image represents the messages of belief, accountability, and guidance that caregivers expressed as far back as I can remember. The image is a handwritten note on the inside cover of a fourth-grade-level mystery book. My mother's twin sister, Kacy Harris, handed me a book that included this note when I was about nine years old, and the book remains one of my most prized possessions to this day. I love you, and I miss you, Kace. Thank you for being my strongest cheerleader, both in person and in spirit.

Solution Tree Press would like to thank the following reviewers:

Michael T. Adamson
Director of Board Services
Indiana School Boards Association
Indianapolis, Indiana

Erica Avila
Assistant Superintendent
Isaac Elementary School District
Phoenix, Arizona

Janet Gilbert
Principal
Mountain Shadows Elementary School
Glendale, Arizona

Lauryn Mascareñaz
Director of Equity Affairs
Wake County Public Schools
Wake County, North Carolina

Craig Randall

Jose "JoJo" Reyes
Chief Administration Officer
Parlier Unified School District
Parlier, California

Ringnolda Jofee' Tremain
K–8 Principal
Trinity Leadership Arlington
Arlington, Texas

Visit **go.SolutionTree.com/diversityandequity** to download the free reproducibles in this book.

TABLE OF CONTENTS

About the Author xi

INTRODUCTION —————————————————— 1

Who This Book Is For 2
About the Author 3
What It Means (and Doesn't Mean) to Combat White Supremacy Culture 6
    What *White Supremacy* Means 7
    What *Antiracism* Means 9
An Administrative Focus on Antiracism 9
Book Overview 11
    Know, Say, Do 13
    Key Vocabulary and Glossary 14
    Call to Action 14

CHAPTER 1
EDUCATE YOURSELF AND COMMIT ———————— 15

Understand the Causes of Disproportionate Racial Outcomes 18
    Find What Has Been Missing From Your Education 19
    Conduct a Literature Review 21
Fear, Learn, Grow 22
    Move From the Fear Zone to the Learning Zone 24
    Move From the Learning Zone to the Growth Zone With the Four Cs 26
    Enrich the Growth Zone 28
Read (Highly) Recommended Resources 29

      Access the Essential Resources 30

      Access the Current Literature 33

   Ask, Reflect, Adjust 36

   Conclusion 37

   Apply Your Learning 38

CHAPTER 2
CAST AN ANTIRACIST VISION ——— 41

   Evaluate Leaders and Systems 43

   Declare Public Intent 44

      Have a Follow-Up Plan 47

      Draft an Open Letter 48

   Use Accurate Vocabulary 50

   Leverage the Use of Storytelling and Visuals 52

      Verbal Analogies 52

      Pictorial Metaphors 53

      Conceptual Diagrams 56

      Digital Media 57

      Your Own Visual Framework 58

   Create Criteria for Leadership Decision Making 59

   Cultivate a Community of Builders 62

   Conclusion 64

   Apply Your Learning 65

CHAPTER 3
PLAN PROFESSIONAL LEARNING EXPERIENCES ——— 67

   Center Learning Progressions 69

      Follow the Steps of the Professional Learning Progression . . . 70

      Create Psychological Safety 73

   Develop Content for Learning Progressions 73

      Chart a Path Toward Sociopolitical Development 74

      Target Critical Consciousness 75

   Evaluate Your Antiracist Practices 75

   Measure the Impact of Professional Learning Progressions 77

Facilitate Connection in Your Community 80
    Strengthen the Facilitator's Toolbox 81
    Prioritize Opportunities for Group Conversations *and*
        Personal Reflections 82
    Build in Structured and Spontaneous Opportunities for
        Learning and Application 84
Elevate Antiracism Across Aspects of School 86
    Use Restorative Practices 87
    Include Personal Connections to Students and Families 88
Support Racial Identity Development 91
    Examine How Whiteness Manifests in Schools 96
    Use Supportive Resources 98
Lean Into Uncomfortable Topics (and Discomfort in General) 101
Conclusion 102
Apply Your Learning 103

CHAPTER 4

ENCOURAGE AND EMBRACE RESISTANCE —— 105

Distinguish Between the Perspectives of Racists, Nonracists,
    and Antiracists 107
    Investigate the Rationale for Resistance 109
    Emphasize the Potential Productivity of Dissent 111
Balance Who Gets Centered 113
    Acknowledge Intersectionality 114
    Recognize and Counteract Forms of Resistance in Real Time ... 118
Reckon With Our Homophily 124
Conclusion 125
Apply Your Learning 126

CHAPTER 5

ELEVATE ANTIRACIST CURRICULUM AND INSTRUCTION —— 129

Review and Design Curricula 131
    Reassess Instruction 133
    Create a System for Assessment and Feedback 137

  Audit Materials 138
 Present Educational Opportunities That Connect to
  Students' Lives 140
   Explore Social Justice in STEM 141
   Practice Historical Responsiveness 142
 Have Educators Interrogate the Roles Race Plays in
  Their Lives 144
   Erase the Idea of the Other 144
   Develop Racial Literacy 145
 Conclusion 147
 Apply Your Learning 148

CHAPTER 6
MONITOR YOUR IMPACT — 151
 Collect Data Intentionally 153
  Essential Varieties of Data 155
 Use Supplemental Supports to Identify Antiracist Target Areas ... 159
  Target Areas for Observation 160
  Organizational Charts for Data Sources 167
 Review and Interpret Data 167
  Root Cause Analysis and Fishbone Diagrams 167
  The Focused Conversation Method 170
  Data Interpretation 172
 Conclusion 173
 Apply Your Learning 173

Epilogue 177

Glossary 179

References and Resources 187

Index 203

ABOUT THE AUTHOR

Daman Harris, PhD, is the manager of the Professional Development Schools Program and the Institutions of Higher Education Partnerships for Anne Arundel County Public Schools in Maryland. He is also the cofounder and codirector of the Building Our Network of Diversity (BOND) Project, a nonprofit that supports the recruitment, development, retention, and empowerment of male educators of color.

Having been an educator since 1996, Dr. Harris has had a wide range of experiences as a teacher, coach, principal, district administrator, adjunct professor, speaker, writer, and consultant. He is a graduate faculty member at the University of Maryland at College Park and an adjunct professor at McDaniel College and the University of Maryland Global Campus, where he leads graduate courses relating to teaching strategies, research methods, and antiracist education.

To book Daman Harris for professional development, contact pd@SolutionTree.com.

INTRODUCTION

Race theory, equity, diversity, inclusion, identity, antiracism, ethnic studies . . . There are a variety of terms used to describe how schools engage with the topics of race and culture. While the content is contested terrain, about seven in ten Americans believe schools should discuss race, racism, and culture as much as or more than they do (University of Chicago Harris School of Public Policy & the Associated Press-NORC Center for Public Affairs Research, 2022). Moreover, upwards of 80 percent of registered voters and K–12 parents prefer that schools teach historical topics such as the Civil War, the history of Indigenous people in the United States, and America's history of enslavement (Echelon Insights, 2021). If you are interested in learning more about how you can use your voice and skills to confront these kinds of issues with your school staff—whether you're a teacher, paraeducator, or administrator—then you're in the right place. In this book, you will learn how to plan, test, and execute a comprehensive antiracist vision to transform the culture, curriculum, and conscience of your school administration.

WHO THIS BOOK IS FOR

I'm going to use the word *you* throughout each chapter of this book. By *you*, I mean the person who is interested enough in the topics of race, culture, and antiracism that you opened the pages of this book. Any member of a school district staff can lead this work. I do not expect you to be an expert on these topics. Most people with whom I discuss these topics consider me an expert because I have studied and taught this content since 2000, yet I still feel I have a lot to learn—in part because antiracist work is constantly evolving. This book doesn't require you to have complete historical knowledge about all systems of oppression that have affected teaching and learning. However, it does require a desire to tackle those issues in partnership with your school staff and community. These topics are critically important to me, so I wrote this book for others who find this content as essential to their work as I do mine.

When I talk to groups of people who have come to learn about maintaining a diverse teaching workforce, they express desires such as the following.

- "I want to learn more about what it means to pursue equity for my students."
- "I want to build a climate of inclusivity and diversity in my department."
- "I want to be an antiracist leader in my school or district."
- "I want to combat White supremacy culture."

Those statements are usually followed by questions such as:

- "Where do I start?"
- "What steps should I take?"
- "What should I consider?"
- "How does that work?"

If you or your colleagues express these viewpoints, then you're reading the right book. With that said, you do not have to approach this book with a total commitment to antiracism. It is OK to read these pages with a healthy skepticism in search of food for thought. Perhaps you'll choose to believe some elements of the book and not others, à la carte style. Take opportunities to visit the references and resources list (page 187) and explore new ideas. Engage in conversations with peers during which you push back on the tenets of the text or its underlying research.

Lean into the content that challenges your beliefs, and spend time considering the possibilities of a truth halfway between your principles and mine. Combine my ideas with yours to deepen your knowledge, strengthen your skills, and lead your staff toward more equitable outcomes for your students and their families.

ABOUT THE AUTHOR

I've been a public educator since 1996, and I've served in myriad roles. Since 2022, I have been the manager of higher education partnerships in a Maryland school district. I am a former principal and a certified reading specialist and special education instructor with experience in academic support, student discipline, community outreach, technical assistance, and program evaluation. I have performed classroom observations, designed and supervised student programs, conducted staff development, implemented crisis intervention, and evaluated schools and school-based programs as a consultant. I earned my PhD in education policy from the University of Maryland, College Park, with a focus on parent involvement in schools.

Additionally, I have served as adjunct faculty for McDaniel College and the University of Maryland, College Park, since 2015, and for University of Maryland Global Campus since 2023; there, I teach courses related to effective teaching methods, conducting research, and cultural proficiency. My students at the university level are typically graduate students looking to earn teaching licenses and current educators learning to establish more equitable and culturally responsive environments where they live and work.

I am also the cofounder and coleader of the Building Our Network of Diversity (BOND) Project, a nonprofit organization dedicated to making schools better places through supporting efforts to recruit, retain, develop, and empower men of color in education. I host BOND's podcast, the *BONDCast*, which features Black and Latino male educators. We use long-form interviews to discuss how they became educators and what drives them to continue.

Through conference presentations and consulting workshops, I speak to groups all around the United States about strategies to acquire and maintain a diverse teaching workforce. To that end, I have promoted the cultivation of antiracist environments in school buildings and districts, drawing on my former role as a building administrator leader, when I practiced the principles of this text with my school community. I promote antiracist environments in my role as district program manager within the division dedicated to professional development, for which I design and facilitate a continuing education course that supports aspiring antiracist school leaders.

The power of antiracist education is deeply personal to me. Before I go into what antiracist education is, picture in your mind two photos (see figure I.1). The first was taken in 1978 on the West Side of Wilmington, Delaware. My cousin, two of my friends, and I are in the foreground. I'm about five years old. There wasn't a swimming pool in my neighborhood, so when the weather was hot and humid, the big kids opened the fire hydrant and splashed around in the spray. Little kids, like me at that time, played downstream as water flowed down the street like tributaries from a major river.

As a young child, I didn't know my family was poor and couldn't afford to go to the pool regularly. I was surrounded by such a tremendous sense of community and nurturing that I only remember my childhood as terrific. At the time that first photo was taken, I was a kindergarten student at a community center that was located right around the corner. My kindergarten teachers, who were also from my community, were special people in the ways that they treated me like a special person. They recognized that I had a skill for reading and writing—even at a young age—and they lifted me up. They praised me and supported me so much that they filled my educational life with joy and pride. They made me think I could do anything, and I've carried that self-esteem with me like a government-issued ID for the rest of my life, despite what some other teachers told me later in my K–12 career.

The second photo is of my three children floating on inner tubes in a large in-ground pool. You can see my feet peeking out from the bottom of the photo as I relax on a lounger. The pool in this photo belongs to a rental home where I went on a vacation. I chose not to build a pool in my yard in part because I don't have great memories of being in a pool as a youngster, but I am able to partner with my wife, Tracie, to provide that kind of experience to my children. This is due to the doors opened by the belief that my early teachers showed in me, which carried throughout my formal education.

The two photos you're envisioning in your mind represent education's importance. The first photo embodies the potential and exuberance of children as they walk into our school buildings for the first time, despite structural forces that contribute to their circumstances. In my case, redlining and other segregation policies probably led my grandmother—who likely snapped the image from her front steps—to purchase a home in a mostly Black, Latino, and poor section of Wilmington, Delaware, in 1978. My grandmother certainly recognized the prominence of segregation in

FIGURE I.1: Two photos from my life.

her town. One of her classmates from Howard High School, a Black high school in Wilmington in the 1950s, was a coplaintiff in the *Brown v. Board of Education* lawsuit. The snapshot of those happy children engaging with each other in an authentic way captures how young children find joy in connecting with their peers and the world around them, which is a critical component of education.

The second photograph symbolizes the outcomes that occur when schools harness children's exuberance and actualize children's potential by providing rich, supportive educational environments. The child playing with his friends in the hydrant-fueled stream against the curb could only dream of traveling to a foreign country with his own children and providing a private pool for the family to enjoy. Not only is education the vehicle that helped bring the dream to fruition, but it is also what generated that dream within that child.

Taken together, the photos exemplify the promise in every child that can be unlocked through the purpose of every educator. The promise is the product of expert knowledge, unwavering commitment, and unconditional love. Children thrive in places full of love and belief, in the face of institutional obstacles. This is true because educators who truly love and believe in their children fight to disrupt structural forces that hurt the children in their charge. Loving, knowledgeable educators teach children how to recognize and disrupt those negative forces as well. Sometimes, well-meaning teachers and leaders can sense the systemic inequities that their students confront, but they might not be able to put their fingers on precisely *what* to blame (notice that I did not say *who*, because this book isn't about blaming people; it's about examining systems). Other times, educators know the problematic issues, but they might not know how to marshal the resources of their school communities to combat multiple systems of oppression. This book is for them: the educators who sense or know that something is wrong, but aren't sure what they can do. This book isn't for people who need to be convinced that racism and White supremacy impact teaching and learning, although chapter 1 (page 15) suggests some background reading if you'd like to do your own research. I won't spend many words justifying the need for antiracist education. This book is for people who recognize the need for antiracist education and would like some guidance on the steps they can take to help their grade-level teams, departments, schools, and districts adopt antiracist orientations.

WHAT IT MEANS (AND DOESN'T MEAN) TO COMBAT WHITE SUPREMACY CULTURE

Antiracist leadership, school leadership that reforms school policies and practices that lead to disproportionate racial outcomes, in our schools is essential. There are scores of books that highlight the issues and delve into the research regarding the impact of inequity, racism, and White supremacy on our schools and the communities they serve. This book answers the question, "So, what do I do about it?" Throughout the text, you will learn things you should know, say, and do to contribute to the solutions.

We look at all the disparate outcomes related to different identity factors, be they race, gender, immigration status, and language proficiency or others. We look at those disparate outcomes for our children, and we can focus on those outcomes, instead of considering the policies and practices that created those racial or other identity-factor discrepancies. If we look closely at the policies and practices that created those disparate outcomes, we should also consider the foundation of those policies and practices: White supremacy culture, the conscious or unconscious belief that White people or things associated with White people are superior to non-White people (people of color) or things associated with non-White people. We must reckon with White supremacy culture. That is the disease; the disparate outcomes related to education are symptoms.

What *White Supremacy* Means

The use of the phrase *White supremacy* is where some people get stuck. Newer participants in antiracism conversations often equate *White supremacy* with *White people*, like they equate *culture* with *race*, *ethnicity*, or *nationality* (Pinder, 2011). They conflate combating White supremacy culture with attacking White people, which is incredibly counterproductive, since more than three-quarters of our teaching corps is White. The confusion about the term also lets people of color off the hook for the times that they uphold White supremacy culture, which can be equally counterproductive (Sullivan, 2014). In fact, although practices related to White supremacy took root as early as the 16th century (Kendi, 2016), the word *racism* probably wasn't in the lexicon until almost four hundred years later (Pinder, 2011). While Whiteness and White supremacy were established to subjugate BIPOC (Black, Indigenous, and People of Color) people, diversity and equity training consultant Tema Okun (2021) explains how White supremacy culture stratifies society and impacts institutions like schools:

> White supremacy culture is the widespread ideology baked into the beliefs, values, norms, and standards of our groups (many if not most of them), our communities, our towns, our states, our nation, teaching us both overtly and covertly that Whiteness holds value, Whiteness is value. It teaches us that Blackness is not only valueless but also dangerous and threatening. It teaches us that Indigenous people and communities no longer exist, or if they do, they are to be exoticized and romanticized or culturally

appropriated as we continue to violate treaties, land rights, and humanity. It teaches us that people south of the border are "illegal." It teaches us that Arabs are Muslim and that Muslim is "terrorist." It teaches us that people of Chinese and Japanese descent are both indistinguishable and threatening as the reason for COVID. It pits other races and racial groups against each other while always defining them as inferior to the White group. (p. 4)

According to Okun (2021), the ruling elite uses White supremacy culture to divide us on multiple layers to do the following:

- Disconnect and divide White people from Black, Indigenous, and People of Color (BIPOC)
- Disconnect and divide Black, Indigenous, and People of Color from each other
- Disconnect and divide White people from other White people
- Disconnect and divide each and all of us from the earth, the sun, the wind, the water, the stars, the animals that roam(ed) the Earth
- Disconnect and divide each of us from ourselves (p. 2)

The division manifests in schools through disparate rates of achievement (National Center for Education Statistics [NCES], 2019a, 2019b, 2019c), graduation (NCES, 2021b), suspension (NCES, 2018), eligibility for free or reduced-price meals (NCES, 2021c), identification for special education services (NCES, 2021a), and myriad other academic metrics. Antiracists believe that superficial changes in curricula or social-emotional learning aren't at the root of the disparities; the disparities are the result of centuries of unresolved White supremacy on which our educational—and labor and housing and employment and health care—systems are founded. Any effective reforms must start here.

We must not overemphasize the symptoms (policies and practices) at the risk of overlooking the disease (White supremacy culture). I understand that it is hard to do. That's why I think we use words like *equity* to make this work less uncomfortable, to add that proverbial spoonful of sugar to help swallow distasteful cold medicine. This is not to say that work on behalf of equity is inherently wrongheaded, mean-spirited, or inaccurate. Cold medicine, to continue the metaphor, can be beneficial in the right circumstances. However, when serious illnesses are suspected or detected, physicians do not prescribe cold medicines in efforts to avoid uncomfortable conversations with their patients. It would be deleterious to their patients' health. Moreover, White supremacy is not a cold; it's a cancer. We don't dole out a spoonful of sugar for cancer; we provide chemotherapy, radiation, or bone marrow transplants. Those treatments are hard on the body as well as the mind. Avoiding challenging content and designing equity work around people's comfort is what Paul Gorski (2019), founder of the Equity Literacy Institute, describes as an "equity detour," a distraction. We must take hard, necessary steps to eradicate this disease, and the symptoms will eventually recede.

What *Antiracism* Means

In her book *Caste: The Origins of Our Discontents*, Pulitzer Prize–winning journalist Isabel Wilkerson (2020) extends the medical metaphor in a way that pushes back on resistance to the topic of antiracism:

> Looking beneath the history of one's country is like learning that alcoholism or depression runs in one's family or that suicide has occurred more often than might be usual or, with the advances in medical genetics, discovering that one has inherited the markers of a BRCA mutation for breast cancer. You don't ball up in a corner with guilt or shame at these discoveries. You don't, if you are wise, forbid any mention of them. In fact, you do the opposite. You educate yourself. You talk to people who have been through it and to specialists who have researched it. You learn the consequences and obstacles, the options and treatment. You may pray over it and meditate over it. Then you take precautions to protect yourself and succeeding generations and work to ensure that these things, whatever they are, don't happen again. (pp. 13–14)

Antiracist school leaders must help their staffs develop appropriate understandings of many terms (including *White supremacy culture*) by facilitating their exposure to additional life experiences. So, I ask you to maintain an open mind about phrases and other information that could trigger uncomfortable emotions for you or your colleagues throughout this book. In the chapters, I'll provide my definitions for a variety of terms, which will provide needed clarification. For now, I'll describe how I began this journey as an elementary school principal.

AN ADMINISTRATIVE FOCUS ON ANTIRACISM

I've read dozens of books on race and culture, but the text that spurred me to reorient my school toward antiracism was *How to Be an Antiracist* by Ibram X. Kendi (2019). Kendi's simple definition of antiracism—the act of identifying and restructuring systems that lead to demographically disparate outcomes—and his descriptions of self-proclaimed nonracist behaviors that are no better than racist behaviors intensely resonated with me. Kendi exposed me as a frequent fence straddler or someone who didn't always have time for what I described as *equity work*. I read this book during the fall of 2019, when I was an elementary school principal, and I realized that I had practiced racist or nonracist behaviors far more than antiracist behaviors throughout my decades-long career. I was compelled to take action immediately, so I began to talk with trusted colleagues, and I determined how I could incorporate my new learning into my school leadership.

During a staff meeting in January 2020, I told my staff that we would have an antiracist focus for the next few school years. I shared that we would audit our curricula and practices, orient professional learning around learning and applying antiracist definitions and principles, reframe our approach to community involvement, and determine ways to evaluate our growth as an antiracist school team. I explained that I didn't know exactly what we were going to learn, how we were going to learn it, or how we would evaluate our progress. All I knew, I said, was that we were going to move forward together. I explained that I was letting them know in January to give them time to get to the school district job fair in February if doing that kind of work made them uncomfortable to the point that they didn't want to be part of our faculty anymore. I added, "I understand I might not be right, but this is where we're going. You can help me shape this vision, you can support this vision, or you can find somewhere more aligned with your values." I was heartened to find that the only people who left the staff that year left because they got promotions or positions that were not available in my building.

During the rest of that winter, spring, and summer, I read everything I could on the topics of antiracism, cultural competence, and equity. At our first preservice week meeting of the 2020–2021 school year, I presented a three-year plan for my school's journey toward antiracism.

Aside from facilitating some of our professional learning conversations, my primary role was to carve out time for our work and give permission to our early adopters. For my school leadership team, that took the form of a book study of *How to Be an Antiracist* (Kendi, 2019), through which the team members took turns facilitating conversations related to the text during each meeting. I also added an extra fifteen minutes to our twice-monthly staff meetings so we could always dedicate at least fifteen minutes to some topic related to antiracism. Several staff members partnered with our district's student of color leadership program to host a student speaker series during which high school students taught our staff about the impacts microaggressions have on students.

We also created a forty-five-minute block of time we rotated each week for different antiracist activities. For example, our assistant principal facilitated conversations about the intersection of racism and trauma. On other days, some staff members, who created their own antiracist work group, used that block for their publicly open meetings or professional learning activities.

In my experience working in educational leadership, I've heard several administrators and other educators explain that there are so many things on which we must focus that they don't have time to focus on antiracism or equity. My response is that there have always been competing priorities. Circumstances continually change. We get new curricula, school or district leadership, social-emotional learning programs, and buzz phrases like *grit* and *productive struggle*. In 2020, we even experienced a pandemic. But you know what hasn't changed? Students with backgrounds like mine are at the bottom of most of the positive outcome categories, and they remain atop most of the negative outcome categories (Modan, 2022).

So, we have two choices: (1) believe there's something inherently wrong with our students and their families that puts them in this position generation after generation, or (2) believe there's something wrong with our system that recreates this demographic hierarchy generation after generation. The folks under my leadership believed the latter, and that is the primary assumption of this book. That assumption is the foundation of a big-picture framework for orienting your colleagues toward modifying our system. The following section will show you how this book is organized by content to bring you that framework.

BOOK OVERVIEW

The chapters of this book take the reader from initial commitment and vision casting to strategy implementation and impact evaluation. This isn't a text that debates the merits of antiracist school leadership. This book operates under the knowledge that the need for antiracist education is a given. This book is designed to help you support your colleagues in acknowledging that need and creating actionable next steps for fulfilling it.

- **Chapter 1, "Educate Yourself and Commit":** In this chapter, you'll review essential information and history regarding antiracism in education. This chapter highlights how school leaders recognize the roles that school policies and practices play in reinforcing systems of oppression that lead to disproportionate racial outcomes. Through the consideration of fear zones, learning zones, and growth zones, school leaders can assess the antiracist readiness of their staffs and themselves to determine entry points that support everyone's learning.

- **Chapter 2, "Cast an Antiracist Vision":** In this chapter, you'll develop a personalized vision for your own antiracist journey. You'll learn how to address the flaws in our disproportionate focus on the inputs (like students, families, and staff) and outputs (like test scores, graduation rates, and discipline referrals) of organizations, at the expense of reflecting on the mechanism that transforms inputs into outputs, which is the system itself. The chapter includes strategies, visuals, and communication practices that antiracist school leaders can use to share their antiracist visions with stakeholders.

- **Chapter 3, "Plan Professional Learning Experiences":** This chapter will share professional learning experiences that give staff multiple opportunities to engage with various media, colleagues, students, and members of the broader school community to achieve the goal of critical consciousness. Early activities will explore Whiteness, White supremacy culture, and historical forms of anti-dark oppression. You will learn how to backward-map to create goals, strategies, activities, and milestones that shepherd learners toward the ultimate target—critical consciousness in students. The chapter will lay out options for developing assessments that help to monitor short-, intermediate-, and long-term progress.

- **Chapter 4, "Encourage and Embrace Resistance":** In your work as an antiracist school leader, you should expect challenges from stakeholders of all categories. This chapter will provide antiracist school leaders with strategies to recognize resisters, understand their triggers, and prescribe measures of support. In addition to learning strategies that antiracist school leaders can use to support stakeholders' fears, deflections, or rejections of antiracist work, you will learn how balancing whose perspectives get centered, recognizing intersectionality, and cultivating allies can reduce the likelihood of resistance.

- **Chapter 5, "Elevate Antiracist Curriculum and Instruction":** History demonstrates that racism influences curriculum selection, instructional practices, stakeholder relationship building, and staff evaluation, among many aspects of schooling (Inoue, 2019; Kendi, 2016; Ranson, 2013; Schultz, 2019). Antiracist school leaders promote awareness of racism's manifestations across areas of schools, and they lead the development of antiracist practices that counteract racism's effects. This chapter shares ideas for how educators can present educational opportunities that are connected to their students' lived experiences and how they should be prepared to confront issues related to race and language. You'll learn how to audit processes related to curriculum selection, instructional practices, stakeholder relationship building, staff evaluation, and other aspects of teaching and learning.

- **Chapter 6, "Monitor Your Impact":** Once you've implemented your strategies and advocated for what's important, you need indicators of your effectiveness beyond a single summative assessment. The final chapter suggests some options for building a system of ongoing assessment that gauges the clarity of your plan and effectiveness of your strategies. This chapter also recommends ideas about the data points that are essential, whose input is critical, and helpful frameworks for analysis. You will hear about ways that school leaders have shared their data about their antiracist efforts in ways that clarified their intentions and motivated their school teams.

Throughout the book, you'll notice a few special features. Each chapter features a review of current research and best practices, which culminates in a final actionable section titled *Apply Your Learning*. The chapters start with a bank of key words to observe throughout the chapter. These words are replicated along with their definitions in the glossary at the end of the book.

Know, Say, Do

I wrote this book to be both inspirational and utilitarian. Each part presents suggested actions that are aligned with current research about leadership, antiracism, or both. The book's subtitle, *What to Know, Say, and Do*, is intended to add balance to the theoretical implications of *The Antiracist School Leader*. My goal is to humanize the theoretical suggestions by embedding stories from my experiences—and those relayed to me by colleagues and friends—that complement the theoretical suggestions in ways that personalize the new information you gather as you read. Each chapter closes on a practical note by explicitly distilling the content into key concepts to remember (know), important statements to consider (say), and essential actions to take (do). These points are meant to confirm your commitment to the work. If you are a beginning antiracist school leader, you might experience significant discomfort as you take in the information presented. Emotional discomfort is often a necessary precursor to intellectual growth in the same way that strenuous exercise leads to muscle growth. The Know, Say, Do sections are designed to center you with some concrete next steps in your growth process. You might not be ready or willing to accomplish each task, but you will be able to move in the right direction.

Key Vocabulary and Glossary

Leading discussions about antiracist work requires a solid grasp on key terms, and having such knowledge up front can also help you to process the concepts in this book. Therefore, each chapter begins with a short set of relevant vocabulary words that might be unfamiliar to new antiracist leaders. You don't have to commit these words to memory prior to reading the chapters (no vocabulary quizzes here); the vocabulary lists foreshadow some of the important concepts contained within each chapter, as well as activate any background knowledge you possess. Toward the end of the book, the glossary provides a single comprehensive vocabulary list that you can reference as needed.

Call to Action

You will also notice that each chapter title begins with a verb. I intentionally use action words because I want every reader to be aware of their personal agency. You don't have to be a principal or superintendent to be an antiracist school leader. Anyone can be a catalyst for positive change in their organization. If you recognize an inappropriate situation, policy, or practice, you have the capacity to make a difference. Will everything you try turn out perfectly? No. Afford yourself some grace. You will learn from each experience.

An important takeaway I want you to glean from this book is there is no end point to antiracist leadership. If you orient yourself and your school in the right direction and try to keep moving forward, even when it's hard (especially when it's hard), then you are an antiracist school leader. The first step is to educate yourself on the topic and commit to the journey.

Chapter 1
EDUCATE YOURSELF AND COMMIT

Key Vocabulary

antiracism	The practice of seeking, deconstructing, or reconstructing systems of oppression that benefit one or more racial groups at the expense of other racial groups.
caste	"A fixed and embedded ranking of human value that sets the presumed supremacy of one group against the presumed inferiority of other groups on the basis of ancestry and often immutable traits, traits that would be neutral in the abstract but are ascribed life-and-death meaning in a hierarchy favoring the dominant caste whose forebears designed it" (Wilkerson, 2020, p. 17).

fear zone	An emotional and intellectual state of being in which one ignores, avoids, or disbelieves the existence of systemic racism.
growth zone	An emotional and intellectual state of being in which one recognizes one's place (advantages and disadvantages) within systemic racism, as well as a commitment to promoting antiracism with a strong sense of self-efficacy.
learning zone	An emotional and intellectual state of being in which one accepts the existence of systemic racism, as well as a commitment to learning more about the topic.
race	A social categorization of human beings by immutable physical characteristics such as skin color, nose width, eye shape, lip fullness, and hair texture, with a heavy emphasis on skin color.
racism	The belief that the social construct of race is associated with inherent physical, intellectual, temperamental, or moral characteristics that position some racial groups as naturally superior or inferior to other racial groups.
racist	Someone who supports racist policies or practices through their actions or inactions (Kendi, 2019).
systemic oppression	A system of advantages and disadvantages based on race. In the United States, oppressive frameworks operate within systems of education, justice, economics, entertainment, and housing, among others.

White supremacy	The belief that the White race possesses inherent physical, intellectual, temperamental, or moral characteristics that naturally position White people as the superior racial group.
White supremacy culture	A set of cultural principles that promotes the superiority of a supposed White racial way of thinking and being.

Race is not a biological phenomenon; it is a social construct (Suyemoto, Curley, & Mukkamala, 2020). However, due to the systems of oppression that were created around skin color, race has very real implications in our society.

I have been an educator for decades, and I have done equity work in one form or another during that time as well—that is, if I do not count all teaching as equity work. I have spent a lot of time trying to educate myself on the content. I have read a multitude of books and articles related to cultural proficiency and antiracism, such as *For White Folks Who Teach in the Hood . . . and the Rest of Y'all Too* (Emdin, 2016), *Stamped From the Beginning: The Definitive History of Racist Ideas in America* (Kendi, 2016), and *White Fragility: Why It's So Hard for White People to Talk About Racism* (DiAngelo, 2018).

Multiple texts informed my thinking, but I don't think most caused me to center my gaze on developing the antiracist school leader within myself. The book that changed my inertia, however, was *How to Be an Antiracist* (Kendi, 2019). Kendi's concept of "antiracist" versus "not racist" strongly resonated with me. I used to view myself as an antiracist, as if it were a static characteristic. According to my interpretation of Kendi's principle, I was more nonracist than antiracist, most times. In other words, according to Kendi, an individual is truly antiracist if they are operating in a way that actively deconstructs systems of oppression.

This shifted the ground beneath my feet. Kendi's argument struck a chord deep within me, and I no longer viewed antiracism as a constant state of being.

> **An individual is truly antiracist if they are operating in a way that actively deconstructs systems of oppression.**

It is a day-by-day, hour-by-hour, decision-by-decision sort of characteristic. Once antiracism became one of my values, and not one of my descriptors, I committed to changing myself and everything within my sphere of influence.

Informing oneself is how a commitment to antiracism begins. To become an effective antiracist school leader, you must first learn the long, difficult history of marginalization that underlies the foundation of the United States and its governing systems, and how that history has filtered through layers of administration to affect the structure and policies of our educational system today.

De jure oppression (for example, legalized segregation of Black and White people) and de facto oppression (for example, segregation implemented by common understanding and personal choice) were overt and explicitly codified from colonization to at least the mid-20th century (Kendi, 2016). Here is a hypothetical example of how de jure and de facto oppression can work in tandem: throughout American history, many leaders who have been framed as champions for justice have explicitly stated their beliefs in the inferiority of people of color (Kendi, 2019). Today's schools are replete with examples of disproportionate racial outcomes that are rooted in our history of anti-dark oppression (Love, 2019). For instance, Black students are more likely to be in schools with teachers who are less qualified, less experienced, and less well paid (U.S. Department of Education Office of Civil Rights, 2014). Black girls are suspended from school at more than five times the rate of White girls (Morris, 2018). To be an effective antiracist leader, you must take responsibility for understanding the complexities of the social and historical realities that have led us to this. In this chapter, you will build a foundation of knowledge by studying the sources and various causes of systemic racism and its effects on the educational system, familiarize yourself with zones of understanding (fearing, learning, and growing), and gather important insights from personal reflection so that you may prepare yourself and your mind to commit to antiracist work.

UNDERSTAND THE CAUSES OF DISPROPORTIONATE RACIAL OUTCOMES

Racism, White supremacy, and White supremacy culture lead to educational, legal, political, medical, and economic systems of oppression that reinforce racist and White supremacist beliefs. Antiracism necessitates more than a disbelief in racism and White supremacy; it necessitates an active posture toward eradicating racism and White supremacy, with a particular focus on racist and White supremacist policies and practices.

Framing the education of students of color as a crisis, as it has been since the 1970s, discounts—if not altogether ignores—the larger context of societal inequities in both law and practice (Lozenski, 2017). Proposed solutions for the crisis are often not based on evidence, which is apparent insofar as interventions have been implemented during the decades without significant reductions in educational disparities related to race (Lozenski, 2017).

Antiracist school leaders recognize the roles that school policies and practices play in reinforcing systems of oppression that lead to disproportionate racial outcomes (Welton, Diem, & Carpenter, 2019). Recognition, however, is only the first step. Antiracist school leaders commit to identifying, modifying, or dismantling problematic policies, as exemplified in figure 1.1 (page 20).

Find What Has Been Missing From Your Education

Additionally, leaders in this work know that they must educate themselves about content that was absent from their teacher preparation programs and administrative leadership courses. Institutions of higher education have opportunities to include discrete courses about equity and antiracism in their educator preparation course pathways and weave antiracism content throughout their courses, but they do not always choose to do so. Irrespective of the reasons for the omission of antiracist content, school leaders must work to fill gaps of those missing topics.

Topics absent from most teacher preparation programs and administrative leadership courses include the following.

- **Definitions related to antiracism (such as definitions of *race*, *ethnicity*, *nationality*, and *culture*):** If you don't have a firm grasp of the vocabulary, it increases the challenge of demonstrating your purpose, articulating your vision, and managing resistance to change.

- **Social group identity development, particularly racial identity development:** Racism is, in part, a function of the in-group–out-group phenomenon, which is supported by the wiring of our brains as well as the rhetoric of our leaders, among other things. Understanding the neuroscience and social science that undergird our inclusive or exclusive choices is helpful in motivating stakeholders in ways that alter the direction of an organization (Corenblum & Meissner, 2006).

Disparate Outcomes for Students	Problematic Policies	How Can Staff Modify the Problematic Policies?	How Can Staff Dismantle or Reconstruct the Problematic Policies?
For the past three years, less than 60 percent of Latinx students achieved mathematics standards.	School administrators review the yearly achievement data from state-mandated assessments, but do not conduct regular, structured root cause analyses to consider disaggregated achievement data.	Incorporate the targeted use of disaggregated achievement data into regular (for example, quarterly) school-improvement planning meetings, during which a variety of stakeholders contribute. If needed, schools should attempt to invite stakeholders to join the meetings—as well as the meetings themselves—in the preferred languages of stakeholders.	The new diverse school-improvement planning team creates yearly goals for improvement, along with quarterly milestones. Data, goals, and milestones are required to be shared in public forums at least twice each year (for example, the beginning and end of each academic year).
Twenty-six percent of Asian students who replied to an end-of-year climate survey indicated that they feel personally connected to the curricular content.	School curricula and instructional materials are not regularly audited for cultural relevance.	School staff regularly (for example, annually) audit curricula and instructional materials for cultural relevance.	School leaders oversee the planning, implementation, and evaluation of mandatory training on the topic of culturally relevant pedagogy.
Two percent of Black students were designated as gifted and talented.	Teachers are not regularly evaluated for culturally relevant pedagogical practices that incorporate elements of enrichment for students who demonstrate mastery of curricular content.	Incorporate aspects of culturally relevant pedagogy into the teacher evaluation system.	Discontinue observational practices that preserve a sole focus on Eurocentric content and instructional practices. With the input of a variety of stakeholders, establish a new set of protocols that train teachers to recognize multiple aspects of giftedness and provide instruction during which students have multiple opportunities to display such traits.
Thirty-five percent of Hispanic caregivers attended parent conferences.	The school staff conduct invitations to parent conferences—as well as the conferences themselves—only in English, and conferences are only held during the school day.	Provide parent conference invitations in the preferred languages of caregivers, provide interpreters during conferences as needed, and include time windows that are before, during, and after the typical workday.	Discontinue the current format of parent conferences, including scheduling, invitations, implementation, and evaluation. Conduct a caregiver needs assessment on which a new parent conference format can be based.

FIGURE 1.1: Examples of how to identify, modify, and dismantle problematic policies.

- **White supremacy culture:** This term is often misunderstood and viewed as scary, both of which can bog down progress on antiracist efforts. Understanding simple facts about this topic, such as "White supremacy culture is not White people," allows leaders to anticipate and circumvent obstacles to the work.
- **Racism's influence on teaching, learning, and school communities:** If you aren't using the right lenses, then racism's influence on teaching and learning can seem invisible. Teachers and leaders need to recognize challenges in order to address those challenges.
- **How to lead student activities related to antiracism:** Whether these focus on social justice, restorative practices, organization for collective voice, analysis of disparities, identification of unfairness, or some other antiracism-related activities, educators must be prepared to plan, implement, and modify instruction in real time. Since teachers need professional learning to support those activities, school leaders should light the way.

Conduct a Literature Review

Part of beginning your journey toward becoming an antiracist school leader involves searching for texts with peer-reviewed research that provide historical facts and statistics (Kendi, 2017; Morris, 2018), as well as peer-reviewed texts that analyze existing literature (Lozenski, 2017). During your search for information, cast a wide net. There might be nearby colleagues who are researching or writing about related topics. Often, these new texts support new learning. Sometimes, a text could cause a radical shift in thinking, as several did for me. If you need a few ideas about where to start, consider the following two options. While these resources are intended for individuals who are new to the study of racial justice, they are helpful to all and should be revisited frequently.

1. The Greater Good Science Center at the University of California, Berkeley (https://greatergood.berkeley.edu/article/item/antiracist_resources_from_greater_good) lists dozens of short articles that are categorized in easy-to-understand ways.
2. The "Racial Justice, Racial Equity, and Anti-Racism Reading List" from the Harvard Kennedy School of Harvard University (https://hks.harvard.edu/faculty-research/library-knowledge-services

/collections/diversity-inclusion-belonging/anti-racist) contains a number of well-researched books that are connected to very strong storytelling.

These sites are relatively easy to read, connected to a wide variety of resources, and accessible to anyone, but there are many others available as well. If you are connected to an ecosystem that meets the same criteria, such as a book club, university research access, or library membership, then by all means leverage those resources to educate yourself. If your colleagues are watching you, modeling your desire for continuous growth could help them navigate the discomfort that comes with engaging with antiracist content. The next section digs a little deeper into how to manage the emotions that can be tied to adopting an antiracist orientation.

FEAR, LEARN, GROW

When gaining new insights into history, politics, and culture that you once thought you knew, you might find yourself experiencing a litany of challenging emotions. This is not unusual. Many who begin learning about the deep systemic inequity built into the United States' educational system experience fear or resistance. Fortunately, antiracist activists and scholars have devised ways to assess, acknowledge, and reframe individual feelings to create a more collaborative mindset for antiracist work. As a school leader, you may want to conduct some preliminary informal assessments of your staff to evaluate their readiness for the subject of systemic oppression and gauge how willing they might be to join you on an antiracist journey. JAMA Network editor Andrew M. Ibrahim (2021) has created a framework designed to informally assess a person's, group of people's, or organization's readiness to engage in antiracist work. The *fear zone*, *learning zone*, and *growth zone* (see figure 1.2) are easy-to-understand categories that allow leaders to quickly predict the willingness of their staff to begin or continue professional learning related to antiracism. It's an effective framework to gauge a starting point and consider the trajectory of initial steps before truly committing to this work.

Before you evaluate your staff on this continuum, I suggest you first conduct a self-assessment. Since there are only three categories, self-assessment might take just a few minutes. I encourage you to be vulnerable and honest with yourself; you don't have to share your findings, but being honest about where you are will help you accurately and effectively determine your next steps. Here's a quick way to get your bearings: if you voluntarily chose to read this book, you are likely in

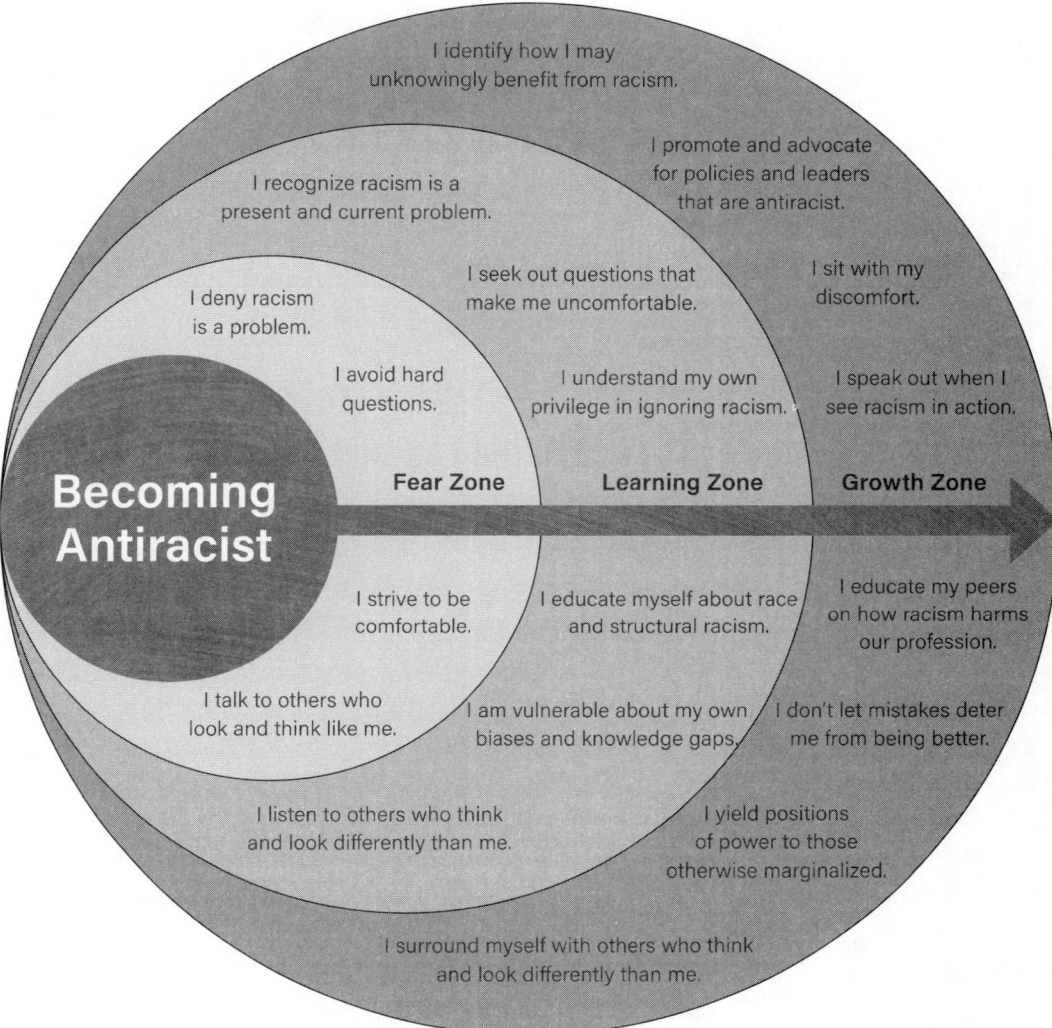

Source: Ibrahim, 2020.

FIGURE 1.2: Fear zone, learning zone, and growth zone.

the learning zone or growth zone. If you are reading this at the request of someone else and feel it was put on you, you might start by looking at the criteria for the fear zone.

In addition to considering your own readiness to begin the journey, committing to antiracist school leadership requires that you estimate the orientation and temperament of your staff, school community, and district leadership. In many cities around the United States, discussing systemic oppression and White supremacy culture as if they are self-evident parts of our everyday lives has led to political uproars and threats of violence. School contexts are always complicated, and those complications are compounded when a leader, staff, and district are in three different zones. For example, what if the locus of power in a school or district were in the fear zone? Would that impede the rank-and-file members of the school district from reaching the learning zone or growth zone?

In order to move from one zone to another, leaders should plan activities that blend the current zone with the next zone in the progression. For instance, if a staff is presently in the fear zone, then the leader should target movement toward the learning zone. The following are some strategies to help you get your staff into the same zone so they can begin to work together.

Move From the Fear Zone to the Learning Zone

Try facilitating active listening conversations between pairs of staff members with significantly diverse life experiences. Since you are beginning antiracist professional development, you could be tempted to pair teammates by race or ethnicity. In a relatively racially homogeneous staff, that could prove exceedingly challenging. Moreover, those conversations could become considerably charged and lead participants to experience emotional retreat or overload and thereby disengage from the experience.

Ask teachers, administrators, and central office staff to indicate the positions of themselves and their schools, departments, and district in the fear zone, learning zone, or growth zone. How you frame the conversation depends on your context and circumstances. For instance, your staff may have been together for years and exhibit a great degree of comfort with difficult conversations. In that case, you might facilitate a whole-group conversation during a staff meeting and ask people to share about themselves as individuals or the school more broadly. On the other hand, if you're new to a building or you have a high percentage of new staff members, you might ask people to personally reflect on the framework and share via an anonymous survey. For many people who identify as being in the learning zone and growth zone, you might hear comments like, "My team knows that some things are wrong, and we know that we should do some things about it; we just don't know exactly what's wrong and what we should do about it."

My recommended use of Ibrahim's (2020) fear zone, learning zone, and growth zone framework is intentionally simplistic. It supports your establishment of a broad orientation; it allows you to locate your starting point and moves you in the right direction. The movement forward takes more knowledge, skill, and commitment, and the more people with you, the more knowledge, skill, and commitment you'll require. If you try to use the framework to dig deeply into the work, you could become bogged down in a way that distracts you from your goals. If you're asking yourself, "How will I know when to move on, assess more deeply, and cast my vision for the deeper work?" you're on the right track. Those questions will be answered throughout the rest of this book.

Spending too much time analyzing where on Ibrahim's continuum each staff member lies can become an "equity detour" (Gorski, 2019), a distraction from the real work (as mentioned in the introduction, page 9). Therefore, when I talked to my school's staff about our beginning, I stated my rationale concisely: *unchanging demographic hierarchies*. I led a school that was predominantly Black and Brown, and most students were eligible for free or reduced-price meals. In addition, more than half my students and their families were English learners, and many were recent immigrants to the United States from Central America or Northeast Africa. I explained that when we considered our national, state, and local data, our students—or students who had similar factors of diversity—tended to be at the bottom of all the good categories and at the top of all the bad categories. I added that we changed curricula, we changed staff members, we changed school leadership, and we even built a brand-new school building in the last four years, yet those disparate outcomes remained.

These data, I implored, forced us into one of two camps of thought. The members of the first camp believed that the problem was rooted in deficits in *our students and their families* that inherently put them at the bottom. The second camp believed that the primary variables were connected to deficits in *our system* that recreated these consistent demographic hierarchies, because systems typically do what they are designed to do, even if it isn't what those systems' users ostensibly desire.

I told my team that I chose to believe my students and their families had the potential to be successful. There must have been things that I was not doing as a school leader, and there were some structural inequities in our systems that were causing these problems, and one of them was the permanence of White supremacy.

During a workshop with school leaders, one of the participants said, "This framework might need a few more categories. Like, what about the *hijack* or *paralyzed zone*, you know, when people are so fearful, they freeze. They might claim that they want to do antiracist work, but when you present them with opportunities, they're beyond scared and can't do anything. They either say or show that you can't talk to them about this because they fall apart. They want to stay in a place where they only talk about the content in ways that are comfortable for them."

Another participant added, "They say, 'What we need to do is buy this new curriculum or focus on using this intervention with fidelity, and that will be what makes the difference. We just need to find the right intervention for these under-resourced kids whose parents can't help them,' or something like that."

After input from other participants in the workshop, we agreed that efforts to avoid actual work for whatever reason are often rooted in the fear zone. Therefore, next steps with people and organizations in that zone can be supported by moving them toward the learning zone.

One way to help people move from the fear zone to the learning zone is creating a psychologically safe environment in which colleagues get to know each other in ways that help them see their personality, social, and cultural differences. For specific ways to create a psychologically safe environment, I recommend reading *Cultural Competence Now* by Vernita Mayfield (2020). Mayfield describes how school leaders can cultivate psychological safety through a cultural and practical infrastructure that promotes emotionally supportive relationships, autonomy, and efficacy. These are key markers of any healthy school culture, not just antiracist ones. If the school staff believe in themselves, the work, and their collective impact, they'll be ready to take on any task, no matter how daunting.

Move From the Learning Zone to the Growth Zone With the Four Cs

Book and article studies are straightforward ways to help a group move from the learning zone to the growth zone. In the learning zone, people have accepted that racism is a real phenomenon that affects teaching, learning, and collegial relationships. Presenting texts from experts adds new information that aligns with the sensibilities of staff who are looking to deepen their knowledge about the topic.

> Antiracist school leaders amplify opportunities to stretch staff members' understanding by providing a psychologically safe, structured space to exchange perspectives on their new learning.

The collegial readings and conversations can take the form of several short articles over the course of several weeks; one book over several months; combinations of articles, chapters, and videos; or any other configuration that suits the staff's time frame and temperament. Such structured learning about key concepts, interrogation of their own beliefs, and inquisition of others' beliefs lead staff to lean into uncomfortable emotions that arise during discussions of racism and White supremacy culture. Antiracist school leaders don't wallow in guilt, shame, or defensiveness; they begin to own their place in our educational system, and they want to share their new learning with others. Transitioning from the learning zone to the growth zone is what activist and abolitionist Bettina Love (2019) calls "freedom dreaming." In *We Want to Do More Than Survive: Abolitionist Teaching and the Pursuit of Educational Freedom*, Love (2019) writes:

> This is why deep study and personal reflection on the history of the US is so important to abolitionist teaching. When an educator deeply understands why meaningful, long-term, and sustainable change is so hard to achieve in education because of all the forces antithetical to justice, love, and equity—such as racism, sexism, housing discrimination, state-sanctioned violence toward dark people, police brutality, segregation, hate-filled immigration policies, Islamophobia, school closings, the school-to-prison-pipeline, and the prison-industrial complex—that is when freedom dreaming begins. . . . We cannot create a new educational system for all with a lack of understanding of what cripples our current system. (pp. 102–103)

Project Zero (2019), an interdisciplinary teaching initiative from Harvard University's Graduate School of Education, promotes the use of a simple yet effective protocol for text discussion: the four Cs thinking routine. The four Cs ask readers to consider key *concepts* that an author is trying to explain, personal *connections* readers are making to texts, statements or implications readers want to *challenge*, and any *changes* that the author is explicitly or tacitly recommending. School leadership teams can focus on one C at a time during a text discussion. In a round-robin format, each participant can share what they noted on a recording sheet, and other group members can comment. If time and interest permit, school leadership teams may discuss anywhere between one C and all four Cs. To close meetings, I sometimes add an element of further reflection by asking participants to journal about new insights they gained from the discussions and how they will apply the new learning to their teaching practices. The four Cs are described as follows (© 2019 President and Fellows of Harvard College and Project Zero):

1. **Connections:** What connections do you draw between the text and your own life or your other learning?
2. **Challenge:** What ideas, positions, or assumptions do you want to challenge or argue with in the text?
3. **Concepts:** What key concepts or ideas do you think are important and worth holding on to from the text?

4. **Changes:** What changes in attitudes, thinking, or action are suggested by the text, either for you or for others?

The four Cs routine offers learners a structured approach for engaging in text-based discussions, with a focus on making connections, asking questions, identifying key ideas, and exploring potential applications. It is a versatile method that can be used after reading a single text or multiple related texts.

Forming small groups for the discussions will help implement the protocol effectively. Before commencing the discussion, allocate some time for group members to locate passages within the text that align with each of the Cs. These identified passages should be underlined or marked in a way that makes them easily shareable during the discussion.

The discussion itself commences with one group member sharing a connection they made from the text. They read the relevant passage aloud and proceed to explain their connection. Other group members can then add their thoughts and comments regarding the shared passage. Subsequently, the next group member shares their chosen passage, and the discussion progresses in a similar manner until each member has shared a connection.

Once the connections have been thoroughly discussed, the group moves on to the next C, following the same process of sharing and discussing text passages. It is essential to ensure that each selected passage is presented and discussed before moving on to the subsequent C.

For more comprehensive documentation of the discussions, you may encourage groups to record the text passages they referenced along with the corresponding insights and comments provided during the discussion. This practice can be valuable for review and reflection.

Overall, this routine works best with small groups and can be adapted to suit the specific needs of the group and the text being examined. Depending on the focus or time constraints, you may choose to emphasize only two or three Cs instead of covering all four in a single session.

Enrich the Growth Zone

When a core group of staff members are in the growth zone, antiracist school leaders leverage the group's growing expertise and enthusiasm to enhance the knowledge of the rest of the staff. One way to do this is through the use of school leadership teams. School leadership teams are groups of school stakeholders who get together to support outcomes for students through their collective actions. In the case of antiracism, schools could have multiple school leadership teams that target diverse strands of teaching and learning experiences.

For instance, more than half of a school's student body might be composed of English learners. Therefore, a significant number of staff members might be interested in supporting their school's policies and practices related to multilingual students and their families. School leaders could meet with potential leaders of the school leadership team and cocreate a vision for how the school leadership team could support the learning of the staff and include voices of the community, which would ultimately lead to improved outcomes for students. Perhaps the school leaders could purchase books for school leadership team members with the understanding that the team members would facilitate quarterly professional learning activities for staff members as well as conduct focus groups that allow parents to express their views. Periodically, the school leadership team could analyze milestone data related to student outcomes (like well-being, engagement, discipline, and achievement). If the school leadership team emphasized the impact of school policies and practices that lead to disparate outcomes for multilingual students and families, then the team members would be enriching their experience in the growth zone, while at the same time helping their colleagues move through the fear and learning zones.

READ (HIGHLY) RECOMMENDED RESOURCES

Like you, I imagine, I skim all kinds of articles, blog posts, videos, and peer-reviewed research. The reason I focus on books here is because books symbolize a different level of commitment. Books are different animals because I have to sit with the content. Other items that I consume, such as TED Talks, podcasts, or blog posts, don't take longer than a couple of minutes to an hour to complete. With books, I spend hours, days, and weeks wrestling with the authors' arguments and exchanging ideas with colleagues and friends. The dedication indicated by committing to books also sends a message to my staff. It signals that this content is central to who I am, how I lead, and where we're headed in the long term.

Each time you share your beliefs about the topic, participate in dialogues, and receive feedback, your message will become clearer and more impactful. You just have to find people you trust because trust creates the environment of psychological safety and encouragement that you need to fully express your viewpoints. Those conversations sharpen your thinking and deepen your commitment. As Macalester College associate professor of urban and multicultural education Brian D. Lozenski (2017) puts it:

> We must fight the fire in our kitchen while realizing that it was started not by grease on the stove but by faulty wiring. We must put the fire out, but a refusal to address the actual cause will result in future fires. In addition, we must search for alternative explanations to educational disparity that do not look to the nation-state as the ultimate protector. . . . Rather, we must ask deeper questions that illuminate holistic contexts for educational analysis. (p. 181)

Applying Lozenski's opinions to school contexts encourages us to use our collective brainpower to identify the problematic policies and systems as well as the disparate outcomes they produce. Sure, we can reduce harm in real time to accomplish short-term goals related to data categories such as achievement and discipline, but we must also carefully examine the roles that school, district, and state policies play in reproducing those outcomes year after year. When searching for resources, you must determine timeless, essential resources alongside more current studies worth adding to your knowledge bank. The following sections detail how to look for knowledge that will help you on your antiracist endeavor.

Access the Essential Resources

Committing to antiracist school leadership is a difficult feat for the individual who decides to do it, but it is not a complex process in itself. The elements of educating yourself and committing are based in five fundamental aspects of learning: (1) reading, (2) listening, (3) viewing, (4) speaking, and (5) writing. These elements are like the standards for English learners, which are also rooted in listening, speaking, reading, and writing. In table 1.1, the elements of educating yourself are listed in two columns. The items in the left column (reading, listening, and viewing) are about immersing *yourself* in an antiracist ecosystem so that you can modify the lens through which you see the world. You become an active consumer of antiracist knowledge. That means reading everything you can get your hands on, listening to everything that your time allows you to hear, and viewing a variety of videos on the subject. The items in the right column (speaking and writing) signify when you begin to become a *producer* of antiracist content. Here is when you exchange ideas with others. It could be through sharing your evolving mindset with people you trust, such as critical friends, family members, staff members, or peers. It's OK to discuss your thoughts with like-minded others who are newcomers to this work.

Of course, the items you consume must fit into the available time in your lifestyle. It isn't possible to read every book, article, or blog; you can't listen to every podcast, audiobook, or webinar; and you won't be able to view every documentary, video clip, TED Talk, or social media post. The point is to put yourself into places where experts are sharing their opinions and facts about antiracism and soak up what you can.

TABLE 1.1: Essential Elements to Educate Yourself and Commit to Antiracist School Leadership

Read	Speak
• Books 　¤ *How to Be an Antiracist* (Kendi, 2019) 　¤ *For White Folks Who Teach in the Hood . . . and the Rest of Y'all Too* (Emdin, 2016) 　¤ *Stamped From the Beginning: The Definitive History of Racist Ideas in America* (Kendi, 2016) 　¤ *White Fragility: Why It's So Hard for White People to Talk About Racism* (DiAngelo, 2018) 　¤ *This Book Is Antiracist: 20 Lessons on How to Wake Up, Take Action and Do the Work* (Jewell, 2020) 　¤ *Caste: The Origins of Our Discontents* (Wilkerson, 2020) 　¤ *The Sum of Us: What Racism Costs Everyone and How We Can Prosper Together* (McGhee, 2021) 　¤ *Complex People: Insights at the Intersection of Black Culture and American Social Life* (Howard, 2015) 　¤ *Culturally Responsive Teaching and the Brain: Promoting Authentic Engagement and Rigor Among Culturally and Linguistically Diverse Students* (Hammond, 2015) 　¤ *Cultural Competence Now: 56 Exercises to Help Educators Understand and Challenge Bias, Racism, and Privilege* (Mayfield, 2020) 　¤ *Cultural Proficiency: A Manual for School Leaders* (Lindsey, Nuri-Robins, Terrell, & Lindsey, 2019) • Websites 　¤ Dismantling Racism Works (www.dismantlingracism.org) 　¤ "Anti-Racism Tools" (Trying Together, n.d.) 　¤ *Anti-Racism Toolkit: How to Talk About Anti-Racism* (Stanford University, 2020) 　¤ "Antiracist Resources From Greater Good" (Greater Good Science Center, 2020) 　¤ *Antiracist Allyship Starter Pack* (Dorrell, Herndon, & Dorrell, n.d.) • Articles and Reports 　¤ "Avoiding Racial Equity Detours" (Gorski, 2019) 　¤ *The Post-Pandemic Pathway to Anti-Racist Education: Building a Coalition Across Progressive, Multicultural, Culturally Responsive, and Ethnic Studies Advocates* (Stuart Wells & Cordova-Cobo, 2021) 　¤ "You Have an Anti-Racist Book List—Now What?" (White, 2021) 　¤ "Detour-Spotting for White Activists" (Olsson, 2011) 　¤ "15 Ways to Strengthen Anti-Racist Practice" (Catalyst Project, n.d.) 　¤ "106 Things White People Can Do for Racial Justice" (Shutack, 2022)	• Share your evolving mindset with people you trust. • Participate in discussions led by more experienced facilitators. • Be sincere, vulnerable, and authentic. • Consult resources that guide speakers, such as the following. 　¤ "Ten Lessons for Talking About Race, Racism, and Racial Justice" (the Opportunity Agenda, 2020) 　¤ "Resources for Talking About Race, Racism and Racialized Violence With Kids" (Center for Racial Justice in Education, n.d.) 　¤ "Want to Talk About Racism With Other Education Leaders? These Are the Important Terms You Need to Know" (EAB, 2020) 　¤ "Talking to Young Children About Race and Racism" (PBS Kids for Parents, n.d.) 　¤ "How White People Can Talk to Each Other About Disrupting Racism" (Allison, n.d.) 　¤ "Talking About Race" (National Museum of African American History and Culture, n.d.)

continued →

Listen
- Attend panel discussions, workshops, and conferences.
- Be a fly on the wall during discussions among more experienced friends, family members, and colleagues.
- Subscribe to podcasts, such as these.
  - *Code Switch*
  - *Momentum: A Race Forward Podcast*
  - *The Anti-Racism Daily Podcast*
  - *Pod for the Cause*
  - *Be Antiracist With Ibram X. Kendi*
  - *Teaching While White*
  - *The Anti-Racist Educator*
  - *Intersectionality Matters!*
  - *About Race With Reni Eddo-Lodge*
  - *Leading Equity*
  - *Anti-Racist Educator Reads*
  - *Time to Act*

View
- "Implicit Bias: Peanut Butter, Jelly and Racism" by *POV* (2016)
- "How to Talk to Kids About Race" by *The Atlantic* (2018)
- "Above the Noise: Understanding Anti-Racism" by KQED (2020)
- "What It Takes to Be Racially Literate" by Priya Vulchi and Winona Guo (2018)
- "The Difference Between Being 'Not Racist' and Antiracist" by Ibram X. Kendi (2020)
- "Ijeoma Oluo: So You Want to Talk About Race" by Talks at Google (2018)
- "Born Good? Babies Help Unlock the Origins of Morality" by CBS News (2012)
- "How Structural Racism Works" by Brown University (2017)
- "Ingroup Bias (Definition & Examples)" by Practical Psychology (2020)
- "Racism Has a Cost for Everyone" by Heather McGhee (2020)
- "How to Deconstruct Racism, One Headline at a Time" by Baratunde Thurston (2019)
- "3 Myths About Racism That Keep the US From Progress" by Candis Watts Smith (2021)
- "The Lie That Invented Racism" by John Biewen (2020)

Write
- Journal about your thoughts.
- Interact in comments sections within internet discussion forums.
- Submit blog posts to self-publishing sites, such as Medium.
- Exchange emails with speakers, researchers, and authors who pique your interest.

Access the Current Literature

A significant part of educating yourself is to seek out information that helps you understand *what* racism is, *why* it exists, and *how* school leaders can combat it. The following books represent the kinds of texts that provide exactly that kind of guidance. This is by no means an exhaustive list, but these books can serve as a good starting point or next step in your education.

ADDRESSING "WHAT IS RACISM? WHAT IS ANTIRACISM?" WITH *HOW TO BE AN ANTIRACIST*

Professor, historian, and activist Ibram X. Kendi (2019) gained mainstream acclaim with *How to Be an Antiracist*, and rightfully so. Kendi's straightforward ideology challenges his audience to recognize that the comfortable stance of "not racist" is an imaginary construct. All people, Kendi opines, are either actively disrupting systems of oppression (they are antiracist) or not actively disrupting systems of oppression (they are racist); there is no "not racist" option.

Kendi adds that racist and antiracist aren't static characteristics like skin color; they are the results of hour-by-hour decisions that either support or resist policies and practices that result in systemic inequities. This decision making is analogous—albeit with much higher stakes—to wanting to improve your physical health (this would be supporting students and families) through diet and exercise (in this case, employing antiracist practices). Some days, you'll eat well and work out, and other days, well, not so much. It doesn't make you an evil person; it makes you human. The more you educate yourself, commit to a long-term approach, and find networks of support, the more likely you will create habits that move you closer to your goal.

Kendi also presents easy-to-understand definitions for various forms of racism and antiracism, which are accessible to newcomers. For instance, here are his definitions for racism and antiracism.

- **Racism:** "A marriage of racist policies and racist ideas that produces and normalizes racial inequities" (Kendi, 2019, p. 18)
- **Antiracism:** "A powerful collection of antiracist policies that lead to racial equity and are substantiated by antiracist ideas" (Kendi, 2019, p. 20)

ADDRESSING "WHY DOES RACISM EXIST?" WITH *THE PERSON YOU MEAN TO BE*, *THE POWER OF US*, AND *THE SUM OF US*

In *The Person You Mean to Be: How Good People Fight Bias*, social psychologist Dolly Chugh (2018) explains how our attachment to race is rooted in in-group and out-group psychology. Members of your in-group are insiders, the people closest to and most like you. They're your community. You take care of each other. The out-group people, on the other hand, are outsiders. They're the people with whom you don't have the most significant characteristics in common. They aren't fellow community members.

The characteristics you and others share bring you closer together, and that closeness filters the way you see the world, especially in regard to your relationship with the out-group. For example, your in-group is complicated and should be explained with nuance; the out-group is simple and can be described with a few basic characteristics. Your in-group earned its place due to its innate greatness, moral clarity, and hard work; that other group might only succeed through handouts from a rigged system. A couple of misguided members of your in-group don't represent the group as a whole, while an example of misbehavior in your out-group indicates the flaws of the entire community.

Generally, in-group and out-group phenomena aren't only about race or ethnicity. In-group and out-group sentiments could refer to any number of groups to which you might belong. For instance, people form in-groups around politics, religions, sports teams, and sexual orientations, among myriad other factors of diversity. In *The Power of Us: Harnessing Our Shared Identities to Improve Performance, Increase Cooperation, and Promote Social Harmony*, psychology professors Jay J. Van Bavel and Dominic J. Packer (2021) explain that group identities can be developed by choice (such as choosing a favorite sports team), assignment (such as being designated as Latinx), or experience (such as surviving trauma). Different group identities move to the foreground and background of your mind depending on the context. For instance, it is possible that you place your gender or socioeconomic status in the background during the workday, while you might associate more with your political affiliations as you listen to talk radio on your commute home. No matter what the origins of our group identities were or when our identities in particular groups dominate our perspectives, there is no doubt that we all see ourselves as members of many groups and those memberships color the way we interact with the world around us.

In the United States, race has become a powerful amalgamation of multiple social groups, and it significantly influences the ways schools operate. Perhaps skin color, facial features, and hair texture are conspicuous physical characteristics that indicate group membership. When you add cultural markers such as clothing styles, dialects, and five hundred years of historical conditioning, it is easy to see how we all get caught in the trap of race. It is so ingrained in us that it has become part of our physical and emotional being. In *The Sum of Us: What Racism Costs Everyone and How We Can Prosper Together*, Heather McGhee (2021), chair of the board of Color of Change, explains:

> The first thing you take in when you see someone is their skin color. Within a fraction of a second, that sight triggers your ingrained associations and prejudices. If those prejudices about a person's skin color are negative—as they overwhelmingly are among White people regarding darker skin—they alert your amygdala, the section of the brain responsible for anxiety and other emotions, to flood your body with adrenaline in a fight-or-flight response. (p. 228)

Ignoring the biological and social causes of racism by pretending to be colorblind will not keep that societal disease from damaging the United States, and everyone therein, just as ignoring the bodily disease of cancer will not keep the disease from spreading from organ to organ. Let's consult some specialists, lock arms, and fight this thing together.

ADDRESSING "HOW CAN SCHOOL LEADERS COMBAT RACISM?" WITH CULTURAL PROFICIENCY

Cultural Proficiency: A Manual for School Leaders (Lindsey et al., 2019) is a must-read for new school leaders. The authors show how all work about culture and equity can be long-term professional learning that is structured in a step-by-step fashion over the course of several years. Each professional development activity should build on previous activities and set the stage for future activities. Randall B. Lindsey and his team use more than fifty coordinated workshop plans to inspire readers to follow their road map or construct a scope and sequence that help teachers as they begin sharing about themselves, learning about their colleagues, and understanding how culture influences teaching, learning, and working in schools.

Consuming texts like these should meaningfully affect how you approach planning strategies to support your staff members during antiracist professional learning.

> You'll come to realize that disagreements between colleagues are often *not* the result of differences in morals or intelligence; they're the result of different life experiences and cultures.

Antiracist school leaders help teammates create new life experiences together, in psychologically safe and informative settings. School staffs grow through the cultural, intellectual, and emotional exchanges that take place as the products of meaningful professional learning opportunities.

As an effective school leader, you understand that such exchanges are based on two-way communication between you and your coworkers. You must be prepared to have your views challenged. Moreover, you should be ready to consider changing some of your views based on your interactions with folks with different perspectives. Very often, people have grown to hold opinions that are just as firm as your views. Why should they be willing to change their minds if you're not willing to change yours?

ASK, REFLECT, ADJUST

The educational system is designed to maintain the equivalent of a caste system (Wilkerson, 2020). We must analyze and deconstruct the parts that aren't working for all our students and their families. The following are a few items I have observed in my experience as an educational leader that are not working for community members.

- Protocols for training that support our interactions with stakeholders
- How we evaluate instructional practices
- The timing and topics of traditional school events
- The holidays we recognize
- The materials we use
- The design of our school-improvement teams or parent-teacher associations
- Our hiring practices
- The timing of our school day

- The myriad other pieces of our schools' systems that explicitly or tacitly signal whose cultures we value

We might intend to support our students and families with our current practices, but intent can never take center stage. Impact always outweighs intention. If our current practices and policies don't deconstruct the historical demographic hierarchy, we must update our practices and policies.

Considering all the elements of antiracist school leadership at once can be overwhelming to someone who is new to the concept. Focusing on one aspect at a time can be an effective strategy to begin your trek toward a place of equity and inclusion for your entire school community. At this point, you only need to say to yourself that you are willing to develop your antiracism knowledge and skills. By reading this book, you've taken a great step in that direction.

CONCLUSION

If you're still reading, then you probably believe that racism wields significant influence on the outcomes of your students, their families, and the communities in which your schools are embedded. You know that disparate racial outcomes that have occurred over time are not merely the result of students' lack of effort, parents' lack of involvement, and educators' lack of knowledge. You understand that the current state of our educational system does not just reflect crises of poverty, violence, or staffing. It is a system that is structured—deliberately or otherwise—to consistently reinforce a demographic hierarchy.

For decades, the leaders of our educational, political, legal, housing, labor, and medical systems have explicitly or tacitly fabricated the narrative that racial differences in effort, intelligence, and morality generated the racial differences in our school data (Kendi, 2016). You know it's a lie. The work you've done with your students, their caregivers, and your colleagues over the years has taught you that. You're trying to figure out how to counteract that narrative, how to push back against the systems that are stacked against the communities you serve.

Thankfully, you're reading the right book, and this chapter articulated the first step: educate yourself. Read about, view, listen to, and speak about antiracism in schools as much as you are able. As you begin this journey, know that you are not alone. There are thousands of educators around the United States who are trying to figure this out. We're trying to move ourselves and our peers to our respective growth zones. We haven't solved the problem, but we welcome you to the conversation. Discuss what you're reading, talk about what you're listening to, and share what you're writing.

Educating yourself on the topic and committing to the work might only be the first step, but it's a significant one. Before you cast a vision to your school community and begin to chart a course for school- or districtwide change, you must first clarify that vision to yourself. Take some time to sit with the media and reflective activities this chapter recommends. Consult with trusted peers, including your supervisor, and solidify your perspective. When you're ready to share your ideas with the broader school community, chapter 2 (page 41) offers guidance in the form of some great next steps.

APPLY YOUR LEARNING

If you're new to antiracist school leadership, the content in this chapter might seem like a lot to process. You might be asking yourself, "What exactly should I know or be able to do with what I just learned?" At the end of each chapter, I'll lay out a few key concepts that you should know, a few phrases that you might want to learn, and a few practices that you should be able to incorporate into your repertoire. These items are not mandates, but recommendations and guidelines that help you to gauge whether you've attained some of the important information in the chapter. Review each bullet and get a sense of what you clearly understand and what you need to review.

There are thousands of resources to support reading, writing, listening, and speaking about antiracist school leadership. The more you read, write, listen to, and view content related to antiracism, the more you are likely to know, and the stronger you are likely to commit. Whether you are very experienced with the topic or this is new to you, here are things that you can know, say, and do to demonstrate your education in and commitment to antiracist school leadership.

 KNOW

- Know your orientation in Ibrahim's fear, learn, and grow readiness framework (page 22).
- Know the definitions of key vocabulary in this chapter.
- Know the texts you've read recently and how they've impacted your thinking. (If you know you felt good about a book but can't remember the key takeaways, perhaps it's time to revisit that text. You will likely need to draw on that knowledge as you shape your vision and engage with others.)

SAY

- Share your evolving thoughts with friends you trust.
- Tell yourself that you are willing to develop your antiracism knowledge and skills. By reading this book, you've taken a great step in that direction.
- Talk to colleagues about texts you have read recently and books you're going to read in the next few months and how you think those texts will influence your thinking or your work.

DO

- Find groups of colleagues or friends to help you digest new information (via private social media chains, conference calls, book clubs, or informal meetings).
- Attend or view school board meetings to hear perspectives related to antiracist content.

- Create a wish list of texts that you plan to read in the next month, the next six months, the next year, or all three.
- Plan activities that blend the current zone with the next zone in Ibrahim's (2020) progression.

Chapter 2
CAST AN ANTIRACIST VISION

Key Vocabulary

allies	People who work "toward something that is mutually beneficial and supportive to all parties involved" (Love, 2019, p. 117). They are advocates for friends of color and racial equality (Fingerhut & Hardy, 2020).
builders	People who commit to examining themselves and systems that surround them, as well as modifying problematic aspects of themselves and social systems (Chugh, 2018).

coconspirators	People who collaborate in ways that reconstruct the current status quo, even if it means giving up their own privilege (Love, 2019).
equity	All students have what they need to reach and exceed common goals (Linton, 2011).
volunteers	People who sustain their efforts to organize in ways that benefit people who might be strangers (Fingerhut & Hardy, 2020); people who support causes when those causes are convenient and nonthreatening to their personal identities or social status.

I became a teacher because I wanted to change the world, especially for poor children of color. My philosophical lens focused on that group of students because I was one of those students, as were most of my friends. As a classroom teacher, I affected the lives of about twenty-five students each year. That was gratifying, but I wanted to make a broader impact on the lives of children. So, I became a principal.

My educational leadership preparation included a variety of courses, trainings, texts, and meetings, each of which offered a different perspective on how to establish and maintain a school culture that improves outcomes for students. Throughout most, if not all, of my professional learning experiences relating to school leadership, I could tease out one common principle, which was school leaders often operate using the following chain of logic: changing the staff leads to changing the students and their families, which (perhaps) leads to changing the world. In other words, to fix the deficits in our school communities, we must address the deficits in our staffs so that they can address the deficits in our students and their families.

Supporting staff deficits sometimes comes in the form of our vacillation between more structured and less structured curricula; supporting student deficits often comes in the form of academic interventions and social-emotional learning programs; and supporting family deficits typically comes in the form of parent information events. In this chapter, you will learn how antiracist school leaders highlight the flaws in our disproportionate focus on the inputs (such as students, families, and staff) and outputs (such as test scores, graduation rates, and discipline referrals) of their organizations. You will learn how antiracist leaders reflect and act on the mechanism that transforms inputs into outputs, which is the system itself. The chapter supports the theory that there is no such thing as "not racist" (Chaudhary & Berhe, 2020), and that either leaders are actively working to reconstruct our educational system in ways that resist historical demographic hierarchies or they are supporting the status quo.

This chapter also includes strategies that antiracist school leaders can use to communicate their antiracist visions to stakeholders. It will provide examples of verbal analogies, pictorial metaphors, conceptual diagrams, and charts that leaders can use to help their audiences understand the new focus on antiracism. You will get opportunities to consider peer-reviewed research on how leaders leverage resources such as digital media (Mislán & Dache-Gerbino, 2018) and personal relationships (Ohito, 2019) to engender buy-in from stakeholders. Members of different stakeholder groups might enter the conversation about racism from different vantage points (Singleton, 2015). Last, this chapter introduces the importance of connecting to stakeholders' life experiences, personal stances, and professional commitments (Chugh, 2018; Ohito, 2019; Singleton, 2015), a key understanding that will be discussed further in chapter 4 (page 105).

> **Systems do not address their users' stated purposes; systems conform to their designs. The U.S. educational system is designed to maintain demographic hierarchies.**

EVALUATE LEADERS AND SYSTEMS

Two key variables are missing from traditional approaches to casting an antiracist vision for change: (1) the leaders themselves and (2) the systems within which all the stakeholders work. Schools have been targeting the deficits in their students, families, communities, and staffs for centuries (Kendi, 2017; Mukherjee, 2016), and the demographic hierarchies of student achievement and other outcomes have not changed. Black and Brown students remain at the bottom for most of the good indicators, such as graduation rates, and the top for all the problematic indicators, such as suspensions (Kendi, 2017; Morris, 2018). The educational system—including content standards, instructional strategies, assessments, funding mechanism, and cultural foci—recreates these hierarchies in each generation.

DECLARE PUBLIC INTENT

Casting an antiracist vision is at best an accountability mirror for yourself unless you share your intent with others. Declaring intent in a public, professional setting makes antiracism part of your professional identity and gives others the opportunity to join you. Consider Marcos's story: Marcos is an administrator in an elementary school in a large suburban school district that borders a major city in the Mid-Atlantic region of the United States. He is also one of my personal friends and sounding boards. Marcos and I discussed my proposal for this book during halftime of a 2021 winter football game. As typical for him, he was very supportive of my premise and offered suggestions. As typical for me, I asked him to help me out, so he offered some insights. I emailed him five broad questions, and he responded in writing.

Over 95 percent of Marcos's students are Black or Latinx. During most years, at least two-thirds of his students are English learners, nine out of ten are eligible to receive free or reduced-price meals, and many families are undocumented immigrants. Marcos describes himself as an aspiring antiracist school leader because, he says, "there is too much at stake for educators to ignore the system that confines the success of the children and families that we serve." He shared with me explicit messages that he delivers to his staff, both new and veteran:

> If you are going to be in front of our students, you will need to have begun your antiracist journey. Our kids deserve teachers who will see them, engage them, and teach them, while being self-reflective antiracist educators. This means school leaders must also be on their personal antiracist journeys to be able to lead staff through this collective journey. Leaders model. Our vision statement describes us as an inclusive, multicultural learning community. So, we need to walk the walk. Our kids deserve it. They should be able to compete on a global scale with peers from wealthy areas in our district, California, or Singapore, regardless of their native language, socioeconomic status, or home countries. (Personal communication, February 2, 2021)

Antiracist school leaders publicly articulate their antiracist visions to a variety of stakeholders, including their staffs, their supervisors, their students, and their school communities. That public articulation could begin as simply as stating an awareness of systemic racism and committing to leading action against it.

Prior to making a public statement at my school, I composed a list of talking points that I planned to include when sharing my vision with my four key stakeholder groups: (1) my staff, (2) my supervisor, (3) my school's parents and community, and (4) my students. I recommend you do the same. Table 2.1 (page 46) is an example of how I organized my ideas. I did not strictly adhere to each talking point during every discussion. These types of lists should clarify your beliefs and anchor your thoughts in ways that prepare you to guide challenging conversations.

I should note that I decided not to share the big vision directly with students during the first year. Since I led an elementary school, students would need guidance from our staff members, particularly their teachers. Staff who are beginners with this content could lead to weak or harmful discussions or policies (Chaudhary & Berhe, 2020). Therefore, teachers should have beliefs, knowledge, and skills to competently support young learners. This means that staff need at least a one-year head start on the journey. So, I decided that my staff should be the first to hear my vision.

I began to cast my antiracist vision to my staff during the winter of 2020. Placing my opening statement at the tail end of an afternoon whole-staff meeting and sending a follow-up email, I felt, were effective ways to send the message to a wide range of staff members. While a follow-up email will allow staff to read the clarity of your vision, an in-person start to your work on this topic will provide an opportunity for staff to hear the conviction in your voice, as well as ask questions and hear responses in real time.

Transparently, I shared this vision with the staff in January because our district's voluntary transfer window opened in February. Prior notice of our upcoming focus on antiracism allowed all staff members to consider their commitment to becoming antiracist educators. It also allowed time for disinterested staff members to search for positions in schools that were more aligned with their personal values. Consider timing the announcement of your vision in a similar fashion.

I told the assembled group that I joined this profession because I wanted to change the world, and it used to be OK for my staff members to join the profession for other reasons, as long as they weren't doing harm to students. The more that I learned about the impacts of racism and White supremacy, I explained, the more that I understood how I had misplaced my focus. Rather than centering on a need to change my students to help them cope with a system that was rife with structural disadvantages, I needed to modify the system itself. For our school to be

TABLE 2.1: Antiracist Vision Casting—Anticipatory Talking Points

TALKING TO STAFF	TALKING TO A SUPERVISOR OR THE CENTRAL OFFICE
<ul><li>We've tried various curricula and interventions for decades, yet the students we serve remain at the bottom of the good categories and the top of the bad categories.</li><li>Our focus has been on fixing the deficits in our students and their families.</li><li>Some of my recent reading leads me to believe that we should turn more of our attention to the policies and practices that support the system that recreates the racial inequities.</li><li>Antiracism is a concept that centers more of our focus on systems of oppression that result in racial inequities, and that is going to be a primary focus for our professional learning and everyday practices for the foreseeable future, starting next summer.</li><li>I don't know all there is to know, so I intend for all of us to grow together.</li><li>Not only would I like you to *walk* with me on this journey, I'd like you to *lead* with me. We can plan and implement our learning activities together.</li><li>We'll remain committed to implementing our curricula and interventions with fidelity. Antiracism should enhance—rather than weaken—our instructional performance.</li><li>I'm telling you now so that you have time to find another school if you prefer not to engage in this learning with us.</li></ul>	<ul><li>My personal value regarding the importance of equity has spawned a commitment to antiracism.</li><li>I'd like your support as I lead my school in an antiracist direction during the next few years.</li><li>There will likely be some pushback from some staff and community members, but I have the theoretical reading, general research, and school data to back up our commitment.</li><li>Antiracism calls on us to intentionally seek out and transform policies and practices that undergird the systems of oppression in our school, and society more broadly.</li><li>I'll tell staff and parents that we remain committed to implementing our curricula and interventions with fidelity. Antiracism should enhance—rather than weaken—our instructional performance.</li><li>What do you think might be some obstacles to my vision?</li><li>What concepts or strategies do you think would be helpful for me to include in my vision?</li><li>(Share staff, parent and community, and student talking points as needed.)</li></ul>
TALKING WITH PARENTS AND THE COMMUNITY	**TALKING WITH STUDENTS**
<ul><li>Racial disparities have been a constant in society, and schools play a role in reproducing those disparities.</li><li>We love your children, so we must change our approach to education in order to serve them better.</li><li>We remain committed to providing high-quality instruction.</li><li>Antiracist pedagogy makes us better educators; it's not a distraction.</li><li>We want the children we share to not just survive or thrive in our world; we want them to transform it into a more just society.</li><li>Social media posts and letters to the community don't make change; we need long-term commitments to action.</li></ul>	<ul><li>The staff work hard to make sure you know that you are capable of doing anything with effective effort.</li><li>We want you to connect your life to almost everything we do in school. That means you need to see, hear about, and learn about people and places that share your cultural and ethnic backgrounds.</li><li>You deserve a fair school and a fair society, but you have to work for it. If you feel like one culture or ethnicity is being valued more or less than other cultures or ethnicities, talk to us about it. Let's work together to figure out a way to make it right.</li></ul>

the best version of itself, I declared, all colleagues must journey toward the same destination: understanding antiracism. I stated this explicitly: "It is not enough for you to just love kids; I need you to change our system in ways that change the lives of our kids. Together, we can improve both their opportunities and their outcomes by improving our policies, protocols, and practices."

I was encouraged to find that no one left my school in 2020 to avoid our concentration on antiracism. That does not mean that every staff member was an early adopter of antiracist pedagogy. My school had its share of resisters, which is common across all schools in the United States. Supporters of the status quo have said that people of color should have stopped needing special support since the end of slavery, if not earlier (Mukherjee, 2016). For modern-day educators, most of whom are White, it could be that a confrontation of racism "is never disassociated from the learners' responsibility to reflect on how they may be complicit in and beneficiaries of inequitable systems and disproportionate power relations" (Ohito, 2019, p. 138).

On the other hand, plenty of staff also self-identified as allies. This may happen at your school as well. These are people who are ready to share ideas, develop professional learning activities, implement antiracist instructional practices, and engage with the school community. Declaring your intent requires courage, conviction, and a plan. In the following sections, we'll develop a follow-up plan for after your public declaration and learn how to draft an open letter.

Have a Follow-Up Plan

Several weeks after declaring your antiracist commitment to your staff, prepare to have a conversation with your supervisor, superintendent, and board of education. I had a conversation with my supervisor because I worked in a district with over 160,000 students and more than 200 schools, so I did not have regular talks with my superintendent or the board of education. I scheduled a meeting with my direct supervisor, who in my district was called a *director of learning, achievement, and administration*. There are two primary goals for the conversation.

1. You must let your supervisor, superintendent, or board of education, or all three, know that antiracism is now one of your core values, which will affect most of what you do going forward.

2. You need them to back you up when you encounter the inevitable pressure from members of your staff, your central office, and the community.

The conversation with my director went well. I shared my early thoughts about my goals, strategies, activities, and potential obstacles. I recommend you do the same. My director listened carefully, asked questions that pushed my thinking, and poked holes in some of my assumptions. For instance, she asked, "Will the professional learning progression for your staff assume that everyone is starting from the same place in this content?" and "How will you manage conversations about intersectionality?" We also discussed potential obstacles to the work that she had encountered earlier in her career.

Draft an Open Letter

With respect to a public declaration to my school's community, I planned to share my vision just prior to the start of the following school year. However, the racial unrest that followed the murders of George Floyd, Ahmaud Arbery, and Breonna Taylor altered my timeline. I emailed an open letter to my community that was linked to text messages and placed on our school's website. The letter explained that I was horrified by the recent murders, but I was not surprised. The letter went on to share that our staff planned to use antiracist pedagogy to help our students improve our society. The following excerpt from the letter highlights how I made sure to point out that antiracism would support our high academic expectations for the students:

> As educators, part of our collective role is to teach our students how to recognize racism and how to work against it. Before we do that, however, we need to recognize and work against the racism in ourselves. . . . We have to commit to continuing antiracist work on ourselves and in our schools in the long term.
>
> Just so I'm clear, our antiracist work will not distract from the high standards that we hold for your children. Antiracism will make us better instructors as well as better citizens. That can only help our students.

When composing your own letter (should you choose to do so), emphasize your dedication to students and be clear that this is done for their benefit. I told my readers that my care for their students had not changed but evolved to serve them better with this new commitment. Keep in mind your purpose as you communicate during this change in direction.

For your reference, I have included the letter in full in figure 2.1.

Once you pledge your antiracist school leadership to your staff, supervisor, and community, there is no turning back. You are obligated to act. Some stakeholders will stand ready to support you, some will have questions, and others might

FIGURE 2.1: Example of an open letter to the community.

begin to push back. Therefore, you should prepare yourself. The next steps involve sharpening the clarity of your vision by outlining specific vocabulary and developing (or locating) explanatory techniques that connect the content to the personal experiences of your staff members.

USE ACCURATE VOCABULARY

Some leaders are reluctant to use the phrases *racism* and *White supremacy*, preferring terms like *equity* and *opportunity*.

Even overtly racist leaders use dog whistles such as "law and order," "crime control," "welfare reform," and "homeland security," which suggest biased policies while avoiding explicit connections to color or race. They use what Roopali Mukherjee (2016), associate professor of media studies at Queens College, calls "permissible narratives of difference." Racist leaders traffic in permissible narratives because those explanations lay the blame on marginalized communities and individuals. Antiracist school leaders do not dance around this issue. They use *equity* when it is appropriate, but they also call *racism*, *White supremacy*, and other problematic phenomena by their names.

Creating personal definitions regarding significant concepts can help antiracist school leaders clarify the content in their minds prior to sharing their thoughts with an audience. My reflections on antiracist readings led me to generate my own understandings of key vocabulary. Those definitions, presented in figure 2.2, clarify each word or phrase in a concise but comprehensive fashion. The figure also provides an opportunity for you to draft your own definitions of these words in the right-hand column. To help you craft your definitions, you could converse with trusted peers and reflect on the audio recordings, videos, and readings presented in chapter 1 (page 31).

> **The use of less threatening vocabulary supports the comfort of members of the dominant cultures.**

If someone gave you a hammer and asked you to describe what it is, you might just say, "This is a hammer." You wouldn't say, "It is a hard pushing tool." Antiracism is the work; educators cannot do the work effectively if they are not ready to use the right vocabulary. Antiracist school leaders show that the descriptive vocabulary is safe to use in their school setting. They put it on their websites, they write it in blogs and social media posts, and they use it in letters to the community. Teachers cannot be expected to become comfortable with the terminology if administrators do not demonstrate comfort with the terminology.

Word	My Definition	Your Definition
racism	The belief that the social construct of race is associated with inherent physical, intellectual, temperamental, or moral characteristics that position some racial groups as naturally superior or inferior to other racial groups	
White supremacy	The belief that the White race possesses inherent physical, intellectual, temperamental, or moral characteristics that naturally position White people as the superior racial group	
White supremacy culture	A set of cultural principles that promotes the superiority of a supposed White racial way of thinking and being	
antiracism	The practice of seeking, deconstructing, or reconstructing systems of oppression that benefit one or more racial groups at the expense of other racial groups	

FIGURE 2.2: Crafting your own definitions.

*Visit **go.SolutionTree.com/diversityandequity** for a free reproducible version of this figure.*

There are a multitude of terms that antiracist school leaders should get to know. *Racism*, *White supremacy*, *White supremacy culture*, and *antiracism* are key vocabulary in every antiracist school leader's lexicon. See the glossary (page 179) for definitions of these terms and many other useful vocabulary words.

For some veteran school leaders, it might be uncomfortable to facilitate meetings with phrases such as *backward mapping* and *disaggregated data*, yet school leaders learn to use them in appropriate contexts. The same can be true for phrases such as *White supremacy culture*. The difference is that some educational leadership jargon is uncomfortable to *say*, while some antiracist leadership jargon is uncomfortable to *feel*. As building and community leaders, if we do not demonstrate comfort with the terms, then we must think hard about what message we are sending to our stakeholders.

LEVERAGE THE USE OF STORYTELLING AND VISUALS

Words alone can be powerful, especially when those words are related to antiracist content. However, effective visionaries leverage their understanding of additional tools. In the case of antiracist vision casting, it is helpful to add clarity by using verbal analogies, pictorial metaphors, conceptual diagrams, charts, and digital media that help an audience understand the new focus on antiracism. Colorful storytelling and visual cues, especially those that link to the audience's lived experiences, make complex phenomena more interesting and easier to grasp (Kao, 2020; Kerby, Brittland, Cantor, Weiland, & Babiarz, 2016). Moreover, there is evidence that members of some cultural groups create stronger personal connections to the content, and to the leaders who describe it, through the use of metaphoric speech (Ondish, Cohen, Lucas, & Vandello, 2019).

Verbal Analogies

Verbal analogies are helpful in adding clarity because they connect the background knowledge of the audience to unfamiliar—and sometimes uncomfortable—concepts such as antiracism. Like the way good teachers activate students' background knowledge during day-to-day instruction, using verbal analogies provides a proverbial cognitive hook on which learners can hang new learning. Since antiracist school leaders are already great instructional leaders, they are familiar with the lived experiences of their staff members, which eases the creation of analogies to which the staff can relate. Analogies can be as simple as phrases. For example, here is an analogy that is sometimes used in antiracist conversations: *For assimilationists, society is a melting pot, while antiracists view society as a tossed salad.* The following two examples could be used to explain why antiracist educators widen their collective focus to include racist systems, going beyond one-on-one racist interactions.

WHITE SUPREMACY AS AN OPERATING SYSTEM

Some school staffs are disproportionately composed of young adults in the millennial age group, so technology-related analogies could be useful. For instance, one could describe racism and White supremacy as the operating system of our society that leads to the racially disparate outcome gaps in our schools. Most of our school-based remedies (like reading interventions, social-emotional learning, and restorative practices) are analogous to applications that must be designed to function within the parameters of the operating system. So school-based interventions, although their ostensible purpose might be to assist students from historically marginalized groups, often reify the principles on which our racist society is based. Therefore, antiracist educators consider the flaws embedded in the systems and policies that structure our institutions just as much as, or more than, they consider the shortfalls of their students and their students' families.

THE GROUNDWATER APPROACH

In another analogical example, Bayard Love and Deena Hayes-Greene (2018) of the Racial Equity Institute composed a white paper that outlines an allegory they call the "groundwater approach," which facilitates recognition of structural oppression based on race. They write the following:

> If you have a lake in front of your house and one fish is floating belly-up dead, it makes sense to analyze the fish. What is wrong with it? Imagine the fish is one student failing in the education system. We'd ask: Did it study hard enough? Is it getting the support it needs at home?
>
> But if you come out to that same lake and *half* the fish are floating belly-up dead, what should you do? This time, you've got to analyze the lake. Imagine the lake is the education system and *half* the students are failing. This time we'd ask: Might the system itself be causing such consistent, unacceptable outcomes for students? If so, how?
>
> Now . . . picture five lakes around your house, and in *each and every* lake half the fish are floating belly-up dead! What is it time to do? We say it's time to analyze the groundwater. How did the water in all these lakes end up with the same contamination? On the surface the lakes don't appear to be connected, but it's possible—even likely—that they are. (Love & Hayes-Greene, 2018, p. 2)

Some who identify as allies or antiracist activists focus almost exclusively on the problems of individual fish and their interactions with other fish. If most of the fish (in this case, the fish are students from historically oppressed groups) in most of the ponds (as in schools in our system) are suffering, antiracist educators should decrease our deficit-based focus on the individual fish and increase our deficit-based focus on what influences the condition of the ponds.

Pictorial Metaphors

Like verbal analogies, pictorial metaphors can add clarity to explanations by connecting the familiar to the unfamiliar. Pictorial metaphors add visual elements that anchor presentations and ensure that all audience members are operating with the same images in mind. The following two pictures have been used to anchor presentations about the importance of equity and antiracism.

THE EQUALITY VERSUS EQUITY BOX STORYBOARD

The image of people standing on boxes outside of a sporting event is likely familiar to many people who have read about equity in schools. University of Cincinnati business professor Craig Froehle (2016) is credited with creating the earliest depiction from which the image evolved (Interaction Institute for Social Change, 2016). (Visit https://rb.gy/x0gfh to see the image and read a blog post Froehle wrote about its reception on social media.) The image simplifies the complex phenomena that are systems of oppression and how educators can respond.

The first snapshot, which represents equality, shows each person standing on a separate box, and the shortest person is unable to see over the fence. The second snapshot, which represents equity, shows the tallest person without a box and the shortest person with two boxes. Now, all three people can see over the fence, because the tallest person did not need a box. The third snapshot, which represents liberation, removes the fence altogether, and now no person needs a box to see the game.

There are some cautions with the use of the box storyboard. For instance, the images problematize more than the fence; they problematize the people behind it. According to this panel, some people need help because they do not have the same skills, abilities, or inherent physical characteristics as other people. That sounds a lot like racism. Other questions also arise, such as the following.

- Why are some people sitting in the stands, while these people stand so far away?
- Why are the people not playing in the game?
- Which people are allowed to make the rules of the game, and which groups of people are advantaged by those rules?
- Why do the people on the outside look like stereotypical males?

The box storyboard serves as an entry-level anchor for conversations about the differences between equity and equality. Additionally, the fence straightforwardly symbolizes the policies and practices that create systems of oppression. School staffs can extend the metaphor to focus on the context surrounding the fence's construction and the controversies that could arise from its removal.

THE *GIVING TREE* PICTURE

Illustrator Tony Ruth (Maeda, 2019) modified the cover of Shel Silverstein's *The Giving Tree* to provide a pictorial representation that delves deeper into the complexity of systems of oppression. Ruth's adaptation highlights a system in need of repair. The four images illustrate how citizens can cope in a system that was designed to privilege some and disadvantage others.

1. We could stay with the status quo, allowing easy access to opportunities for some while limiting access for others (inequality).
2. We could implement colorblind standards of equality, enhancing the opportunities for the already privileged while providing limited help to others (equality).
3. We could implement equitable standards that focus on getting people what they need to survive in a system that is designed to oppress them (equity).
4. We could repair the broken system so that, by design, everyone has access to opportunities (justice).

Ruth's images go further than the box storyboard in indicating the sophistication of systemic inequities, but they—like the box storyboard—have their limits. Diversity, equity, and inclusion consultant Richard Leong (2020) posted a blog that draws attention to two major limitations.

1. The tree metaphor suggests that our inequitable system naturally occurred, as if the tree just happened to bend that way. We know our social, economic, legal, educational, and medical systems are not natural occurrences. The racial inequities we experience are not accidental; they exist by design.
2. Reconstructing systems of oppression is not as simple as putting up a couple of braces. All stakeholders have to participate in a lot of self-examination, public discourse, renouncement of privileges, and consistent effort in order to dismantle the various systems of oppression in our society.

Moreover, Ruth's images do not examine the literal or metaphoric roots of racism, classism, and other forms of oppression, or their interconnected existences. By narrowly focusing on the outer aspects of the phenomena, the images miss opportunities to extend the metaphor to include broader systems of marginalization, like the following.

- Someone comes over to "discover" that tree, thereby deserving ownership, taking half the apples, and leasing the tree to the apple pickers.
- A "leader" or group of leaders comes along to take most of the apples, requiring the pickers to share fewer apples. The leaders might also support conditions in which the pickers blame each other for the scarcity and fight among themselves.
- If either picker complains about their perceived mistreatment, perhaps law enforcement gets involved, resulting in negative outcomes for the protesting picker.

Conceptual Diagrams

If a phenomenon to be explained has multiple steps or parts, conceptual diagrams can be effective means of communication. I used the following diagrams to share my antiracist vision with my school staff during the summer of 2020.

I used figure 2.3 to justify our focus on racism and White supremacy. After discussing historical trends related to our students' achievement and disciplinary data, I asked staff to read the arrows from right to left. "If racial inequities are caused by racist policies, and racist policies are based on racism and White supremacy," I offered, "then we should spend more time fighting the disease rather than solely focusing on the symptoms." The diagram made my argument more comprehensible to everyone, even if not everyone agreed with my argument.

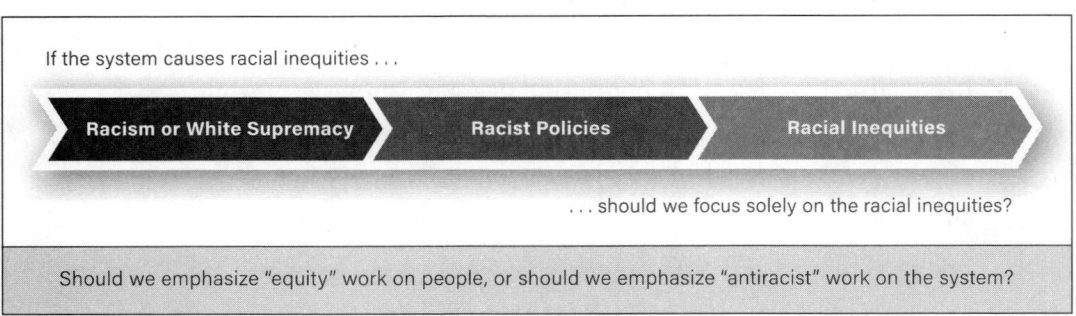

FIGURE 2.3: Racial inequities logic model.

Cast an Antiracist Vision   57

I shared figure 2.4 a few slides later, during the same presentation. I used it to illustrate my vision for our professional learning targets for the next few years. I shared the scope of what I planned for us to learn and the sequence of each major topic area. I outlined the approximate number of meetings that we would spend in each area, and I chose that particular diagram to explain how each step moved us toward our ultimate goal: the development of critically conscious students. Like the use of the arrow diagram, the step diagram was employed to ensure that everyone knew what was coming, even if they might disagree with my premise.

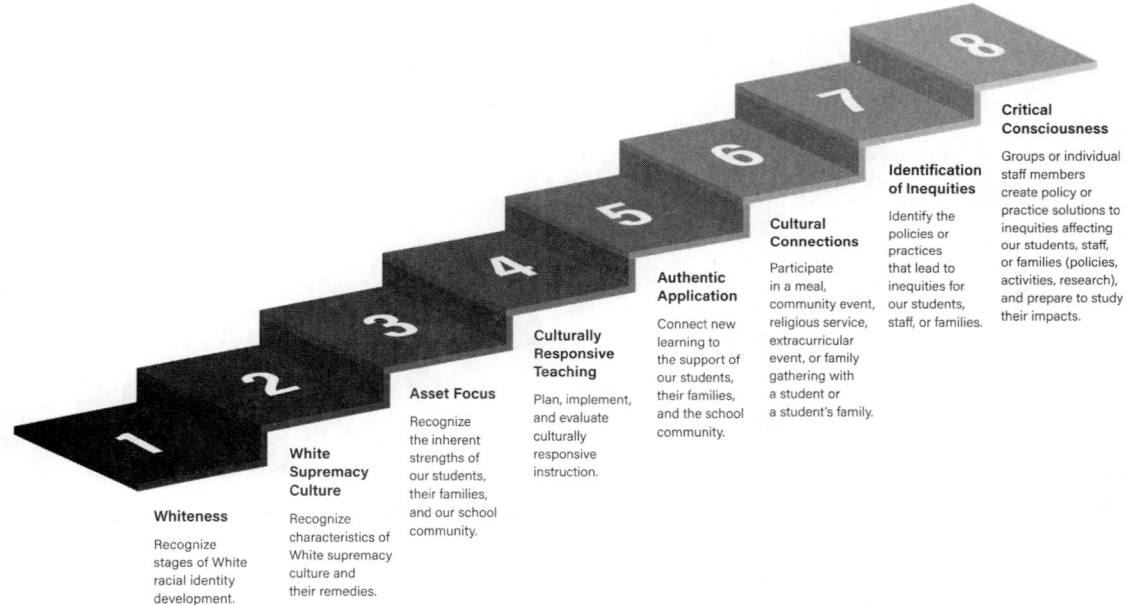

FIGURE 2.4: Professional learning progression diagram.

Digital Media

Digital media, such as video-sharing sites and social media platforms, have allowed what used to be considered isolated or lesser-known incidents to be viewed in the context of a larger web of events, which sometimes sparks or nourishes social movements (Mislán & Dache-Gerbino, 2018). In addition to connecting school staff to activities that link prevalent issues across our society, digital media can bring national or international audiences to local issues. The Arab Spring, Occupy, Make America Great Again, QAnon, and Black Lives Matter exemplify the types of movements that benefit from representation in digital media.

Antiracist school leaders can leverage digital media resources to elevate the need for antiracist work in their communities, including a specific focus on schools. This leveraging could be as simple as sharing an article via the school's social media account. It could be as complicated as supporting the production and distribution of a student-created film that raises awareness about systemic oppression. The goal is to use digital media in ways that build multidimensional flows of information between the school staff and the broader community of antiracist activists.

It is important to keep in mind that communication techniques are not quests for perfection. I point out the shortcomings in the metaphors, diagrams, and other clarity tools to underscore that there are no perfect forms of communication; there are only effective forms of communication under particular circumstances. Antiracist school leaders do not make perfect the enemy of good. All metaphors do not have to be perfect; they should add clarity. All clarification techniques do not have to be flawless; they should increase comprehension.

Your Own Visual Framework

Antiracist school leaders and rank-and-file educators are not limited to preexisting metaphors and conceptual diagrams. Perhaps they would benefit from opportunities to create their own visual frameworks. Psychologist Chen-Yao Kao (2020) has found that college students are more engaged and creative when they are asked to create their own analogies. Early childhood education expert Catherine M. Capio and colleagues' research suggests that novice young adults might grow the most from the use of analogies (Capio, Uiga, Lee, & Masters, 2020). Research scientist Peter Ondish and colleagues' (2019) study indicates that Spanish-speaking Latinx people form stronger connections to leaders who use metaphoric speech. Many supportive teachers and administrators will be at the beginning stages of their antiracist educations. Thus, using culturally connected, appealing, and clarifying visuals and stories could engender a greater, more effective commitment.

Using the form in figure 2.5, try drafting your own verbal analogy, pictorial metaphor, or conceptual diagram.

Generating innovative ideas to articulate your antiracist views can be a real challenge. It's OK to have awkward moments in collaborations with colleagues, misspeak during brainstorming conversations, scribble tough-to-decipher images on sticky notes, and use any other practices that support your imaginative process. Creative communications aren't easy for all of us. Allow yourself grace as you get started.

Framework	My Idea
Verbal analogy: Verbal analogies are helpful in adding clarity because they connect the background knowledge of the audience to unfamiliar—and sometimes uncomfortable—concepts such as antiracism. Create a verbal analogy about racism and White supremacy.	
Pictorial metaphor: Like verbal analogies, pictorial metaphors can add clarity to explanations by connecting the familiar to the unfamiliar. Pictorial metaphors add visual elements that anchor presentations and ensure that all audience members are operating with the same images in mind. Create your own pictorial metaphors about how the following concepts relate to one another. • Inequality • Equality • Equity • Justice • Broader systems of marginalization	
Conceptual diagram: If a phenomenon to be explained has multiple steps or parts, conceptual diagrams can be effective means of communication. Create a conceptual diagram that justifies your focus on racism and White supremacy or illustrates your vision for your professional learning targets.	

FIGURE 2.5: My own verbal analogy, pictorial metaphor, or conceptual diagram.

*Visit **go.SolutionTree.com/diversityandequity** for a free reproducible version of this figure.*

CREATE CRITERIA FOR LEADERSHIP DECISION MAKING

Borrowing from an existing bank of antiracist communicative practices may be helpful to those who struggle to start from scratch. Many of us prefer itemized criteria by which we can frame the choices we make as leaders and learners. Ecologists V. Bala Chaudhary and Asmeret Asefaw Berhe (2020) published an editorial titled "Ten Simple Rules for Building an Antiracist Lab." These principles target science laboratories, but they can be applied to most educational institutions. The following ten rules could be components of an antiracist vision.

1. Lead informed discussions about antiracism in your lab regularly. **School application:** Antiracist school leaders establish environments in which people feel comfortable talking about race and reporting racism at all levels.

2. Address racism in your organization's guidelines. **School application:** Antiracist school leaders encourage regular examinations of school policies, protocols, and practices to weed out those that lead to racial inequities.

3. Publish papers and write grants with BIPOC colleagues. **School application:** Antiracist school leaders collaborate with BIPOC colleagues to share antiracist information in public forums such as conferences, blog posts, interviews, and op-eds.

4. Evaluate your organization's mentoring practices. **School application:** Antiracist school leaders ensure that every staff member—with a particular focus on those from historically marginalized groups—has access to high-quality mentors within or outside of the school building.

5. Amplify the voices of BIPOC individuals in the field. **School application:** Antiracist school leaders amplify the voices of BIPOC colleagues, students, families, community members, and others in the field.

6. Support BIPOC individuals in their efforts to organize. **School application:** Antiracist school leaders support BIPOC colleagues in their efforts to organize.

7. Intentionally recruit BIPOC students and staff. **School application:** Antiracist school leaders intentionally recruit BIPOC staff and community partners.

8. Adopt a dynamic research agenda. **School application:** Antiracist school leaders encourage staff and students of color to contribute in creative, novel, and nontraditional ways.

9. Advocate for racially diverse leadership. **School application:** Antiracist school leaders advocate for racially diverse school and district leadership.

10. Hold the powerful accountable and don't expect gratitude. **School application:** Antiracist school leaders:

> recognize the difference between performative action and action that doesn't bring personal glory. We should educate ourselves on effective bystander intervention techniques for addressing issues of inequity, harassment, and discrimination. We should also be able to use accountability mechanisms in our own institutions (if we don't have them, work to set them up) and hold our colleagues and ourselves accountable for creating healthy workplace climates. (Chaudhary & Berhe, 2020, p. 7)

The lab recommendations and their corresponding school applications are potential actions that might be taken in hypothetical contexts. They are not hard-and-fast necessities for every aspiring antiracist school leader. Advanced antiracist leaders who are more stable in their roles might be able to attempt each of these guidelines simultaneously. Newer antiracist leaders—or leaders in less stable circumstances—can choose particular strategies in an à la carte fashion. Try not to be overwhelmed by the number of strategies. Like the rest of the recommendations in this book, these strategies can be viewed as an adoption of a mindset rather than an immutable adherence to a set of rules.

Marcos, the elementary school administrator introduced earlier in the chapter (page 44), explained that personal presence, relationships, and vision are necessary—but insufficient—elements of antiracist school leadership. He described to me an important understanding that he gained early on in his work with staff:

> I am confident in my leadership. I have spent years cultivating relationships, deepening my learning, and improving my craft. Casting an antiracist vision is proving to be more challenging. It is difficult to enact change when it is not curriculum, pedagogy, or even becoming culturally proficient. Becoming antiracist is everyday work. It is being committed to challenging ourselves and confronting our biases. In fact, the first step is acknowledging our biases. Diving into this work can be unsettling for some people. Changing mindsets takes time and effort. You are challenging people's long-held beliefs and core values. That is the challenge of this work. (Personal communication, February 12, 2021)

As Marcos's statements suggest, antiracist school leaders, despite their vision and charisma, cannot by themselves move a building full of educators and students. Identifying, disrupting, and reconstructing systems of oppression is a heavy lift, and not even the most dynamic visionary can accomplish this task alone. The good news is that antiracist school leaders rarely operate in isolation. There are usually people on staff who share the commitment to examining themselves and the systems they support. Some call those people "allies," Bettina Love (2019) calls those people "coconspirators," and Dolly Chugh (2018) calls those people "builders."

CULTIVATE A COMMUNITY OF BUILDERS

A focus on equal rights and access is not sufficient to transform societies. There is often a racial backlash to social justice campaigns, as members of historically dominant groups resist potential loss of status. Across the Western Hemisphere, Black and Indigenous rights discussions have led to a consolidation of power and partnership among groups who, on the surface, do not fight racial fights, such as religious groups and groups that want national security. This emphasizes the need for partnerships among antiracist stakeholders who can help you cast your antiracist vision.

Perceptive school leaders differentiate between key types of supportive partners, such as *allies*, *volunteers*, *coconspirators*, and *builders*.

- Allies are advocates for friends of color and racial equality (Fingerhut & Hardy, 2020).
- Volunteers are people who sustain their efforts to organize in ways that benefit people who might be strangers (Fingerhut & Hardy, 2020).
- Builders, according to Dolly Chugh (2018), are people who accept that they have biases and that systemic biases have implications across all sectors in our society.
- Coconspirators, as defined by Bettina Love (2019), collaborate in ways that reconstruct the current status quo, even if it means giving up their own privilege.

While important partners might exist outside of the school building, such as nonprofit organizations and universities, teachers are key partners, so antiracist leaders must analyze their staff to consider which partnership levels their teachers each occupy and how teachers might be moved into progressive levels. The following vignette describes conversations among a group of builders who emerged from my staff after I shared my antiracist vision. We developed a plan that allowed them to lean into their personal missions, provide professional development opportunities for our staff, and directly support some high school students in our school district (Harris, n.d.). An idea for a book study began to circulate among several of the teachers at my school. They considered eliminating our school's academic content committees, which would allow us to sharpen our focus on a book study related to antiracism. The following was my reply.

> Hey team,
>
> I'm encouraged by your enthusiasm. Everyone will be doing antiracist work, and I'm cool with book studies. This is not a one-year type of plan. We will need a three-to-five-year plan. There are scores of books and hundreds of articles that would benefit our staff and, therefore, our students. We'll likely engage with pieces of different texts throughout this year to take people on a journey through understanding their racial identities to recognizing the impacts of racist/White supremacist policies on our beliefs. One of my target outcomes for our staff will be for each person to identify an inequity in our building, community, and/or district. The next step will be to develop and implement a plan to interrupt the inequity and measure the impact of the plan. We'll be looking to change practices and policies, in addition to hearts and minds. We'll need to keep in mind that antiracist work can come in many forms, at least according to Ibram X. Kendi, one of the hot names right now. We'll also consider intersectionality and other forms of discrimination.
>
> I don't agree with the wholesale replacement of our content focuses. Instruction should also be an antiracist practice, so we should blend those concepts. Additionally, it will be our first year with [a new ELA curriculum] and second with [a new mathematics curriculum]; we'll also need some of the basics for each program. However, those learning spaces might take place during staff meetings. We're also going to need to have math and reading nights in the fall to support families with the new form of school, so we'll need committee work on that.
>
> In terms of how it will look, I'm still thinking. We'll likely use seventy-five minutes in our staff meetings twice each month, with twenty to forty minutes on antiracism in some fashion. So, the staff will get a "core curriculum," so to speak. I plan to have a supplemental list of resources that people can read and/or watch in between our meetings. Perhaps you could each lead book studies with different texts, and we could spend time at some staff meetings comparing the concepts. If we used four books [school leadership teams], each person in

> each grade level (mostly) could read a different text, which would color the conversations in planning meetings.
>
> With that said, I'm open to your ideas.

The teachers and I met during the following summer to brainstorm potential initiatives that they could spearhead. We decided to create a partnership with our school district's Minority Scholars Program, a group led by high school students of color who fight to reduce the opportunity gap. Members of the Minority Scholars Program created a student speakers series through which high school students led quarterly workshops for our staff on the topic of microaggressions. The students helped us to see microaggressions from a high schooler's perspective. The conversations were revelatory for our staff members. Students shared firsthand accounts of harmful interactions with staff and students, many of which would have seemed benign to inexperienced observers. Those students' stories educated and motivated my staff in ways that helped staff members push through more challenging aspects of our journey. The students touched on emotional chords and explained impacts that were hard to deny.

In this story, my leaders—adults and students—were builders. They identified injustice, recognized the role that they and their peers played in supporting injustice, and took action to combat the injustice. An assumption of this book is that builders like these are present in every school building; sometimes, they just need guidance and acceptance from a leader.

CONCLUSION

Throughout the course of this chapter, you've learned the importance of evaluating your school's or district's leaders and systems, not just the students and their families. I encouraged you to collaborate with your trusted team members and representative stakeholders to develop a collective vision for your antiracist work.

At some point, you'll need to publicly declare the intent of your efforts. Prior to that, you should consider some anticipatory talking points for each stakeholder group so that you take everyone's views into account. A subsequent step is to draft an open letter, email, blog post, or web posting that incorporates talking points and lays out your early thoughts about your end goals. In the opening declaration and subsequent interactions with your community, be sure to use accurate vocabulary, including definitions that you clearly understand.

You should also leverage the use of storytelling and visuals that enhance the comprehensibility of your major communications. Verbal analogies that connect antiracist ideas to concepts that are familiar to your stakeholders are strategic tools. Pictorial metaphors and conceptual diagrams are also helpful in communicating where you are and where you want to go. Analogies and metaphors, like the ones presented in this chapter, are available, but the most influential tools might be the ones you create to suit your context. You and your team know what elements of your culture could be effectively symbolized and leveraged for outreach.

Begin to cultivate a community of builders, people who recognize that our personal biases—along with systemic biases—influence teaching, learning, and everything else in school buildings. They will help you shape your vision, craft professional learning activities, and manage the resistance that is surely headed your way.

This chapter has prepared you to articulate your vision to your potential builders and everyone else on your team. In the following chapters, you'll learn how to develop professional learning activities, embrace resistance to the work, advocate for what's important, and determine ways to evaluate the impact of your efforts.

APPLY YOUR LEARNING

Now that you have a sense of how you can share your antiracist vision with your school community, here are a few next steps you can implement to demonstrate your progress to yourself and others. Some of these items might seem like steps too far in your development, or you might outright disagree with their application. Share your ideas with colleagues or friends who would engage in honest conversations about your views on each item, and about how the items could affect your educational philosophy.

 **KNOW**

- Know your broad vision for what antiracism should (or will) manifest in your school.
- Be able to explain key concepts and definitions in your own words (see figure 2.2, page 51).
- Know the stakeholders who need to know your vision, and consider efficient ways to share your vision statement with each subgroup.

 SAY

- Make a public declaration of intent using your antiracist vision statement for your school.
- Share customized versions of your vision with key stakeholder groups.
- Communicate to your students' caregivers, "Our antiracist work will not distract from the high standards we hold for your children. Antiracism will make us better instructors as well as better citizens. That can only help our students."

 DO

- Draft your own verbal analogy, pictorial metaphor, or conceptual diagram related to your thoughts about antiracism (see figure 2.5, page 59).
- Brainstorm a list of talking points that should resonate with each subgroup of stakeholders (see table 2.1, page 46).

Chapter 3

PLAN PROFESSIONAL LEARNING EXPERIENCES

Key Vocabulary

backward design	Deconstruction of learning objectives at each level of a learning progression to determine the prerequisite knowledge and skills necessary to engage in the learning. Those prerequisite elements become the objectives of the prior level of the progression, and the planners repeat the protocol until the prerequisite knowledge and skills reflect the current school context (Bowen, 2017).

critical consciousness	One's understanding that systems of oppression are effectively resisted when marginalized populations recognize inequities, can reconstruct the systems, and are motivated to make use of their knowledge and skills to force change.
critical Whiteness	A thoughtful interrogation of Whiteness's impact on social contexts.
cultural proficiency	An understanding of one's own identity, others' identities, and the ways cultural lenses impact teaching and learning.
professional learning progression	A step-by-step set of learning targets that build on each other to move staff from their current levels of knowledge and skills to desired levels of knowledge and skills (Jin, Mikeska, Hokayem, & Mavronikolas, 2019).
racial identity	A social perspective about group patterns, physical characteristics, sociocultural patterns, racialized group interactions, and one's place in a racialized society (Mims & Williams, 2020; Syed, Juang, & Svensson, 2018).
sociopolitical development	Understanding of the forces that affect society, with a particular focus on groups that exist toward the low end of the power spectrum, those who occupy lower castes (Zion, Allen, & Jean, 2015).

chools are places where White supremacy exists, just like many other places in society, and schools reinforce White supremacy culture through their racially disparate outcomes. Despite the existence of consistent demographic

hierarchies, there remain those who say that a focus on racism is unnecessary and divisive (Matias, Henry, & Darland, 2017). Without an explicit focus on antiracism, some schools' missions emphasize factors such as individual responsibility as the primary determinants of our societal status quo, without noting the systemic inequities that have been more determinant in our current demographic hierarchies (Zion et al., 2015). Antiracist school leaders keep the spotlight on the policies and practices, undergirded by racism, that foster racial disparities. Moreover, antiracist leaders oversee the development of professional learning progressions that build the capacity and motivation of their staffs to create personal and systemic change.

Antiracist education builds critical consciousness by treating schools as places where stakeholders learn how to challenge the institutional status quo in systems that reach beyond the walls of the school building. Antiracist educators are not looking to symbolically fit students into the existing school and societal frameworks. Antiracist educators expose the White supremacy culture that undergirds the construction of said frameworks, demand the reconstruction of those systems, and teach their students to do the same.

This chapter points out that if the critical consciousness of students is the goal, then critical consciousness of staff is necessary. You will learn how to plan learning experiences that backward-map to create goals, strategies, activities, and milestones that shepherd learners toward critical consciousness (Wiggins & McTighe, 2005). This chapter will also lay out options for developing assessments and monitoring tools.

This chapter emphasizes the need for a strategic focus on the impacts of racism and White supremacy that forces learners to interrogate their own perspectives and engage with the perspectives of others (Matias et al., 2017). You will read peer-reviewed research that encourages the use of a variety of media, texts, and symbols that elicit emotional responses as well as represent stories that are counter to race-based stereotypes (Matias & Mackey, 2016).

CENTER LEARNING PROGRESSIONS

A learning progression is a thoughtfully crafted sequence of steps designed to enhance a learner's knowledge, skills, and beliefs (Jin et al., 2019). Each new piece of content knowledge or skill builds on the previous piece in the progression. There is not one correct way to draft a learning progression. Learning progressions can be composed by one person, they can be cocreated by a pair or group of people, or they can be modifications of previously existing learning progressions.

In schools, learning progressions typically target the knowledge and skills of the students. In student learning progressions, the goal is usually mastery of one step prior to moving toward the next step. The parts of the progression serve as interconnected pieces of the curricular puzzle. The more knowledge and skills gained with each step, the more the larger enduring understandings come into focus.

Professional learning progressions are based on a similar premise to student learning progressions. The leaders of a school staff set knowledge or skill targets based on the mission, vision, and values of the school. In any given year, a school could have multiple professional learning progressions, each of which focuses on a significant strand of a variety of growth needs. For instance, one school might have a learning progression focused on elements of mathematics instruction, a learning progression dedicated to supporting social-emotional learning, and a learning progression centered on concepts related to new science standards. However, it is rare to come across schools that have professional learning progressions centered on antiracist pedagogy, a topic whose significance is overlooked in numerous institutions of learning—hence the composition of this book.

Follow the Steps of the Professional Learning Progression

The three steps to creating a professional learning progression are as follows.

1. **List broad concepts and skills:** The creation of a professional learning progression aligns with Stephen Covey's (2020) second habit of highly effective people—*begin with the end in mind*. Antiracist school leaders consider how their current school contexts relate to their desired states (that is, their antiracist school visions). The school leaders then mentally or physically list the knowledge, skills, and beliefs that are necessary for the staff to help realize the antiracist school vision of the leader.

   This is the time for broad concepts and skills. Detailed plans of action come later in the process. Think about the progression like the story arc of a television series. Each school year is a season, and each staff, student, or community learning session is an episode. When planning the series, the writer does not need to include detailed scenes and dialogue; they just have to have a vision regarding the storylines and major events that will transpire throughout the life of the series, which are rooted in the climax of the season or series.

Professional learning progressions are the storylines and major events that take place throughout the learning, which are rooted in the antiracist vision of the school leader.

In order for students to achieve critical consciousness, they need to be taught by critical pedagogues. Therefore, a one- or two-year professional learning progression, in this case, could target critical consciousness among the staff.

2. **Implement backward design:** Next is the implementation of what Grant Wiggins and Jay McTighe (Bowen, 2017) describe as *backward design*, during which planners deconstruct the objectives of each level of the progression to determine the prerequisite knowledge and skills necessary to engage in the learning. Those prerequisite elements become the objectives of the prior level of the progression, and the planners repeat the protocol until the prerequisite knowledge and skills reflect the current school context.

3. **Determine optional versus essential content:** While professional learning progressions are laid out in a linear fashion, antiracist school leaders do not have to rigidly adhere to each element of the progression, much like a classroom teacher does not have to adhere to every element of a structured curriculum. In some cases, antiracist school leaders might set up learning modules or pathways that staff members have options to explore independently, such as history lessons related to various civil rights movements. Other content may be deemed essential content in which all staff members must engage, such as racial identity development and an interrogation of personal cultural traits and values. Antiracist school leaders have discretion in determining which content and activities are required to orient the staff toward the ultimate vision and motivate them to travel the path.

When casting my antiracist school vision to my staff, I included a possible learning progression in my presentation. The sample professional learning progression in figure 3.1 (page 72) is based on the antiracist school vision shared in the previous chapter (page 57). The vision targets the critical consciousness of students, meaning students can recognize policies and practices that lead to inequities, they have the skills to redress those policies and practices, and they are motivated to take action. The long-range target is placed at the bottom of this figure, but it was at the top of my thinking. I envisioned how students' critical consciousness could

Three-year goal (June 2023): Students will develop, implement, and evaluate solutions to inequities affecting themselves and their communities (critical consciousness).

Two-year goal (June 2022): Staff will develop, implement, and evaluate policy and/or practice solutions to inequities affecting our students, staff, and/or families.

One-year goal (June 2021): Staff will develop, implement, and evaluate culturally responsive practices that support all areas of school, such as instruction, assessment, relationship building, discipline, and parent engagement.

School staff will be able to:

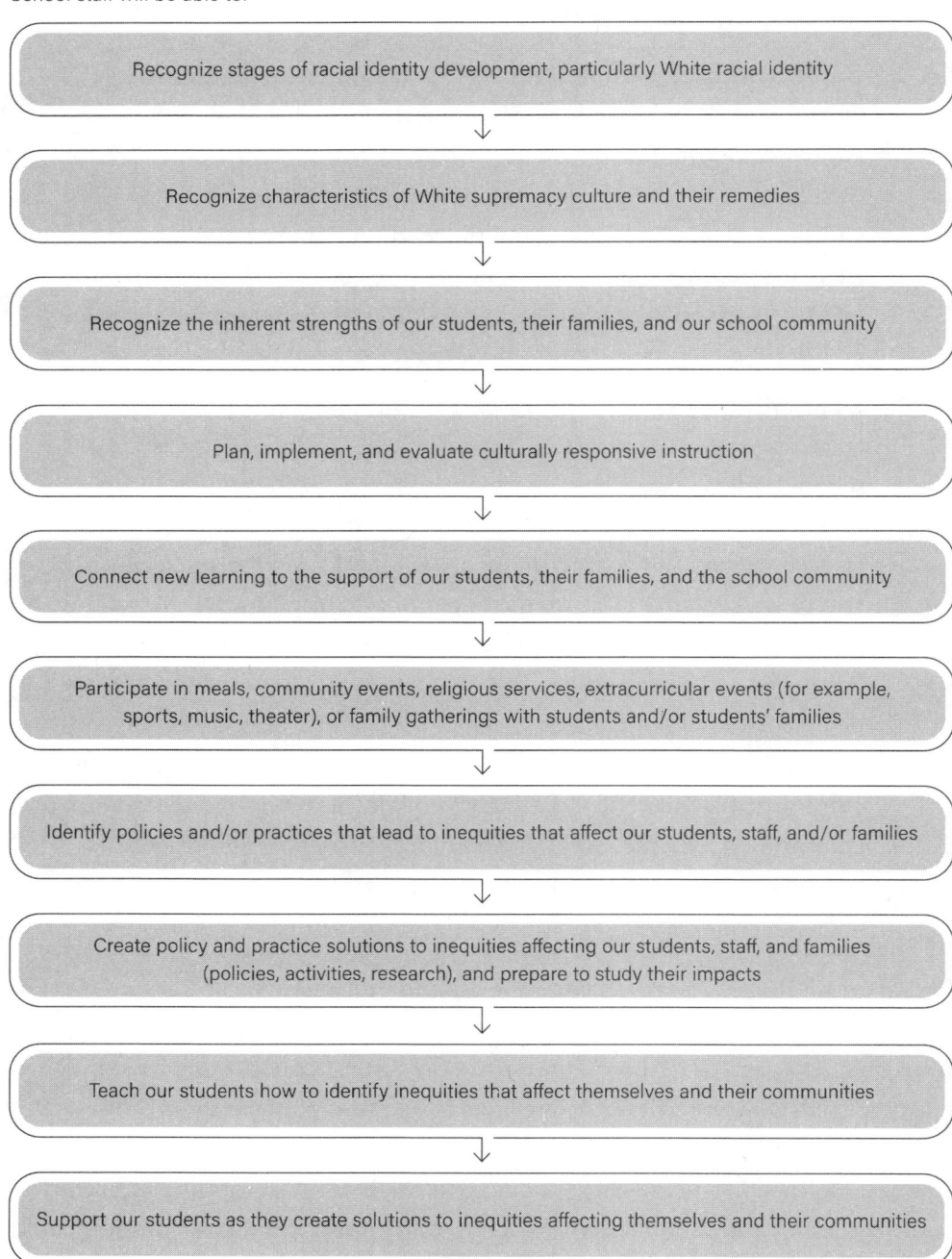

FIGURE 3.1: Antiracist professional learning progression, 2020–2023.

look, and then I listed prerequisite knowledge and skills, which are listed in the space second from the bottom. I continued to list prerequisite knowledge and skills for each step until I reached the point where my staff possessed the knowledge and skills necessary to take the next step.

Create Psychological Safety

Great educators of all kinds, including antiracist school leaders, prioritize the development of psychological safety within the learning environment. They spend time establishing norms for conversations to prepare learners for future discussions that might elicit discomfort or strong emotional reactions. In *Courageous Conversations About Race: A Field Guide for Achieving Equity in Schools*, Glenn E. Singleton (2015) presents four agreements that he recommends for the start of racial equity conversations.

1. Stay engaged.
2. Experience discomfort.
3. Speak your truth.
4. Expect and accept non-closure.

Committing to agreements like these during the early parts of the professional learning progression builds camaraderie on which colleagues will draw as they exhibit vulnerability and hold each other accountable during more challenging activities down the road. Effective antiracist professional learning progressions build in early opportunities for staff members to bond as they get to know each other through low-risk activities, such as sharing aspects of themselves and their families.

DEVELOP CONTENT FOR LEARNING PROGRESSIONS

This is the time when you must ask yourself, What content should be considered for inclusion in antiracist professional development progressions? With professional learning in schools, like instructional standards for students, leaders tend to set targets that move from the known to the unknown, from the familiar to the unfamiliar. Antiracism content is slightly different because it often attempts achievement metrics that have indicated racial disparities for centuries. Antiracist school leaders ask staff to *reconsider* their beliefs about the nature and causes of those disparities. In another example, we know students of color are more likely to be disciplined for the dress code violation of wearing a hat in school (Morris, 2018). Antiracist school staffs examine the cultural significance of wearing headwear indoors, for both staff and students.

Chart a Path Toward Sociopolitical Development

The ultimate target of antiracist professional learning progressions is the critical consciousness of students. Sociopolitical development is a precursor to critical consciousness. It is about recognizing the forces that shape a society. It is about who is in power, whose narrative is canon, whose cultures are deemed mainstream, and how those power dynamics came to be. Conversely, sociopolitical development is also about understanding which groups exist toward the low end of the power spectrum, those who occupy lower castes (Zion et al., 2015).

Teachers who overtly buy into antiracist professional learning often view themselves as "not racist," or without prejudice, but they usually enter the learning with "internalized ideologies that justify the racial status quo, devalue cultural diversity, and fail to account for White people's beliefs and attitudes that have long justified societal oppression and inequity" (Zion et al., 2015, p. 919). Sociopolitical development helps White teachers view themselves, schools, and society through a racialized lens (Zion et al., 2015). Sociopolitical development requires educators to identify and take action against local systems of injustice. After all:

> if students are to develop the skills, mindsets, and ability to act against oppression, then educators must have the support and opportunities to learn and practice acting as agents of change against oppression in the educational system. . . . In order to cultivate those attributes in their students, educators must have the opportunity to reflect critically on their own thoughts and practices as well. (Zion et al., 2015, p. 915)

Sociopolitical development also targets the growth of students. Students are significantly impacted by a system that creates discrepancies in academic attainment that can be seen in graduation rates, test scores, discipline, and identification for special education. They should be empowered through schooling, and perspectives of who has power in schools and whose cultures are centered should be challenged (Zion et al., 2015).

One way to support the sociopolitical development of educators is to present small groups with opportunities to read current paper or online news articles that reflect mainstream values and a traditional power structure. Facilitators can ask questions that push participants to connect with notions of roles that people of various races should have in our society. Considering the races of the authors or people quoted, how people of different races are depicted, or how the systemic power structure is more or less apparent will ground conversations in authentic views of humanity, be they in schools or otherwise.

Target Critical Consciousness

We want students and staff to be aware of the inequities that stem from racist policies and practices. But what good is awareness if students and staff do not have the knowledge, skills, or motivation to change the system? Change is the goal, and critical consciousness is an effective mechanism.

Critical consciousness is a concept that was introduced by educator and philosopher Paulo Freire (1970) in the 1970s. Freire opined that systems of oppression are effectively resisted when marginalized populations recognize inequities, can reconstruct the systems, and are motivated to make use of their knowledge and skills to force change. Within a school context, the most marginalized groups are our students of color, English learners, and students in poverty (Nieto, 2008). Therefore, the critical consciousness of students should be the ultimate target, despite the grade level. The critical consciousness of students is a worthy goal. However, developing the critical consciousness of students requires the critical consciousness of teachers. Most educator preparation programs do not require future teachers to engage in antiracist concepts, so antiracist school leaders should first target the professional learning of their staff members.

Researchers have shown how schools can use multiple strategies to develop the critical consciousness of students. For instance, schools can create a climate that focuses on inclusiveness and social justice, community engagement, and social-emotional functioning (Heberle et al., 2020). Additionally, schools can provide opportunities for students to discuss current events, their experiences with racism, and their intersectional identities to support critical consciousness (El-Amin et al., 2017; Mosley et al., 2021). Table 3.1 (page 76) shares a few examples of how to create this climate and these opportunities in your institution.

EVALUATE YOUR ANTIRACIST PRACTICES

Dr. Alana Murray, a friend and colleague of mine, co-taught a graduate course that taught participants how to conduct research to evaluate their antiracist practices. During our semester together, from February to May 2020, we exchanged numerous thoughts about all things antiracism, especially how to create learning progressions that would resonate with our staffs. At the time, she was a middle school principal, and she talked to me about how she developed and shared a professional learning progression with her staff.

TABLE 3.1: Goals and Actions for Developing Students' Critical Consciousness

GOAL	ACTIONS
Create a school climate that focuses on inclusiveness and social justice.	Sponsor student clubs that target social justice learning and actions. Include social justice goals and metrics in your school-improvement plan.
Create a school climate that focuses on community engagement.	Create a team of staff who focus on creating, maintaining, and evaluating partnerships with stakeholders outside of the school building. Regularly convene a roundtable of community members who represent various stakeholder groups (for example, caregivers, business owners, religious leaders, nonprofit representatives, and politicians).
Create a school climate that focuses on social-emotional functioning.	Establish staff positions, request central office supports, or use contractors that support student and staff well-being (for example, mental health, physical activity, trauma-informed practices, and community celebrations). Require instructional practices that incorporate mindfulness, collaboration, and physical activity.
Provide opportunities for students to discuss current events, their experiences with racism, and their intersectional identities to support critical consciousness.	Establish the practice of class meetings, during which students can reflect on current events and share their experiences via a structured conversation protocol.

Dr. Alana Murray is the principal of Shady Grove Middle School in Gaithersburg, Maryland, and author of *The Development of the Alternative Black Curriculum, 1890–1940: Countering the Master Narrative* (2019). She is also the cofounder and co-coordinator of McDaniel College's Equity and Excellence in Education (EEE) program. EEE is a master's degree or certificate sequence of courses that requires participants to use the antiracist knowledge and skills gained through coursework to document their impact on social justice causes in their schools, districts, or surrounding communities. Program completion certifies participants' critical consciousness because it confirms their understanding of issues related to racism and White supremacy culture, reflects their examination of racial and ethnic disparities in their schools and communities, and details their implementation of interventions designed to interrupt systems of oppression.

Dr. Murray discovered the need for the antiracist pedagogy during the first fourteen years of her teaching career, despite an "educator preparation [that lacked] a sufficient introduction to equity issues," and she wanted to be "more responsive to the diverse students that [she] served" (personal communication, July 24, 2023). She shared her thoughts with her local teachers' union and coedited *Putting the Movement Back Into Civil Rights Teaching* (Menkart, Murray, & View, 2004). The teachers' union asked her to develop an equity training program for teachers, and Dr. Murray enthusiastically agreed.

When she planned the arc of learning and activity necessary for educators to gain critical consciousness, she took a collaborative approach. She consulted the leads of her district's equity office, the teachers' union, contacts at McDaniel College, and her other cofounder and co-coordinator, Dr. Heather Yuhaniak. Dr. Murray says that the wide range of experience and expertise resulted in a "more thoughtful multicultural, antiracist, and culturally responsive approach to thinking about closing the opportunity gap in [her school district]" (personal communication, July 24, 2023).

Dr. Murray lets students lead the way with her professional learning progression targets. She says, "I usually speak to my students to determine what my staff needs. Students are honest and they share what they feel the adults in their lives (including me) need to do to give them the best environment" (personal communication, July 24, 2023). Students are also the primary arbiters of the professional learning progression's impact on the staff. Dr. Murray says, "I measured the impact of my professional learning activities with my staff having greater efficacy in adjusting lessons to meet the needs of our students. Our staff's critical reflection should lead to better relationships with students and a more enriched narrative to teach our students" (personal communication, July 24, 2023). The following section dives deeper into evaluating the impact of professional learning activities.

MEASURE THE IMPACT OF PROFESSIONAL LEARNING PROGRESSIONS

Irrespective of the choices between optional and essential subject matter, antiracist school leaders monitor the impact of all professional learning activities. Therefore, learning progressions incorporate milestones of performance at regular intervals. Benchmarks could focus on the sentiments or behaviors of the staff, but some benchmarks must concentrate on students. Educational consultant Thomas R. Guskey (2016) devised a straightforward stratification of five types of professional learning measures.

- **Level 1:** Participants' reactions
- **Level 2:** Participants' learning
- **Level 3:** Organizational support and change
- **Level 4:** Participants' use of new knowledge and skills
- **Level 5:** Student learning outcomes

Guskey's levels progress in complexity and importance, with the lowest level centered on self-reports from the staff and the ultimate stage highlighting outcomes for students.

1. **Participants' reactions:** The first level of assessment, *participants' reactions*, represents the baseline of evaluation. Level 1 asks how staff members feel about the professional development experiences. Soliciting the sentiments of participants is usually a simple process through which facilitators can find out basic information such as, "Do you feel that the outcomes were relevant to your work?" Guskey (2016) also suggests that leaders ask about the physical location of the learning with questions like, "Was the room the right temperature?" or "Were the chairs comfortable?" (p. 32).

   The simplistic quality of information gathered at level 1 can cause some leaders to undervalue collecting these data. To the critics of this level of evaluation, Guskey (2016) offers this reply:

   > Some educators refer to these measures of participants' reactions as "happiness quotients," insisting that they reveal only the entertainment value of an experience or activity, not its quality or worth. But measuring participants' initial satisfaction provides data that can help improve the design and facilitation of professional learning in valid ways. In addition, positive reactions from participants are usually a necessary prerequisite to higher-level evaluation results. (p. 33)

2. **Participants' learning:** The second level of measurement, *participants' learning*, "focuses on measuring the new knowledge, skills, and perhaps attitudes or dispositions that participants gain" (Guskey, 2016, p. 34). At this stage, the leader takes a step beyond

whether participants enjoyed the experience, seeking to find the value that was added to each individual. Because the outcomes are generally determined in advance of meetings, Guskey suggests that facilitators develop criteria that indicate attainment of the outcomes in advance of meetings as well.

The first two levels of evaluation can take place during and immediately following professional learning activities. They essentially ask the participants how they feel about the professional development that occurred as well as what knowledge they gained. Likert-style surveys, multiple-choice items, open-ended written responses, observations of participation, and verbal statements during or after the event could be used to assess staff members' learning and personal feelings about activities.

3. **Organizational support and change:** The third level of measurement represents the transition from a focus on the individual to a consideration of the collective. At this level, staff indicate how the professional learning experiences support the creation or modification of systems that align with the staff's antiracist school vision. The staff consider how building or district policies (for example, policies on planning, instruction, discipline, academic tracking, relationship building, and mental health) promote or constrict practices that reduce racial disparities among students and staff. Guskey recommends methods such as questionnaires, document reviews like meeting minutes, and structured interviews to assess levels of organizational support and change. At an antiracist school, a level 3 assessment could involve an audit of school policies and practices. School staff could compare past practices to current practices as one method to measure systemic change.

4. **Participants' use of new knowledge and skills:** Changes in practices are also measured through Guskey's fourth level of assessment, *participants' use of new knowledge and skills*. Level 4 requires the collection and analysis of data captured a significant amount of time after the professional development activities. Educators need time to learn new knowledge and practice new skills before being evaluated. Leaders might establish a practice-feedback-practice loop that measures key indicators of knowledge

and skills at multiple points throughout the school year, because growth could ebb and flow over the course of several months or years. Observations, interviews, questionnaires, and portfolios can all be effective ways to measure level 4 effects, according to Guskey. Antiracist schools could develop a peer observation protocol to look for key instructional indicators (for example, wait time, calling patterns, questioning practices, and feedback delivery) as a form of level 4 assessment.

5. **Student learning outcomes:** The final level of assessment, *student learning outcomes*, lies at the heart of all schools. The purpose of adults' growth in schools is to affect children's growth in schools. Schools have been measuring student performance since their beginning. Antiracist schools attempt to connect student outcomes to professional learning about antiracism. Guskey (2016) warns against relying on a standardized test score to be the sole gauge of student learning; instead, he says evaluators should examine "multiple measures of student learning" and "multiple sources of evidence" (p. 35). Social-emotional learning and mental health indicators are also considered student learning outcomes, in Guskey's opinion.

FACILITATE CONNECTIONS IN YOUR COMMUNITY

The bonds built through shared experiences and consistent agreements are critical in cultivating a community of care and connection. There is evidence that feeling emotionally connected to peers increases the likelihood that all members of the group will wade into uncomfortable discussions and empathize with colleagues, through whose cultural lenses they can more easily recognize systems of oppression and privilege (Ohito, 2019).

Building trust also includes the public acknowledgment of the degree of difficulty related to the topic of antiracism. Antiracist school leaders foreshadow the challenges ahead. Leaders do not expect the path to be a simple journey. In fact, they don't shy away from uncomfortable emotions related to discussions about racism and White supremacy to avoid the topics. Facilitators should be prepared to manage emotional deflections like crying or verbal dismissals (Matias et al., 2017). The first time the group broaches some topics might be the first time some staff members have ever considered those topics, which can trigger latent feelings such as anger or guilt. Educators should be prepared for the sensitive and potentially triggering content of antiracist professional learning (Matias & Mackey, 2016). Skilled leaders set the stage for thorny issues that will inevitably arise in this arena.

Strengthen the Facilitator's Toolbox

Professional learning about antiracism takes a tactful leader, so antiracist school leaders must acquire and develop social skills for understanding, defusing, and redirecting the emotions of individual members of their cohort. I call these tenets of emotional intelligence and responsiveness the *facilitator's toolbox*. Understanding the content is paramount, and recognizing their own emotional triggers is almost as important. Leaders also need to be ready to employ traditional facilitator strategies such as the use of humor, active listening, and verbal redirection.

Educational leadership expert Randall Lindsey and his team (2019) describe antiracist work as:

> not the kind of work that can be done well from a script or from an inauthentic place. Know your material so well that you have information, answers, and anecdotes that are not part of your lesson plan, which you can use as needed and appropriate. (p. 184)

This does not mean that antiracist school leaders are expected to be preeminent experts on the subject matter; however, their levels of knowledge are clear indicators of commitment to the work. Knowledge is necessary, but insufficient on its own. True authenticity shines through when leaders are knowledgeable, committed, and open minded. The following are some examples of the kinds of emotional tools a facilitator should work to develop.

- **Awareness of emotional triggers:** Skilled facilitators of antiracist content must also be aware of their emotional triggers and how those affect the interplay between them and their learners. The occasional teardrop or intense verbal exchange can be useful in creating a sense of urgency about important topics. The occasional sobbing emotional breakdown, personal insult, or physical altercation is extremely counterproductive. Conversations about racism and White supremacy culture touch emotional chords that are central to our personal identities. Antiracist school leaders are aware of topics or lines of thought that trigger intense emotional responses within themselves, and they learn about those same triggers among their staffs.

- **Humor:** Not all emotional reactions are negative. Laughter can be a sign of positive feelings connected to the humor of a leader or a group of learners. Facilitators can use "humor to tear through tension that arises in uncomfortable conversations, with the understanding that laughter is an embodied expression of a slew of feelings" (Ohito, 2019, p. 139). "Laughter can be an audible reminder that under the crushing confines of racial oppression, it is possible—necessary even—to feel more than pain" (Ohito, 2019, p. 139). There is an art to deciding how long and how often to let learners sit in their discomfort and when to reduce the tension in the room with a funny facial expression, perception, or anecdote associated with the subject matter.

- **Validation or redirection:** There is also a necessary balance between leaning into listening when learners need to be validated and redirecting when learners try to avoid deeply considering topics that challenge their values and beliefs. Building community through shared activities makes striking that balance easier. Growth through these collective experiences is a collaboration between the facilitator and the members of the group, and members from all sides come with nuanced perspectives that sometimes need to be acknowledged and other times need to be challenged (Ohito, 2019).

Prioritize Opportunities for Group Conversations *and* Personal Reflections

Conversations about racism and White supremacy often question the core values of the discussion's participants. Core values are central to each person's identity. So, when a meeting facilitator requires people to interrogate their personal values, the meeting participants can feel personally attacked by the facilitator. Since antiracist school leaders typically build professional learning into group settings, such as staff meetings, perceived personal attacks in public settings can amplify the emotional rigor of professional development activities.

Discussion or reflection group size should be inversely related to how intensely an activity asks staff members to interrogate aspects of their core identities. Highly challenging activities require smaller group sizes, at least during the initial phases of reflection. Leadervation Learning president Vernita Mayfield (2020) articulates it this way:

> It is absolutely vital to provide time for rich discussions. Some are more appropriate in partners. In some cases, small-group discussions are recommended, and in others whole-group discussions are suggested. I make this distinction based on the nature of the questions. Questions that are more personal are likely facilitated in pairs or small groups where people can connect more intimately. (p. 61)

Varying group sizes means that sometimes staff members will reflect individually. It is important to build opportunities for self-reflection into antiracist educator training because it supports the self-examination of personal biases (Gorski & Dalton, 2020; Matias & Mackey, 2016). Antiracist professional learning action plans offer chances to journal in paper or electronic logs, write in responses to structured questions, or simply sit quietly and think in response to new learning. Educators' self-reflections are important steps toward more regularly implementing antiracist practices (Alaca & Pyle, 2018).

> **Antiracist school leaders must carefully consider the level of intimacy needed to support the learning of staff members involved in activities.**

While personal changes can occur in isolation, systemic policy and practice changes require group exchanges of ideas. A strategic focus on the impacts of racism and White supremacy forces learners to interrogate their own perspectives and engage with the perspectives of others (Matias et al., 2017). Professor of education Shelley Zion, educator Carrie D. Allen, and educator Christina Jean (2015) created a yearlong professional learning progression oriented toward critical consciousness through what they describe as *critical civic inquiry* (*CCI*). Here is how they explain the variety of individual and group structures for learning that occurred in their exploratory study:

> [The course] guided teachers through a combination of trainings, readings, peer discussions, and teaching observations. Teachers completed an autobiography of themselves in relation to privileged or oppressed identity groups to which they belonged, a curricular unit that integrated CCI activities with their course content and facilitated an action research project that is documented through field notes, reflections, and student artifacts. (Zion et al., 2015, p. 916)

Complementing group discussion structures with personal reflection opportunities may not always seem like an easy balance to strike, but it is essential to optimizing the growth of inexperienced antiracist educators. Creating opportunities for staff members to converse with peers about the content is critical, and those types of conversations are unusual for many staff members. Therefore, antiracist school leaders must build the capacity of staff members to engage in these conversations (Singleton, 2015; Zion et al., 2015). Capacity can be built through engagement with incremental levels of content intensity and gradual steps toward the public interrogation of one's core cultural values.

For example, Buffalo State University associate professor Jennifer Ryan-Bryant (2018) taught a course about the literature of lynching, an emotionally charged subject. She supported her students through gradual steps of intensity and conversation, and she encouraged learners in the class—herself included—to lean into constructive conflict. Here, she describes what she and her class learned from the experience:

> My students and I sought to increase our consciousness of our own positions relative to the topics that we studied, examining our motivations in making statements about race and racism, social justice, and movements toward public change. We confronted the moments of conflict that arose in discussion and in the texts we studied, rather than turning away from them. Conflict, we found, is a necessary precursor to change, even—or especially—when it is painful and unpleasant to work through. (Ryan-Bryant, 2018, p. 54)

Build in Structured and Spontaneous Opportunities for Learning and Application

All professional learning plans are structured pathways toward greater capacity in some arena. Staff meetings, webinars, structured conversations, book studies, asynchronous web-based modules, and other coordinated learning activities ensure that staff are exposed to critical content, conversations, and reflections regarding antiracist pedagogy and the development of critical consciousness within students.

There is no doubt that professional learning should:

> embed opportunities to engage in explicit conversations and teaching about power, privilege, and systems of oppression in course and internship experiences, throughout teacher training programs, induction, and professional learning opportunities. Move away from the "one multicultural education course" model that is prevalent in many programs. (Zion et al., 2015, p. 931)

However, that does not mean that teachers will not converse in hallways and parking lots once they walk out of the room. Colleagues often spontaneously share reflections and insights through phone calls, lunch talks, and social media exchanges, among other unstructured learning experiences. In my experience, staff members sometimes learn as much from a long exchange of text messages with a group of trusted colleagues as they can from a half-day staff development training from an outside consultant, particularly when it comes to recognition of their personal biases. Effective professional learning progressions acknowledge this reality, and great professional learning progressions leverage it.

Take advantage of spontaneous teachable moments that occur in meetings and classrooms; great professional learning progressions intentionally create the conditions for reflection and growth from spontaneous teachable moments that occur in meetings and classrooms. For example, you might overhear colleagues having a conversation during a break in a meeting, interject a few questions that solicit deep connections to the colleagues and the content, ask for permission to share the topic, and discuss the exchange with the larger group with the help of the participants in the original conversation.

Leaders can also build time into the plan for think-aloud reflections and circulate through the room and halls during breaks to join sidebar conversations and capture model thinking. Combining structured and spontaneous learning opportunities maximizes the engagement and growth of all learners.

In these ways, staff members get chances to authentically connect their personal insights to the public discourse in their school buildings. Teachers operate in similar fashions as they work through the scopes and sequences of their various curricula and classroom standards. With respect to structured antiracist practices in classrooms, some teachers publicly recognize significant events, such as holidays or heritage months. Educators also implement spontaneous practices that embed antiracist practices. For instance, a teacher might pause a planned lesson to facilitate a conversation that takes advantage of a teachable moment when a student expresses a sentiment with racist undertones.

> **Antiracist school leaders cannot rely on teachers to consistently incorporate antiracist content and instructional strategies without guidance.**

Antiracist school leaders are aware of the expertise and values of their staff, and their staff may be replete with well-meaning, caring instructors. Even the most superficially nurturing educators can need help structuring the antiracist practices in their classrooms.

In one example, Betül Alaca and Angela Pyle (2018) of the Ontario Institute for Studies in Education interviewed six kindergarten teachers. Five of those kindergarten teachers said that students' cultures should be considered when planning, but less than half the teachers included students' cultures regularly. When teachers did include students' cultures in the classroom, those experiences were more likely to be spontaneous than planned in advance.

In the Zion and colleagues (2015) study mentioned earlier in this chapter, structured learning activities helped teachers to identify their roles within systems of oppression, make connections to how systems of oppression hurt students, and understand how educators could take action to reconstruct those systems. In describing the impact of organized learning activities on teachers and students, the researchers write the following:

> Each [teacher] was able to identify how their cultural backgrounds or group memberships instilled particular values and biases. Each was able to understand how those group memberships created levels of privilege (or oppression) for themselves. All developed deeper understanding of systems of oppression, and through conversations and interactions with their students, could see the immediate and pernicious influence of those systems on the lives and opportunities of children and families. (Zion et al., 2015, p. 929)

The Zion and colleagues (2015) and Alaca and Pyle (2018) studies exemplify how antiracist pedagogy will likely be inconsistently implemented in the absence of structured opportunities for learning and application. Consequently, professional learning action plans must embed activities that require staff members to personally reflect on—and apply—antiracist knowledge and skills as well as hold their colleagues accountable for consistent application of the content.

ELEVATE ANTIRACISM ACROSS ASPECTS OF SCHOOL

When I shared my antiracist school vision with my community, several builders on my staff stepped up to provide moral, vocal, and programmatic assistance. As stated in chapter 2 (page 63), one group of builders asked if we could substitute work with antiracism for our typical academic professional learning committees, such as our reading and mathematics committees. During our discussion, I shared that—from my perspective—antiracist work lives *within* every area of a school. Therefore, I went on, our job was to elevate the presence of antiracism on our academic and well-being committees, not replace those topics as if antiracism were a stand-alone focus.

Because of my local school context, some connections to racial disproportionality were easy to make. We all knew that learning about personal biases was key (Gorski & Dalton, 2020), and our district required all staff members to take asynchronous training about implicit biases. Additionally, our district made race and socioeconomic status requisite components of every school's improvement plan. Over 95 percent of our school's students were Black or Latinx, and over 80 percent of our students were eligible to receive free or reduced-price meals.

Spotlighting explicit racial connections to our school's work was low-hanging fruit. I told my early builders that antiracist work underpinned our curricular choices, our implementation of interventions, protocols for identifying students for special education and giftedness, and so on. The thread of antiracism should weave through all our staff meetings, data chats, grade-level meetings, parent conference preparation, and everything else we did at school.

I needed those builders, I said, to help me maintain antiracism on our collective front burner because we could not count on the societal focus on racism that arose from George Floyd's murder in 2020 to persist. New events were sure to inhabit the news headlines, and new district mandates were sure to compete for our professional attention.

Use Restorative Practices

One example of a district mandate that elevated antiracism across aspects of school was a shift to using *restorative practices*; these are exercises and behaviors meant to strengthen relationships between individuals and communities to maximize social connection (Ferlazzo, 2020). My district decided that my school should pilot the use of restorative practices with students to prevent and heal issues related to student discipline. I became concerned that teaching, learning, and applying new protocols for staff-to-student and student-to-student interactions would obstruct teaching, learning, and applying antiracist pedagogical practices. So, I reached out to a restorative practices contact in my district's central office, and I asked her to help me make the connection between restorative practices and antiracism. She sent me several documents that laid out clear connections between the two concepts, and she followed up with a call to ensure that I understood. From that point on, I was able to show my staff how restorative practices supplemented our antiracism work; it was not an added responsibility.

I also learned that sometimes our obstacles would come from beyond the district's central office; community issues or natural disasters could also vie for our attention. For example, the rise of COVID-19 in 2020 occurred just as I began rolling out my antiracist school vision. The pandemic did not shift our focus from antiracism; it underscored the need for our antiracist work. Attendance, engagement, virtual instructional practices, access to technology, transportation, food insecurity, academic interventions, curricular enrichment, childcare, physical and mental health care, employment, and housing were all issues facing my students' families. All those aspects of physical, social, psychological, and academic well-being were also intricately linked to race in my district. Consequently, different teams on our school staff worked to support each of those areas. Part of my role as an antiracist school leader was to illustrate vivid connections between the various school factions and our building's work with antiracism (see figure 3.2).

Include Personal Connections to Students and Families

It is essential that professional learning progressions embed opportunities for educators to personally connect with students and their families. After all, the cultivation of critically conscious students who have the tools and motivation to change the lives of themselves and their families is the end goal of the long-term learning progression. It makes sense that school plans elevate the need to deepen understanding of those key stakeholder groups.

However, navigating antiracism content can be tricky for even the most experienced facilitators. Also, there might not be very much difference in diversity among the staff, students, and families in some school communities. Therefore, antiracist school leaders must carefully consider how and when to place connections with students and families on the timeline.

Some challenges with engaging with the content are related to educators' perceptions about obstacles, such as the age of the students. For instance, some teachers say that explicit conversations about culture are not developmentally appropriate for young children because they are too young to express biases or recognize racial differences (Alaca & Pyle, 2018). However, research indicates that preschool and elementary school students already notice and discuss children's physical differences, including race (Hagerman, 2019; Kemple, Lee, & Harris, 2016). To support this challenge, schools can conduct professional learning focused on implementing

Issue	Connections to School Stakeholder Groups	Connections to Antiracism	Questions to Consider During Professional Development
Attendance and engagement	**Students:** Students attend and engage at high levels when curricula are relevant to their lives. **Staff:** Classrooms are happier and more orderly when students are present and engaged with their learning. **Caregivers:** Students who are happy to go to school are likely to be happier at home after school. Students who are eager to go to school are less likely to stay home unnecessarily, leaving caregivers more opportunities to develop their own skills, work, or exercise self-care. **Community members:** Students with high levels of engagement and attendance are less likely to engage in troublesome behaviors in the community during or after the school day.	Traditionally, schools have maintained Eurocentric and middle- to upper-income frameworks for curriculum, instruction, discipline, and well-being, which have contributed to racially disproportionate attendance, graduation, and dropout rates.	How do we define attendance and engagement? What goals and metrics do we use to assess our attendance and engagement? What staff and protocols are in place to monitor and support attendance and engagement? How can we get to know about the lives of our students outside of the school building? What attendance and engagement strategies have worked for schools that are demographically similar to ours? How can we leverage relationships with families and community members in ways that support attendance and engagement?

FIGURE 3.2: Examples of connections between school factions and antiracism.

continued →

Issue	Connections to School Stakeholder Groups	Connections to Antiracism	Questions to Consider During Professional Development
Instructional practices	**Students:** Students engage and achieve at high levels when expert educators tailor instruction to meet their needs, interests, and backgrounds. **Staff:** Effective educators combine their knowledge of pedagogy with their understanding of their students to deliver culturally responsive instruction that lifts the spirits and achievement of all students. **Caregivers:** Students who receive high-quality instruction are more likely to achieve at high levels, leading to enhanced college and career opportunities after high school. **Community members:** Powerful instructional practices contribute to a high-performing school, and high-performing schools contribute to increased property values and employment opportunities in their surrounding communities.	Historically, schools have implemented one-size-fits-all instructional and curricular frameworks that are based on middle- to upper-class Eurocentric principles or values (for example, individualism, competition, and centering Whiteness).	What staff performance and student outcome data do we collect that indicate the quality of our instructional practices? What are the recent historical and current levels of performance for our various student subgroups (for example, race and ethnicity, socioeconomic status, and language proficiency)? Which student subgroups are performing at disproportionately low rates? What instructional practices—including both initial instruction and evidence-based interventions—are correlated with the success of our student subgroups who are not succeeding? What do our stakeholder surveys tell us about the cultural relevance of our curricula and instructional practices? What professional learning do our staff members need in order to enhance their instructional skill sets?
Physical and mental health care	**Students:** Students are more likely to thrive in environments that support their physical and mental health. **Staff:** Student engagement and achievement levels are likely to be higher when students are physically and mentally healthy. **Community members:** Communities with physically and mentally healthy students are likely to have higher-performing schools and lower rates of crime, both of which contribute to higher property values and a better quality of life for residents.	Historical trauma from our country's legacy of enslavement and other forms of racism continues to have a lasting impact on every member of our society, with people of color and poor people harmed at disproportionate rates. Current policies that support outcomes such as limited health care options, environmental pollution, food insecurity, and employment discrimination significantly contribute to relatively higher levels of physical and mental illness among poor people and people of color.	What data do we collect regarding the mental and physical health of our students, staff, and families? How have we embedded supports for mental and physical health into our curricula? How can we provide extracurricular physical and mental health care supports in our school—for both students and staff? How can we partner with other community organizations and political leaders to support mental and physical health care supports in our community?

a schoolwide class meeting protocol during which students can participate in semi-structured conversations about concepts such as classroom climate, home cultures, and their perspectives about race.

Teacher capacity is an additional obstacle to antiracist pedagogy. Conversations about racial and social justice can be stressful for both students and staff, and staff should be ready to facilitate such conversations (Ryan-Bryant, 2018). Like with other forms of pedagogy, educators need both content knowledge and instructional skills to make meaningful impacts on outcomes for students and families, and capacity building at scale for an entire staff takes time (think years). A book study about using culturally proficient instructional practices or combating antiracism would support educators' needs for professional learning of theories and applications that make a difference for their students.

Moreover, some teachers come from backgrounds of privilege, with little firsthand experience on the receiving end of racial bias. Students can have many more encounters with racial and social injustice than school staff. To compensate for those differences, staff must diligently focus on listening to students and learning about related topics (Ryan-Bryant, 2018). Establishing teacher-student dyads, with a common listening and speaking protocol, as well as some thought-provoking questions requires educators to listen to and directly address the needs of their students and families.

Additionally, teachers tend to focus on the cultures of students who are in their classrooms, resulting in the exclusion of other cultures (Alaca & Pyle, 2018). If the demographics of a classroom or school community are relatively racially or culturally homogeneous, then activities related to appreciating cultures other than one's own and a handful of others must be intentional and required by all staff members.

SUPPORT RACIAL IDENTITY DEVELOPMENT

When asked to define "race," people often lean on physical characteristics, such as skin color. However, when asked to describe what their race means to them, people typically add a social perspective about group patterns. The process of learning to associate physical characteristics, sociocultural patterns, racialized group interactions, and one's place in a racialized society is called *racial identity development* (Mims & Williams, 2020; Syed et al., 2018). Developing one's racial identity is a necessary step toward becoming an antiracist educator, particularly for White educators (Zion et al., 2015).

Young people develop their ethnic-racial identity in part by the way they are treated by other members of society during their elementary school years and adolescence, and stereotypes have a significant impact on how children are treated at that age, particularly children in marginalized groups (Mims & Williams, 2020). Families play the largest role in the formation of racial identity, followed by peer groups, and class discussions of race and racism (Nelson et al., 2018). Schools, and the educators therein, are at the nexus of all three major influencers and therefore have an opportunity to exert a sizable influence on students' racial identity development. For example, schools can support systems that counteract negative stereotypes by impacting how students view the places of their races in society (Mims & Williams, 2020), or schools can offer curriculum that elevates the profiles of marginalized groups of people within historical content (Piper, 2019).

Educators' racial identity development is a precursor to healthy student racial identity development. This is particularly the case for White, middle-class educators. White teachers might discuss institutional racism, but they often lack understanding of the interplay between their racial identities and their teaching practices (Utt & Tochluk, 2020), so they will likely need guidance from their leaders. Leading this work can be difficult, in part because adults, like children, develop their racial identities through cultural immersion that is heavily influenced by their families and peers (Mims & Williams, 2020), and White supremacy dominates our culture. Trying to help people understand their Whiteness, while at the same time operating within a White supremacist system, is uniquely challenging (Matias et al., 2017).

Because concepts related to Whiteness and White supremacy can be particularly uncomfortable for many educators, antiracist leaders must demonstrate the need for educators to "embrace ambiguity and not-knowing through an attitude of humility, and to work and mutually puzzle through challenges always in community and relationship with others" (Malott et al., 2019, p. 97). This is necessary because "a more tolerant perspective toward the trial-and-error nature of antiracist action may increase White learners' openness to ongoing self-reflection, critical feedback, and change, to enhance self-compassion and a willingness to take risks and make mistakes along the way" (Malott et al., 2019, p. 93). Some tactics such as emotional regulation strategies (like mindfulness) could be tried as coping mechanisms for staff as they manage their reactions to critical self-reflection and feedback from others.

Identities are complex. Each person has a different identity, and therefore, racial identity development is unlikely to be a linear, one-size-fits-all process (Shim, 2020). It's complicated work, so it might be helpful for you to use concise structures for vision casting and planning activities. In their journal article titled "White Teacher, Know Thyself," Jamie Utt and Shelly Tochluk (2020) offer a six-step pathway toward racial identity development:

1. Analyzing privilege and microaggressive behavior
2. Exploring ethnic and cultural identities
3. Engaging with history of White anti-racist and multicultural struggles for justice
4. Developing intersectional identity
5. Building White anti-racist community
6. Demonstrating accountability across race (pp. 130–131)

Although the authors emphasize the need for White teachers to engage in the work, these areas can help all educators understand themselves and act in their communities.

Take a deep dive into the concept of privilege. Unpack the unearned advantages that accompany membership in certain preferred groups in our society, with a particular focus on race. These advantages may manifest in overt or covert fashions, depending on the context, and they are often closely linked to other factors of diversity. An intense interrogation of privilege, especially by White teachers, "is necessary to recognize distortions and understand how subconscious enactments of racial privilege negatively impact communities, injure students of Color, and display poor modeling for White students" (Utt & Tochluk, 2020, p. 133).

The next step on the pathway to racial identity development, according to the authors, requires staff to consider how their ethnic and cultural identities fit within the system of White supremacy (Utt & Tochluk, 2020). Some cultural identities are privileged in our society today, as they have been since the origin of the United States. White teachers, in particular, experience dissonance because it's hard to simultaneously view oneself as a proponent of antiracism and a proponent of Whiteness. Therefore, some White teachers try to distance themselves from Whiteness in ways that overidentify with their European ancestry or people of color. Continuing the lean into the discomfort yields at least two benefits:

> White anti-racist educators who enjoy a healthy racial identity that includes self-acceptance are able to build relationships with, and influence, White

> educators around them. Second, students benefit when White teachers are able to admit their relationship to Whiteness and White culture, own their responsibility to work for justice, and avoid enacting microaggressions. (Utt & Tochluk, 2020, p. 136)

Opponents of antiracism have zeroed in on how curricula represent the history of the United States and other parts of the world. Antiracist school leaders agree with Utt and Tochluk (2020) that educators must do their best to present a holistic view of our past, which includes reckoning with the parts that are uncomfortable. Like with many aspects of antiracist education, White educators should resist the temptation to settle in a space of guilt or distance themselves from Whiteness. Students and colleagues need clearheaded facilitators to help them review facts, interpret salient events, and make connections to the present. Moving through the discomfort to a place of acceptance is a healthy part of one's racial identity development.

The struggles of the past were not just those of people of color. There are people within a diverse range of identities who have struggled for recognition and equality in communities around the world. While antiracism intentionally elevates our awareness of the outsized role that race plays in our lives, with a particular focus on systems, policies, and practices in our society, it by no means reduces the presence of intersectionality, the multiple identities that we all recognize within ourselves. Some of those identities are chosen (political party), while others are assigned (race and gender), experienced (survival of trauma), or with us from birth (sex). Each of those various identities comes with particular advantages or disadvantages depending on a person's cultural context. For example, a person might be White, which comes with some advantages in a White supremacist culture. However, that person might also be gay, Latina, and from a lower socioeconomic class, all of which are disadvantaged identities in the United States. Intersectionality recognizes that our webs of identities are complicated constructs of privilege and disadvantage. People with healthy racial identities recognize that as such in themselves and others.

Creating and sustaining peer groups that push a person's thinking and hold that person accountable are the final two ingredients for supporting a healthy racial identity. For White educators, one of those critical friend groups should be composed of White people. Utt and Tochluk (2020) explain:

> This kind of group allows White teachers to (a) value learning opportunities offered by White people, (b) embrace a role as a potential influencer of other White colleagues, and (c) receive the critical feedback needed to increase awareness of subconscious enactments of microaggressions and privilege. (p. 143)

Another accountability peer group should contain people of color. White educators should lean into the discomfort rather than avoid challenging conversations; they should actively listen rather than center themselves; they should reflect on what they hear rather than defend against it; and they should take action on what they learn rather allow the status quo to remain. Working through these six strategies for racial identity development helps educators understand themselves, others, and ways they can act in their communities.

Ms. Mary Hart is an instructional specialist in Montgomery County Public Schools' Office of School Support and Well-Being. On at least four occasions, Mary has also been my co-instructor in the Equity and Excellence in Education (EEE) program as adjunct for McDaniel College in Maryland. During one of our exchanges between classes, Mary described how her connection to multiple accountability groups powerfully impacted her antiracist outlook.

> Community is essential. As White women, we have both suffered from patriarchy and used it to oppress women of color. And, some of us, like me, have a history of family trauma, so this can be viewed from multiple angles. We talk about how oppression and trauma can be similar in that they are generational, yet they also seem entirely different in other ways. We push each other to consider all the sides of these issues without falling into the trap of assuming we totally understand everything.
>
> I wouldn't say only build a White antiracist community, though that is important. I think building a multiracial antiracist community has helped me grow. I have built trust across racial lines, which helps my friends of color hold me accountable and share their experiences with me. This helps me understand how we are all connected in this fight for justice. It is no longer something I am doing "for" someone else: paternalism. It is essential for all of us. I felt that before, but I didn't totally understand how justice is deeply intertwined. There's just lots to think about, so collaborating with a variety of partners is helpful.
>
> I plan to stay in these communities. I maintain friendships with people who will challenge me and invite me to grow. Professionally, I make sure that I am part of communities that foster learning and hold me accountable for speaking up. There's a ton to read and listen to as well, but even when I am not reading, I have my community, and their voices are in my head encouraging me to continue the work. Also, teaching in the EEE program allows me to regularly hear from teachers that are doing the work and learn from them. It also helps me remember that I am not alone in my district, and I can call on others when needed. (M. Hart, personal communication, June 2, 2023).

Mary's experience exemplifies the ways committed, non-judgmental fellowship among colleagues and friends can spur self-interrogation of our values, beliefs, and behaviors that undergird the policies and practices that support or constrain the students we share. Humans are social animals, and knowledge can be enhanced through social interactions. When we provide psychologically safe environments to socially construct knowledge, school staffs can take on even the scariest aspects of antiracist concepts, one of which is an examination of Whiteness itself.

Examine How Whiteness Manifests in Schools

Whether school staffs are composed of self-identified allies, White teachers who proclaim colorblindness, White teachers who possess a savior mentality toward the students, or teachers of color who have internalized racism, antiracist professional learning progressions must at some point journey through Whiteness. The rationale for reckoning with Whiteness is simple: most teachers are White, and many of them have not been required to examine how Whiteness manifests in school contexts as well as society writ large (Matias & Mackey, 2016). If educators' respective life experiences have socialized them not to believe that race—let alone racism—is a topic for polite, constructive conversations, then those educators might believe that they don't see the world through racialized lenses. Research—and probably most antiracist school leaders' experiences—suggests that race is always present when educators are asked to think about diversity (Alaca & Pyle, 2018; Matias et al., 2017; Matias & Mackey, 2016).

When considering cultural implications of teaching and learning, teachers can focus on students' ethnic backgrounds as primary markers of diversity. For instance, Alaca and Pyle (2018) found that teachers give ethnicity far more consideration than gender, religion, or socioeconomic status; even when teachers consider other factors of diversity, they connect those factors to ethnicity.

A thoughtful interrogation of Whiteness's impact on social contexts, what some researchers call *critical Whiteness*, is sure to cause discomfort among school staff members (Matias et al., 2017; Matias & Mackey, 2016). To mitigate the discomfort of learners in their urban teacher preparation course, Cheryl E. Matias and Janiece Mackey (2016) organized their course into three emotional phases: (1) critical reading, (2) critical reflection, and (3) discussion. Matias and Mackey (2016) incorporated multiple texts, media, and "other symbolic representations of society" (p. 37), and "each pedagogical activity and text was given space for reflection on part of the teacher candidate's learning journey" (p. 38). Here's how you can apply their research to the work with your staff.

- Provide readings to staff members that elevate the existence of Whiteness ideology.
- Assign tasks that require readers to think critically about the content.
- Facilitate structured discussions that allow participants to apply their new learning in ways that move beyond guilt and defensiveness and extend toward social justice.

An essential focus on Whiteness does not exclude the possibility of exploring the racial identity development models related to BIPOC communities. All stakeholders should be able to see themselves in the professional learning progression. Antiracist school leaders may choose if, how, and when to center various identities. Because of the prevalence of White teachers in the teaching corps, the historical and current presence of institutional racism, and our societal avoidance of conversations about race, interrogating Whiteness is a must-do.

Dr. Alana Murray, the principal introduced earlier in the chapter (page 75), was supported by an active teachers' union that represented a progressive school district. Dr. Joseph Stephens (pseudonym) works in a far less supportive environment. Dr. Stephens is a deputy superintendent in a rural district in the Mid-Atlantic region of the United States. There is no official statement about the topic of equity and no office in the district dedicated to examining racial disparities in academic or well-being data. Equity is an invisible issue in the district. Dr. Stephens, a former student within the district, expected nothing more than the district provides. Here is how he phrased it:

> As a lifelong resident and graduate of this school district, I am too intimately acquainted with the [deep-seated] racism that permeates this community. Schools are a microcosm of the community. Many of the school leaders are also lifelong residents of this community. Most graduated from high school, traveled about thirty miles to a local university, and returned to teach and eventually lead schools. [With] the lack of diversity school leaders have experienced along with their White privilege, antiracist leadership was needed to, one, help the White administrators understand their dimensions of identity and, two, understand how this school system was infected with structural and systemic racism. Though this district has been beleaguered by opportunity gaps, there have been no intentional efforts to disrupt the existing narrative. As a result of the aforementioned, I am assured my thinking is correct about the need for antiracist work. (J. Stephens, personal communication, July 24, 2023)

Nevertheless, Dr. Stephens recognized the need for antiracist pedagogy, and he took action. Early on, he relied on his personal research. In this statement, he explains how he developed one of his professional learning progression activities:

> At the beginning of antiracist work, one must begin with the self. I asked school leaders to do a lot of self-reflection to understand their dimension of identity because it colors how you see things. I engaged the Pacific Educational Group led by Glenn Singleton. He started with the racial autobiography and constantly reminded us to begin with racializing yourself as you state your perspective. For example, as an African American cisgender man, I noted White administrators struggled with naming race, which speaks to the research about how White people [prefer] being colorblind. (J. Stephens, personal communication, July 24, 2023)

When planning evaluation milestones for professional learning progressions, Dr. Stephens leans into school leader knowledge. He expresses the following:

> Because I supervised principals, it was expected that they would carry out the directives from my office. The explicit directive for principals was to center antiracism and as such they had a responsibility to comply. Additionally, doing administrative evaluations, antiracist work was one of the performance goals. Principals had to be able to speak to their antiracist work and cite specific examples with impact. The Courageous Conversations (Singleton, 2015) training provided through the Pacific Educational Group provided much-needed support for principals.
>
> I plan to measure my impact with the degree to which principals are able to identify equitable and antiracist instructional practices in their schools. Oddly enough, I also measure my impact by the degree of pushback I get when I hold school leaders accountable for closing existing gaps and dismantling long-standing procedures that further disadvantage marginalized students. (J. Stephens, personal communication, July 24, 2023)

Use Supportive Resources

Antiracist school leaders can be visionary and innovative, but they do not have to reinvent the wheel. There are myriad books, articles, websites, and videos that contain strategies and activities related to identity, culture, and racism. A simple search of your favorite internet search engine, online book retailer, or video curation website will generate myriad options for exploration. You can select texts or exercises based on your level of knowledge and the status of your staff.

If you or your staff are new to conversations about equity, cultural proficiency, and racism, you would likely benefit from texts that explicitly explain the importance of the work and provide structured plans that facilitators can use to help groups recognize their own identities, gain awareness of others' identities, and understand how cultural lenses impact teaching and learning. In addition to outcomes, procedures, and handouts, these types of texts provide tips for facilitation, anticipated misconceptions of the audience, and potential follow-up tasks.

- *Cultural Proficiency: A Manual for School Leaders* (Lindsey et al., 2019), which I referenced in chapter 1 (page 35), is one such text. *Cultural Proficiency* aims to show all educators the powerful influence that culture has on teaching and learning. After setting the stage by presenting research-based theories related to cultural proficiency in schools, the authors spend the next part of the book providing step-by-step directions that support the cultural identity development of every educator in the building. The book's publisher, Corwin, states that the audience should "use this book as a workbook for small groups, or as a guide for improving the cultural competence of [their] teaching (Corwin, n.d.)."

- *Culturally Proficient Leadership: The Personal Journey Begins Within* (Terrell, Terrell, Lindsey, & Lindsey, 2018) takes a similar stylistic approach to coaching school staff. It pushes readers to understand the impact of culture on teaching and learning. Readers review research that promotes the need for cultural proficiency, and chapters provide activities—albeit more structured activities—that encourage readers to become introspective, as they connect with their own personal lenses.

There are myriad books written for similar purposes and using similar frameworks for beginners, such as *Cultural Competence Now: 56 Exercises to Help Educators Understand and Challenge Bias, Racism, and Privilege* (Mayfield, 2020); *Equity 101: The Equity Framework* (Linton, 2011); and *Building Equity: Policies and Practices to Empower All Learners* (Smith, Frey, Pumpian, & Fisher, 2017). In addition, websites such as Dismantling Racism Works (www.dismantlingracism.org) and Culturally Responsive Leadership (www.crsli.org) provide comparable content.

If your staff are more experienced with cultural proficiency, perhaps you could target particular aspects of your school-improvement plan, based on your data related to student achievement, school discipline, stakeholder voice, and staff performance. The following texts might be helpful in that regard.

- *Equity Visits: A New Approach to Supporting Equity-Focused School and District Leadership* (Roegman, Allen, Leverett, Thompson, & Hatch, 2019) is a guidebook that supports school leaders who want to envision different instructional practices that take place within their classrooms. It provides activities, discussion questions, data collection documents, and other tools that underpin a structured approach to addressing pedagogical underperformance that constrains the growth of historically marginalized groups of students. The premise of the text is that great instruction improves learning opportunities for all students and, therefore, reduces the achievement gap.

- *Grading for Equity: What It Is, Why It Matters, and How It Can Transform Schools and Classrooms* (Feldman, 2018) is another book that aims at a specific area of institutional racism in schools: grading. The author, Joe Feldman, lays out the problem of racial disparities, and he recommends that schools take a professional learning community approach to teacher, school, district, and state assessment policies and practices. Feldman points out common biases and misconceptions that affect student evaluation, and he articulates dozens of specific practices that educators can use to counteract bias, demonstrate a growth mindset, cultivate positive relationships, and deepen their understanding of students' knowledge and skills.

- In *Culturally Proficient Coaching: Supporting Educators to Create Equitable Schools*, Delores B. Lindsey, Richard S. Martinez, Randall B. Lindsey, and Keith T. Myatt (2020) present a "personal journey map" to support educational leaders as they strive to develop themselves and their colleagues. The authors present data about the impact of coaching, strategies to mitigate bias, experiences retold by educational coaches, and case study examples, among other forms of guidance. A text such as this would fit well as a book study for an experienced administrative team or other core group of school leaders.

Other helpful texts present general thoughts about leadership in diverse contexts, case studies, and reflections on policies.

- *Anti-Racist Educational Leadership and Policy: Addressing Racism in Public Education* (Diem & Welton, 2021) guides educational leaders as they consider prominent topics in 21st century schools (like school choice and high-stakes testing). Each chapter focuses on a different issue, combining research with authentic examples. The text helps school leaders recognize and address the racial undertones of mainstream policy issues that often claim to be colorblind or race neutral.

- In another example, *Leadership for Increasingly Diverse Schools* (Theoharis & Scanlan, 2020) is like the previous book in that it focuses on school leaders, it presents research-based theories and practices to help schools support historically marginalized groups of students, and each chapter focuses on a different topic.
- *Transforming Sanchez School: Shared Leadership, Equity, and Evidence* (Isola & Cummins, 2019), a third example of this kind of general equity leadership text, is a case study that examines the shared leadership model employed by a transformational school leader. The text tells the story of how elevating the voices of all stakeholders can increase the achievement of all students.

While equity and cultural competence texts are plentiful, there is not a wide selection of antiracist school leadership books, articles, and websites available—hence the composition of this book. Therefore, at some point, you will need to blend your antiracism reading with your individual school context.

LEAN INTO UNCOMFORTABLE TOPICS (AND DISCOMFORT IN GENERAL)

Antiracist education builds on critical pedagogy by treating schools as places where stakeholders learn how to challenge our institutional status quo in systems that go beyond the walls of the school building. Antiracist educators travel beyond the philosophy of symbolically placing students into the existing school and societal frameworks, like what is asked in multiculturalism. Antiracist educators expose the White supremacy culture that undergirds the construction of said frameworks, demand the reconstruction of those systems, and teach their students to do the same.

Professional learning progressions provide blueprints for monitoring and evaluating the impacts of professional development activities on both students and staff. Planning learning progressions begins with articulating the knowledge, skills, and dispositions students need in order to become critically conscious. Once the targets are set, effective professional learning progressions use a backward design model to identify prerequisite knowledge, skills, and dispositions for each step toward students' critical consciousness.

Perhaps most of all, antiracist school leaders must lean into uncomfortable topics in the plan, such as analyzing Whiteness. When considering professional development activities about some antiracism content, facilitators can be tempted to dance around controversial subjects. Antiracist school leaders understand that educators' growth, in large part, is bolstered by joining hands and wading through those topics together.

CONCLUSION

Chapter 3 has explained how you should collaborate with your school leadership team to create at least one learning progression, a carefully constructed scope of learning that outlines how you are building interconnected concepts and skills that will move your school or district from its current state to your desired state. You can begin with the broad concepts and skills that will lead you to your vision and use a backward design model to tease out the requisite knowledge and skills to achieve each step along the way. The sample learning progression in the chapter presented a one-year target within a three-year plan, but your target distance may be as long or short as you deem necessary. For instance, your team might determine that a six-month goal fits the needs of your staff and the capacity of your planning team. As this book states repeatedly, there are no hard-and-fast rules and there are no perfect practices. Your primary goal is to develop a mindset that helps to orient your community in an antiracist direction and move toward it.

> **Antiracist school leaders ensure that professional learning progressions include assessments that track staff feelings about the activities, alignment with the organizational mission, application in authentic contexts, and improvements in student outcomes.**

At some point, you're going to need to create learning progressions for your students. For now, it's OK to focus on the growth of your staff through the use of learning progressions. In order for your students to move forward, they're going to need capable and willing educators to support them, so the growth of staff should be your early target. You'll need to build the capacity of yourself, your team members, or both to deftly facilitate whole and small groups that cultivate psychological safety, support racial identity development, and make Whiteness visible.

Antiracist learning progressions should aim for critical consciousness because critical consciousness ensures that people have the knowledge, skills, and motivation to identify and counteract injustices that operate at individual and systemic levels. The development of critically conscious students necessitates critically conscious adults, so that reinforces the need to begin with an eye on staff development. Should you feel ready to dive into developing the critical consciousness of students, this chapter provided some examples for identifying injustice, cultivating community engagement, highlighting social-emotional functioning, and blending understandings of intersectionality and current events.

Every good lesson plan includes assessments for how you'll know if you met your objectives. Learning progressions call for the same line of thinking. This chapter presented Thomas Guskey's (2016) levels of evaluation of professional learning, and chapter 6 (page 151) presents a more comprehensive framework that accounts for the entire school environment.

No matter how well you articulate your vision, craft your learning progressions, or evaluate your progress, the journey toward an antiracist school culture inevitably encounters headwinds. Not all resistance is due to ignorance, lack of intelligence, or bad intentions. In fact, you might find that none of those reasons cause the opposition you face. The next chapter discusses some of the causes for pushback and how you might manage resistance in ways that support your entire school community, resisters included.

APPLY YOUR LEARNING

As a current leader in your school, antiracist or otherwise, you have experience with developing and facilitating professional learning. The things to know, say, and do for this chapter ask you to refine your thinking about professional development to narrow the focus on antiracist content. Even if it's not a current practice in your district, you should construct a leadership team representative of various stakeholder groups to identify disparate outcomes in your school achievement and well-being data. Ensure that disparate outcomes are highlighted in your school-improvement plan, and consider the elements of critical consciousness necessary to act on potential biases in your practices at the individual and systemic levels.

KNOW

- Understand how the elements of your current school-improvement plan relate to antiracism.
- Determine the builders on your staff who can help you create and implement your vision.

SAY

- At a school leadership team meeting and a staff meeting, share your drafted learning progression, one that moves your staff from the current state of knowledge, skills, and motivation to the desired state.
- Reach out to the builders on your staff who can help you develop and implement your professional learning progression.

DO

- Consider potential obstacles that could obstruct your focus on antiracism and the proactive steps you can take before those obstacles overtake the front burner.
- Create quantitative and qualitative metrics that evaluate each of Guskey's five levels of professional learning evaluation.
- During your review of school achievement and well-being data, brainstorm structures and practices that encourage or discourage the development of staff and students.

Chapter 4
ENCOURAGE AND EMBRACE RESISTANCE

Key Vocabulary

cognitive diversity	A collection of team members from various backgrounds who are more likely to view the world differently, approach challenges differently, and build community differently.
constructive dissent	A push to interpret visions, purposes, strategies, or metrics from alternative viewpoints.
heterophily	Interest in connecting with activities or individuals that elevate perspectives that are counter to our demographic characteristics or current beliefs.

homophily	Interest in connecting with activities or individuals that elevate perspectives that are similar to our demographic characteristics or current beliefs.
intersectionality	The recognition and support of the multiple identities of each person, with a specific focus on historically marginalized identities (Mims & Williams, 2020).
Whiteness	Privileged ways of thinking, doing, and being that are attributed to a generic White racial identity.

Contemporary White supremacy may appear different than it did in the past, but White supremacy remains (Hall, 2018). However, many educators, a majority of whom are White, are resistant to learning about Whiteness, White supremacy, and antiracist pedagogy (Shim, 2020). To some extent, the reproduction of this belief is a function of teacher preparation programs and educational leadership programs, whose faculty are often unmotivated and underprepared to teach antiracist concepts to preservice teachers (Matias, Montoya, & Nishi, 2016; Shim, 2020).

Many educators believe that our society has *racists*, people who openly state that racial hierarchies are natural and inevitable, and *nonracists*, people who view existing racial hierarchies as a combination of historical events and contemporary choices. Those same educators often contend that openly racist people rarely choose careers in K–12 education.

Often, self-proclaimed nonracists use deliberate strategies to avoid working through antiracist frameworks, such as the following.

- **Proclaiming ignorance:** "I don't talk with a lot of racist people or read books about race. I'm not sure that I know enough about the topic to fully participate in these conversations."

- **Requesting additional facts:** "Where did you get that information? Are you sure we can trust that source? Can you point me to additional sources that confirm those facts?"
- **Elevating intersectionality:** "Our students are poor; they are immigrants and are English learners. We have a lot more to consider than race."

Expressions of shame and guilt can also obstruct antiracist professional learning opportunities (Matias et al., 2016; Tanner & Berchini, 2017). In some cases, nonracists go further by explaining that antiracism is divisive because it focuses on race in a noncolorblind way (Hall, 2018; Shim, 2020), and therefore, they outright refuse to engage.

This chapter explores the techniques of resistance, outlining *what* nonracists might do to interrupt antiracist work, as well as considering *why* nonracists resist antiracist work. Additionally, you will learn strategies antiracist school leaders can use to support nonracists' fears, deflections, or rejections of antiracist work. This chapter asks antiracist school leaders to consider a seemingly counterintuitive question: *What if opponents of antiracist pedagogy are right?*

DISTINGUISH BETWEEN THE PERSPECTIVES OF RACISTS, NONRACISTS, AND ANTIRACISTS

Race is not a biological construct. It has only been a social, cultural, and pseudoscientific concept for the last four or five hundred years, and its function has been to justify the subjugation of Black people across several continents (Hall, 2018; Kendi, 2016). It was created by a vicious cycle of cultural biases reflected and enhanced by the general public, individuals in public office who perpetuated and believed in those biases enough to write them into law, and political policy reflecting those bigoted beliefs over centuries to form a social hierarchy based in large part on observable physical characteristics such as skin color, hair texture, lip thickness, and nose width. A racist infrastructure that elevates Whiteness is at the center of our institutions of law, labor, housing, health care, and education.

When race is viewed through the lens of education, the teacher workforce remains overwhelmingly White, despite calls for diversification. Educator preparation programs "continue to practice in a manner such that they replicate themselves, while positioning diversity as a hopeful thought instead of an actual reality"

(Matias et al., 2016, p. 2). The lack of diversity leads decision makers and practitioners to use Whiteness as a primary lens in all areas of teaching and learning, including curriculum, instruction, discipline, hiring, and evaluation (Matias et al., 2016). Within educator preparation programs, stakeholders center Whiteness in decisions regarding admissions, counseling, course selection, faculty selection, and mentoring (Matias et al., 2016).

Kendi (2019) argues that racists and nonracists are two sides of the same racist coin, insofar as both groups work toward segregation or assimilation of historically subjugated people of color, with a particular focus on Black people. Self-identified racists and nonracists both agree that group characteristics are what maintain the racial hierarchies across American society; there is a subtle difference in that racists might believe the group characteristics are inherent, and nonracists believe that the group characteristics are choices. For instance, racists could say that Black people are less successful in our society because they are inherently lazy, violent, or less intelligent. Meanwhile, nonracists might say that it just so happens Black people are less successful because they have been socialized to invest less in education, they are more likely to grow up in poverty, and they need more support with parenting skills. Therefore, both racists and nonracists argue mitigating racial hierarchies necessitates a change in the groups of people who are consistently at lower rungs of the societal ladder, rather than changes to the systems and policies that consistently reproduce racial inequities (Hall, 2018).

In contrast, others maintain that simplistic frameworks such as *racist*, *nonracist*, and *antiracist* do not possess the capacity to capture the nuance inherent in concepts related to the human condition (Carbado & Harris, 2019; Hall, 2018; Tanner & Berchini, 2017). One-dimensional descriptors or simplistic dichotomies that ascribe monolithic characteristics to groups of human beings can hinder antiracist school leaders' attempts to diagnose sources of resistance and provide appropriate support.

Skeptics equate antiracism with White racism, in that antiracism also seeks to dominate the discourse based on race. Critics of antiracism sometimes describe antiracism as a "covert abuse of power for race group gain by oppressing others when more civil actions would be equally effective" (Hall, 2018, p. 64). They regard antiracism as another form of reverse racism, which shifts the focus from the racial equality that is colorblindness (Hall, 2018).

Requiring staff members to self-reflect about issues of privilege or race could uncover uneasiness and ambivalence (Shim, 2020). Both not knowing about the perspectives of members of marginalized groups and interrogating the origins of their own viewpoints can be very off-putting for members of dominant social groups. Adding the additional layer of Whiteness or White supremacy to antiracist content can be a productive entry point for White people (Tanner & Berchini, 2017), but it also compounds the challenge of mitigating discomfort.

Investigate the Rationale for Resistance

My wife Tracie and I were eating lunch in a Boston restaurant when we overheard the conversation of a family eating in the booth next to us. "Kids that age shouldn't want guns. Don't get any ideas," the man said. We both raised our eyebrows at a statement that was explicitly pushing back on gun enthusiasm. I whispered to Tracie, "Imagine if we were visiting from Alabama or Texas or Mississippi," places where we both thought gun ownership was a more socially acceptable social norm.

Social norms that form common identities, like supporting the right to carry firearms or supporting gun control, are sometimes explicitly stated from those closest to us. These life experiences could be different for each of us. They shape the lenses through which we see the world. They don't make any of us ignorant or unintelligent or evil. Those experiences make us different, but not necessarily in a bad way. We have to combine and share our life experiences with our colleagues, students, and school communities in ways that elevate common identities or form new ones—identities that encourage us to fight for each other and view circumstances through a collective lens.

Activities relating to racism and White supremacy can appear daunting because educators—especially White educators—can become defensive when they are presented with antiracist training about Whiteness. There could be a psychic instinct for antiracist school leaders to spend a disproportionate amount of time trying to formulate what *English Journal* editor Ken Lindblom (2017) calls "a gentle approach to racial awareness" (p. 74). After all, the prevailing discourse of Whiteness communicates that teachers can be colorblind and not racist while not examining systems of oppression that privilege some and disadvantage others (Lindblom, 2017). Further, discussions about racism can have negative, intensified, and emotional responses with unconscious triggers (Grinage, 2019).

Sometimes, stakeholders use techniques to avoid collegial exchanges and critical self-reflection about topics related to antiracism, such as appealing to ignorance or elevating intersectionality. Antiracist educators think about the lenses through which they view adult-to-adult and adult-to-child exchanges because the successes and failures of those interchanges might not be as clear-cut as they initially appear.

There are opportunities for adults and children to grow as a result of each interaction. How much each participant, witness, and organization *should* grow is a matter of interpretation (Grinage, 2019).

Resistant staff members are typically invested in Whiteness; this is the case because most of us—including me—are socialized to elevate Whiteness (Shim, 2020). For example, when we consider achievement and opportunity gaps, White students comprise the group to which all other groups of students are compared. Some might push back on the premise that comparing groups to the highest-achieving population means that we're elevating Whiteness. I'd respond by pointing out that, in many cases, White students are not the highest-achieving group, yet they're viewed as the default demographic. Continuing the practice of Whiteness as the norm is one way that educators tend to elevate Whiteness. The manifestations of that investment could include shame, deflection, projection, and rage, among other things (Tanner & Berchini, 2017).

> **Actively listen to resisters, and assume they have positive intentions. Don't attack the person; dialogue about the construct of their arguments, which better supports your work together (Hall, 2018).**

On the surface, it appears that resistance might originate from several possible sources, such as colorblindness, fear, guilt, ignorance, selfishness, or outright disbelief. A closer look reveals that these potential origins each are different aspects of a person's life experiences. If staff members grew up in families or surrounding communities where people avoided conversations about race, then they are more likely to be ignorant of antiracist issues. If they have never conversed with anyone who has been adversely affected by systemic racism, or they regularly consumed media that preached against antiracism, then they are more likely to disbelieve racism's existence. Guilt may stem from an upbringing that explicitly recognized systemic racial or ethnic privilege (Matias et al., 2016). Notice these forms of resistance are not based on intelligence, ethics, or lack of information. People's life experiences significantly influence the way they view all topics, and emotional issues like racism amplify those influences.

Emphasize the Potential Productivity of Dissent

Cognitive diversity, or "differences in perspective or information processing styles" (Reynolds & Lewis, 2017), is a business principle that is growing in acceptance (Tuff & Goldbach, 2021). It's grounded in demographic diversity. People from varied backgrounds are more likely to view the world differently, approach challenges differently, and build community differently. Effective leaders convene cognitively diverse teams who constructively collaborate in ways that leverage the best elements of many perspectives. Great ideas—and the ones that are more likely to be embraced by the widest audiences—are born from these environments.

To a school that is committed to antiracism, resistance can appear as a violation of social norms. Even questioning an aspect of your collective work (like the overall vision, or a particular strategy) can seem like wholehearted dissent. Researcher Francesca Gino (2018) uses the moniker "rebels" to label group members who intentionally go against agreed-on norms of belief or behavior. However, instead of roundly condemning those who present alternative ways of thinking and acting, Gino recommends that leaders inspect resistance to identify aspects of *constructive dissent*—a push to interpret visions, purposes, strategies, or metrics from alternative viewpoints. She has found that rebels add essential elements to their organizations.

- Novelty
- Curiosity
- Perspective
- Diversity
- Authenticity

In her examination of companies such as Time Warner, Deutsche Bank, and Pixar, Gino (2018) has found numerous examples of how effective organizations encourage and leverage dissent in ways that invigorate their teams and spur the growth of their companies. The benefits of dissent can also be accrued within school contexts.

Dissent might be resistance to thinking about or behaving regarding a particular element of the plan, but it isn't always a push against the agreed-on mission of the organization. For instance, many schools declare missions that are some iterations of the following: *We will cultivate capable learners, critical thinkers, and knowledgeable citizens who are prepared for both college and career.* Nowadays, as this book recommends, schools might also add explicit antiracist elements to their missions, perhaps replacing *knowledgeable* with *antiracist*.

If a teacher questions the study of a book by an author who previously made statements that the teacher believes were anti-Semitic, that doesn't mean the teacher doesn't accept the concept of structural racism. If a paraeducator thinks that teaching first graders about the enslavement of Africans in North America is inappropriate, that doesn't mean the paraeducator believes that primary students should not learn how to think critically about the historical stories they are told. Psychologically safe groups recognize this, and they interrogate behaviors to discern the difference.

Obediently following the chain of command isn't always the best course of action. When encouraging devil's advocates on my staff, I often make statements such as, "I'm good at saying things and making clear decisions. However, I'm not good at saying the best things and making the best decisions. Our ideas are at their best when we all contribute to the thinking. Alternative viewpoints are often the most helpful to our thinking. Let's make this a safe, encouraging space to share them."

For his book *The Culture Code: The Secrets of Highly Successful Groups*, Daniel Coyle (2018) researched scores of organizations to identify practices that lead to strong organizational cultures. During one of Coyle's interviews, a Navy SEAL articulated the need for divergent perspectives in decision making:

> The problem here is that, as humans, we have an authority bias that's incredibly strong and unconscious—if a superior tells you to do something, by God we tend to follow it, even when it's wrong. Having one person tell other people what to do is not a reliable way to make good decisions. So how do you create conditions where that doesn't happen, where you develop a hive mind? How do you develop ways to challenge each other, ask the right questions, and never defer to authority? We're trying to create leaders among leaders. And you just can't tell people to do that. You have to create the conditions where they start to do it. (p. 139)

Coyle suggests that in addition to inviting diverse perspectives, leaders should establish narratives that highlight the organization's priorities and articulate behaviors that lead to desired outcomes. Moreover, he says, those narratives are best when they connect to heuristics, simple this-leads-to-that kinds of phrases. For instance, Coyle (2018) lists several heuristic statements from KIPP charter schools, such as, "Work hard, be nice" and "No robots." He also lists statements from the

New Zealand All Blacks rugby team, like, "If you're not growing anywhere, you're not going anywhere." Narratives that lead to catchphrases that highlight the purpose, strategies, or desired practices or outcomes of the organization are critical to the existence of high-functioning organizations.

The existence of resistance can reveal positive aspects of a school's culture. It indicates a degree of openness and psychological safety among staff. Productive discussions are signs of health, not symptoms of disorder. Dissenting opinions can make ideas stronger, and there might be less passive-aggressive subterfuge.

BALANCE WHO GETS CENTERED

Schools—and the classrooms therein—are racialized spaces (Acuff, 2019; Grinage, 2019). Effective teachers embrace the diversity of their students (Holland & Mongillo, 2016). Race, particularly Whiteness, must be an ongoing, intentional discussion (Acuff, 2019). Effective antiracist teachers recognize that their relationship with Whiteness is an element of their own diversity (Lindblom, 2017).

Whiteness is the set of norms that outlines preferred beliefs, practices, and communications that are invisible components of curricula, instructional techniques, disciplinary practices, behavioral dispositions, and so on that undergird the foundation of our schools. The topic of Whiteness goes "beyond White privilege to prepare teachers to engage in more critical analyses of context and power" (Berchini, 2019, p. 176). Societal norms (that is, Whiteness) dictate that discussions about Whiteness in a pejorative sense are inappropriate because Whiteness is colorblind and fair (Acuff, 2019; Crowley, 2019; Lindblom, 2017).

"Whiteness" is not the same as "White people," so an exploration of one's orientation to Whiteness is an understanding that all educators need, not just White educators (Acuff, 2019). Part of the art of antiracist leadership is balancing how much professional learning opportunities and educational infrastructure center Whiteness or White people.

Some antiracist education advocates contend that the narratives of Whiteness and White people have dominated societal discourse for so long—and so intensely—that antiracist school leaders should use professional learning platforms and other teachable opportunities to center the experiences of Black people, Indigenous people, and other people of color (DiAngelo, 2018; Love, 2019). After all, those groups have been the most harmed by our systems of oppression, and their experiences are regularly devalued by schools and society writ large.

Antiracist school leaders must spend considerable time centering Whiteness and White educators for two primary reasons: (1) White educators continue to comprise most of the teaching corps in the United States, and (2) White educators, on the whole, do not interrogate the effects of Whiteness on themselves or their students, unless they are prompted (Crowley, 2019). Like with any effective pedagogy, instructors must align the learning targets and activities with the cultures of the learners. In order to combat the harmful effects of White supremacy, antiracist school leaders must make Whiteness visible, especially to White people.

Think back to the professional learning progressions from chapter 3 (page 67). Racial identity development was one of the concepts to cover. It could be as simple as discussing a prompt such as, "Why do you think that 'White students' is the group to which other groups are compared when we analyze gaps?" Perhaps it could be writing individual reflections about clips from a video such as the documentary *Mirrors of Privilege: Making Whiteness Visible* (Butler, 2006). Making Whiteness visible could also be a guided conversation through which staff members take introspective views at how current events affect them and those they love (Helms, 2017).

The resistant behavior of White teachers is not the primary problem; the primary problems are our collective and individual investments in the system of Whiteness (White supremacy), and divestment is a complex process. Antiracist school leadership is problematic insofar as it labels teachers—irrespective of race or ethnicity—who try to do the work as failures, without considering the context of school structures, district mandates, collegial support, and other variables (Berchini, 2019).

Research suggests that school administrators can be the most significant influence on teachers' use of antiracist instructional practices and materials (Holland & Mongillo, 2016). Researchers Karen F. Holland and Geraldine Mongillo (2016) have found that "strong and supportive leadership" has a stronger connection to antiracist instructional practices than district mandates or a teacher's ethnicity (p. 22). This speaks to the need for school districts to empower well-trained antiracist administrators who are well connected to—and trusted by—their staffs and school communities.

Acknowledge Intersectionality

During the summer of 2020, Tracie and I visited a winery in Napa, California. On the fourth pour into a tasting, I smiled and giggled to my wife, saying, "The sommelier poured more into my glass than yours." Her deadpan expression didn't match my silly smirk. "He poured more into your glass every time . . . ha ha . . . sexism. I hope you're including something about that in your book." I hadn't noticed because it didn't affect me, even though it affected one of the people I love most in the world.

I said that we should share our observation with the sommelier. Tracie matter-of-factly replied, "Don't bother. He probably won't understand, and the stress would strain our vacation visit. Men often have difficulty recognizing obstacles that are not in their paths." Had this experience been related to race, I'm confident that I would have recognized the problem easily. Since it was related to gender, and I was privileged in that circumstance, I didn't notice the pattern until it was explicitly brought to my attention.

For Tracie, that experience was simply another in a long line of microaggressions; it just happened to be about gender in that case. For me, that experience underscored how "racial identity cannot be disentangled from the experience of gender, sexual identity, wealth or class, citizenship, religious identity, ability or disability, body size, or any other core or peripheral aspect of social identity" (Utt & Tochluk, 2020, p. 139). For this reason, *intersectionality*, which is the recognition and support of the multiple identities of each person, with a specific focus on historically marginalized identities, is a key consideration in antiracist work (Mims & Williams, 2020). In school settings, "an intersectional approach perceives the diversity of students' characteristics and seeks to understand their funds of identity—their ways of being, knowing, and experiencing—with the goal of improving learning outcomes for all students" (Whitenack, Golloher, & Burciaga, 2019, p. 37).

One way to manage those considerations is to highlight the connections to race and other factors of diversity. Kendi (2019) elevated intersectionality by combining several factors of diversity into separate strands of antiracism. For instance, instead of describing discrimination against people who identify as nonbinary as *homophobia* or *sexism*, he labels it *gender racism*, which means the fight against it would be *gender antiracism*.

Bias still plays a significant role in educators' consideration of intersectional support. For instance, when analyzing low student achievement, teachers are more likely to consider outside-of-school factors, such as poverty, than instructional or disciplinary practices. Culturally responsive pedagogy training is not enough to interrupt teachers' complicity in systems of oppression (Whitenack et al., 2019), so antiracism must remain a front-burner issue.

Superficially, intersectionality can seem like a crude form of "whataboutism." When asked to confront issues of racialized spaces, resisters might respond, "What about English proficiency?" "What about poverty?" or "What about special education?" as if racial bias doesn't impact their conversations about any other demographic indicators. To the contrary, intersectionality and antiracism can be used as mutually supportive frameworks.

Various forms of biases influence educators' thoughts about intersectional issues, and there are myriad factors of diversity, so it can be difficult to keep the staff focused on the vision. When dealing with the thoughts and interactions of human beings, there are no monoliths. School leaders might not have the expertise to delve deeply into detailed facets of social science. So, whether frameworks lean toward simplistic or complex should not be our primary focus; it should be whose voices are valued and whose voices are overlooked or excluded (Carbado & Harris, 2019).

> Antiracist school leaders must watch out for those discussions of non-racial diversity being used as techniques to avoid the less comfortable and omnipresent topic of race in their buildings.

Intersectional and antiracist frameworks are not inherently good or bad. Both lines of thinking can be helpful in certain contexts, if they avoid single-axis centering of one specific group for the entirety of their work (Carbado & Harris, 2019; Whitenack et al., 2019). There should certainly be platforms for discussions regarding the treatment of people who represent all factors of diversity. Schools can provide some of those platforms. For instance, in Montgomery County, Maryland, a suburb of Washington, DC, all secondary schools are required to sponsor at least one club that is overtly supportive of LGBTQ+ students, such as a Gay–Straight Alliance. Additionally, the board of education drafted policies that explicitly articulate the district's stance on the treatment of LGBTQ+ stakeholders and issues. Queer issues that relate to race, gender, and religion are certainly complex (Pender, Hope, & Riddick, 2019; Wernick, Espinoza-Kulick, Inglehart, Bolgatz, & Dessel, 2021); however, they are not drastically unlike other discussions related to oppressive institutions. Therefore, an antiracist orientation would be helpful when considering such frameworks (Shelton & Barnes, 2016).

For example, a staff member might express the need for an emphasis on a "culture of poverty" in Black and Brown communities—a deficit-based theory about individual responsibility or group characteristics at the expense of a focus on structurally racist elements of our society (Ladson-Billings, 2017; Seale, 2020).

Some researchers caution antiracist school leaders to pay careful attention to who is centered in their antiracist efforts because antiracism can easily slide into centering the experiences of Black men and White women, de-emphasizing the discriminatory experiences of women of color (Carbado & Harris, 2019). Additionally, because of phobias present in communities of color, LGBTQ+ people do not always see themselves as welcome in the antiracism struggle (Clarke, 2019).

School administrators are key to leading the building-level work of intersectional antiracist work, as they are uniquely situated to remodel school structures, galvanize their communities, interact with policymakers, and develop the capacity of their staffs. However, any staff member can advance intersectional issues to the forefront of the staff's collective agenda. They can make statements and facilitate activities that bring shared identities to the forefront and cast spotlights on examples of intersectional oppression.

Antiracist school leaders can support intersectional antiracism by including and promoting the following approaches to support students' learning, according to education professor David A. Whitenack and his colleagues (2019).

- Having sociocultural consciousness (the understanding that different people can have different worldviews)
    - » Facilitate activities during which participants reflect on a wide range of perspectives, particularly when the varied opinions are about a particular topic.
- Affirming views of diversity
    - » Facilitate activities that allow students to share their backgrounds, discuss perspectives, find commonalities, and embrace their differences.
    - » Make statements such as, "Our diversity is one of our strengths."
- Committing to acting as change agents
    - » Facilitate activities that encourage students to take action when they recognize inequities or wrongdoing.
    - » Make statements such as, "Change starts within each of us."

- Understanding how learners construct knowledge
  » Facilitate learning opportunities that balance student-centered and teacher-centered activities, employ static and active instructional techniques, incorporate inquiry-based and project-based elements, and provide opportunities for listening, speaking, reading, and writing.
- Knowing about their students' lives

The culture of White supremacy within our society results in racially disproportionate achievement, disciplinary, engagement, social, and psychological outcomes for students in our schools (Chin, Quinn, Dhaliwal, & Lovison, 2020; Dunbar, Mirpuri, & Yip, 2017; Gershenson & Papageorge, 2018; Hung et al., 2020; Jones et al., 2021; Merolla & Jackson, 2019; Young, 2019). Similar gaps exist across a wide variety of student demographic groups, including English learners, students with special needs, and students who are eligible for free or reduced-price meals. To support the broad range of needs among students, should schools target language acquisition strategies, special education goals and interventions, or socioeconomic supports? Absolutely. Schools should focus on all the above and more, but not at the expense of an antiracist focus.

Recognize and Counteract Forms of Resistance in Real Time

During the fall of 2020, as part of the discontent with antiracism in schools, some community members of my school fought against the inclusion of Toni Morrison's novel *Beloved* in the curriculum. Opponents of the book explained that required readings for high schoolers should not contain explicit sexual content, and *Beloved* depicts a rape of an enslaved woman.

On the morning of October 26, 2021, Qasim Rashid, a talk radio host, tweeted, "If you want to ban fiction novels about slavery because they're traumatic to White kids but praise Confederate statues despite their trauma on Black kids, then it isn't children you're protecting, it's White supremacy." Someone replied, "You don't know what you're talking about. You aren't even close. For those of us whose families have been here for 200 years, those statues mean something. Its [sic] OUR history. I know it isn't yours."

The tweet exchange is emblematic of why we need to have real-time conversations with people who are interested in learning together. Direct conversations in a psychologically safe environment—particularly in schools in which people have formed collective identities—can widen the aperture of perspective from both sides.

Some might view Rashid's message as dismissive of anyone with an opposing point of view. One could argue that Black children aren't traumatized by statues and that some Confederate icons made people proud for reasons other than the Civil War and the enslavement of Black people.

The reply to Rashid's tweet suggests that Confederate statues resonate only with people whose families have been in the United States since at least the 1800s, and that the history of the Confederacy belongs only to those people who appreciate Confederate monuments. That line of reasoning is also problematic. Black people, for example, have been in the country for four hundred years. Confederate statues do "mean something" to many Black people; it's just that the resonance evokes negative emotions. The Confederacy's waging of the Civil War and the reasons they fought are American history.

The Twitter exchange was unproductive because neither party grew from the interaction. Both individuals may feel that the other person's growth wasn't their concern. However, school leaders don't have that luxury. School leaders are responsible for supporting the development of all school stakeholders, with a particular focus on students and staff. Resistance in the form of dissent or presentation of alternative viewpoints is essential to the optimal functioning of the school. Unproductive talking *at* each other rather than talking *to* each other doesn't benefit anyone, least of all students.

Despite the proactive strategies mentioned up to this point of the chapter, some forms of unproductive resistance are bound to surface. Therefore, antiracist school leaders should be prepared to counter unproductive resistance in real time as examples present themselves.

A common form of unproductive resistance is an overt disbelief in systemic or structural racism. School leaders could connect the content to the resisters' beliefs in forms of bias that the resisters might have an easier time understanding. For example, since the K–12 educator workforce is dominated by women, discuss the participants' views on sexism, patriarchy, or gender bias at the systemic level. Lead the conversation toward the ease with which some women might recognize disparities in treatment or policies because they face the obstacles. Men, who might not face the obstacles in the same way, if at all, might not see the roles that sex and gender play in their everyday interactions and life outcomes.

You could have similar discussions about how obstacles might be obscured for people who are wealthy or thin or able-bodied. If a resister recognizes the "those who face the obstacles see them more easily" dynamic, it's easier to connect to how members of a dominant group (in racism's case, White people) are less likely to identify—or believe the existence of—discrimination against minority groups:

> Humans are pack animals. Belonging is a primary need. People are neurologically wired to feel good when people in their in-groups succeed, perhaps even more than themselves. Since we are social animals, our views of the world are framed by the norms of the groups with which we most strongly identify. (Van Bavel & Packer, 2021)

Perhaps a key to connecting with someone who has a nonracist or segregationist ideology is to meet with them privately and exchange information at times when the nonracist identity is in the forefront. For instance, the school leader might use lunch conversations to solicit the perspectives of nonracist colleagues who were quiet or oppositional during a race-focused staff meeting conversation about trends in school disciplinary data. In another example, some staff members might have never participated in direct conversations about White supremacy, so tying antiracist content to Whiteness could be a productive entry point for those people (Tanner & Berchini, 2017).

For some people, family history can trigger reactions to antiracist content (Tanner & Berchini, 2017), so antiracist school leaders might *prime* discussions in ways that prepare staff to cope with—or temporarily disassociate themselves from—past experiences that could interfere with their engagement in antiracist work. For instance, researcher Brené Brown (2020) spoke with Ibram Kendi on her podcast, where Kendi offered a metaphor to help teachers consider their impending feelings about race discussions:

> IK: If we talk about racist ideas, to grow up in America is to grow up and for racist ideas to constantly be rained on your head and you have no umbrella and you don't even know that you're wet with those racist ideas, because the racist ideas themselves cause you to imagine that you're dry. . . . Then someone comes along and says, "You know what? You're wet, and these ideas are still raining on your head! Here's an umbrella!" You can be like, "Thank you. You know, I didn't even realize I was drenched." . . . This is why I don't think people should feel ashamed. There were other people—and very powerful people—and a history that was constantly raining those ideas on your head. So, what that means is that, for instance, if you're a White American who has racist ideas, and then let's say perpetuated

those ideas [by], let's say, not hiring a Black person because you thought they were lazy, you were simultaneously victim and victimizer. So, I think it's critical for people to recognize that literally. . . . As I talk about in *How to Be an Antiracist*, there's a specific reason why you had so many powerful Americans trying to convince White Americans that Black people were inferior. It was out of their own self-interest. . . . Americans were tricked into believing that Black people should be enslaved in 1855. Then, meanwhile, poor Whites—whose poverty was directly the result of the riches of White slaveholders—were like, "Yeah, it should be this way." So . . . those people were able to get richer and richer. So, me coming to that poor White person who believes Black people should be enslaved, and men who have even sort of worked on slave patrols and brutalized Black people trying to run away, I'm basically coming to them and saying, "Here is the way you were a victimizer, and here is the way you were a victim." It's critically important for people to understand people have been tricked. They've been manipulated. They've been hoodwinked. That's what I want people to realize.

BB: Yeah, thank you for the umbrella. I didn't know I was wet.

At my school, we played this podcast episode during the early part of our antiracist vision arc. It so happened that the year prior, we read Brené Brown's (2018) *Dare to Lead*, and one of my staff members thought her conversation with Kendi would help us transition to our antiracist focus.

In her work with White preservice teachers in educator preparation programs, education professor and researcher Cheryl E. Matias and colleagues (2016) uncovered multiple examples of emotional deflection and projection. Deflection could take the form of mentioning other factors of diversity, such as sexual orientation, while projection could take the form of gaslighting, where "the *real* victims are White people." Deflection, projection, and other forms of passive aggression are forms of unproductive resistance.

Matias recommends that antiracist school leaders take clear actions to counteract staff who passive-aggressively take little to no action, waiting for this phase of the school's professional learning cycle to pass. One way to combat the passive-aggressive approach, she explains, is to make explicit commitments to antiracist education. When resistant folks understand that this focus is not a passing fad but a new value that will affect school norms moving forward, they lose the crutch of trying to outlast the leader's focus.

The possible forms of resistance to antiracist education are too numerous to list here. Table 4.1 (page 122) offers sample kinds of resistance to antiracism and potential countermoves.

TABLE 4.1: Sample Forms of Resistance and Possible Countermoves

POTENTIAL EXPRESSIONS OF RESISTANCE	POSSIBLE COUNTERMOVES
People express disbelief in anti-dark racism. *"I know some people can be racist, but that doesn't mean that the whole system is set up against people of color."*	Connect to or discuss the participants' beliefs in a form of bias that the participants might have an easier time understanding. *"Some of my female colleagues have explained their experiences with discrimination to which I was totally oblivious. I've since learned that it is harder to recognize the obstacles that I myself don't face. Have there been times when you have experienced discrimination based on one of your characteristics?"*
People angrily shout clichés in public forums. *"Teaching about racism makes White children feel guilty, and it encourages Black children to hate White children!"*	Ask measured questions about their information sources and connections to empirical research, historical trends, or district data. *"I'd like to learn more about your concerns. Can you point me to some examples where hate was created by teaching about racism?"*
People say they don't feel like they can make missteps for fear of being labeled racist. *"I'm uncomfortable joining conversations. What if I say the wrong thing? I don't want to be labeled a racist just because I have a different point of view or I make an incorrect statement."*	Facilitate activities to build trust and connection, thereby increasing feelings of psychological safety. Begin with low-risk exchanges of information, such as table or partner conversations about interests or family structures. Later, move on to reading or viewing content that could be closer to participants' core values. Model vulnerability by sharing personal mistakes and how missteps should be considered teachable moments. Make explicit statements expressing the belief that no one member of the staff knows all and mistakes are not only supported but also expected. *"I'd like us to see this team as a cohesive group of learners. No one of us knows everything about this topic. No one of us has a monopoly on meaningful life experiences. We are going to make mistakes, but we are not going to condemn each other. We will look at mistakes as teachable moments. We will add value to our collective conversations in ways that lead us to enrich the lives of our students."*
People say their life experiences haven't indicated the need for antiracism. *"I know slavery used to exist, but I've never seen anyone commit a racist act. Every successful person I know has gotten there through hard work, and every unsuccessful person I know has done the opposite."*	Share and jointly analyze research that compiles the life experiences of others. Ask people what conditions, evidence, or criteria would change their minds; then share that information (Grant, 2021). *"What kind of information could possibly cause you to change your opinion?"*

continued →

People demonstrate passive-aggressive reluctance to participate in antiracist professional learning activities. *[Silence]* *"I'm not sure I understand where we're going with all this conversation."*	Make public statements about the school's long-term commitment to the work (Matias & Mackey, 2016). Engage in one-on-one conversations to gain the perspectives of nonparticipative staff members.
People stress competing priorities, such as the needs for new instructional skills, curricula, tools to fight a pandemic, and social-emotional learning strategies. *"I believe antiracism is important, but I think we have to put some other things on the front burner. We have to focus on the things that have larger effects on student achievement."*	Explain that antiracism encompasses all aspects of schooling because racism affects all aspects of schooling. For instance, students might be less engaged with texts, videos, or other content that is bereft of their cultures, which impacts their ability to learn the material. In another example, teachers who don't culturally connect with students might view a benign behavior (for example, shouting out a connection to the statement of a peer or disagreement with a teacher's viewpoint) as a disruption or as disrespect.
People make statements that imply their family history has triggered reactions to antiracist content (Tanner & Berchini, 2017). *"White people have never cared about the well-being of people of color, so I don't expect things to change now."*	Prime discussions in ways that prepare staff to cope with—or temporarily disassociate themselves from—past experiences that could interfere with their engagement in antiracist work (Tanner & Berchini, 2017). For instance, Glenn E. Singleton and Curtis Linton (2006) created four agreements that could serve as ground rules for these conversations. 1. Stay engaged. 2. Experience discomfort. 3. Speak your truth. 4. Expect and accept non-closure. Singleton and Linton (2006) also use what they call the Courageous Conversations About Race (CCR) Compass, which is a tool that suggests people filter these experiences through one of four temperaments: (1) believing, (2) thinking, (3) feeling, or (4) acting. Introducing this concept during an early conversation encourages participants to empathize with colleagues, and it heightens their self-awareness.
People post provocative statements on social media platforms. *"Why are you spending my tax dollars to teach Hispanic and Black children that they don't need to work hard to be successful?"*	Ignore them. Like educator Fred Jones and colleagues (2014) say about school discipline, if you are lured into an emotional exchange by someone who is clearly disinterested in what you view is a productive outcome, then you are agreeing to costar in a play that is written, produced, directed, and marketed by the provocateur (Jones, Jones, Talbott, & Jones, 2014). Don't take the bait!

Above all, assume positive intent and actively listen to alternative perspectives. Taking in new information, reflecting on the clarity of your expression, and examining your assumptions can only strengthen your ideas.

RECKON WITH OUR HOMOPHILY

During teacher interviews for my school, I developed several informal practices. I required the members of my interview panel to complete an online training module about the effects of implicit bias in hiring; I selected applicants to interview based on the recommendations of referrers I trusted; and my panel posed questions that candidates received verbally, in real time. Once, one of my staff panelists explained that people who were cerebral introverts, like her, might be at a disadvantage because they might not stand out to previous employers, and they might need more time to think about their responses to questions posed by the panel. During our discussion, my staff panelist said, "It looks like you are advantaging people who are similar to you. Is that what we're doing?"

In researching her book *The End of Bias: A Beginning—The Science and Practice of Overcoming Unconscious Bias*, Jessica Nordell (2021) found that we all have a strong bias toward homophily, which is *like of the same*. Homophily anchors us to people, places, music, situations, and other aspects of culture. Nordell says we should intentionally seek out divergent circumstances that challenge us to interrogate our assumptions, review our data, and rethink our conclusions. We should regularly consider the question, "What if opponents of antiracist pedagogy are right?" I try to keep that question in my mind as I'm planning and facilitating activities related to antiracist practice. For others, it might help to journal or regularly discuss this reflection with trusted colleagues.

> **Antiracists must be willing to change their minds when new facts warrant a change. If not, then why should racists or nonracists be willing to change their minds after a conversation with antiracists?**

In his book *Think Again: The Power of Knowing What You Don't Know*, organizational psychologist Adam Grant (2021) lays out common roles that leaders use when they face resistance: preacher, prosecutor, and politician. The preacher and prosecutor both adopt the posture that others need to change, but not themselves. The politician may tell people what they want to hear at the risk of avoiding reality or what needs to be faced. Those are not the only available roles. Grant says leaders should think more like scientists. Scientists form hypotheses based on what previous data suggest, and they develop conclusions based on what current data support. Scientists are looking to pursue particular beliefs; they are looking to answer particular questions.

Kendi (2019) contends that antiracist practitioners should consider approaching disbelievers with an open mind. It is possible that the beliefs of people who disagree are just as central to their identities as antiracists' beliefs.

Grant (2021) takes Kendi's open mind practice a step further. Grant recommends that strong leaders actually cultivate groups of people who express disbelief and other forms of dissent. He says that while support networks are important, leaders also need challenge networks, people who critique and push our current levels of best thinking and make them even better.

Intentionally seek heterophilic activities—those that elevate perspectives that counter your current beliefs, which tend to broaden your life experiences—and individuals who push back against your current ways of thinking. Both approaches push you to examine your current beliefs and practices at deeper levels. You might decide to redouble some efforts while eliminating others. Either way, you develop a stronger version of your vision and more effective strategies to achieve it.

CONCLUSION

My mother has Crohn's disease, caused by an autoimmune condition in which her immune system attacks her digestive tract. I remember when she found the right course of treatment, when she was around the age of forty-five. We sat together on her front porch on a crisp autumn morning, with her cocker spaniel Buddy lying at our feet. We spoke about several topics, not the least of which was her excitement about an effective new treatment she had recently begun. After decades of constant discomfort and multiple surgeries, her body seemed to have righted itself. She gently smiled and remarked, "I forgot what normal feels like."

The uproar about antiracism, whether from the view of a proponent or an opponent, is analogous to the fever, severe pain, or other symptoms from an autoimmune disease; there are intense, sometimes debilitating feelings, but ultimately, one part of a body is attacking another. For either side to win, a part of the body must be removed. Treatments for such illnesses teach the immune system which part of the body has the disease without attacking other parts of the body. Racism and White supremacy have always been part of the United States, so we can't know what "normal" feels like; we need to be prepared for feelings of disequilibrium.

The members of a school staff—and the citizens of the United States more broadly—are parts of our body. Through dialogue, we can come to agree on commonalities, and we can jointly confront the problems that our districts face. That doesn't mean that we will always agree, but we can disagree without being disagreeable. We can discuss the worth of an idea and build on it without condemning the worth of the people who present it. This is what Grant (2021) calls *productive conflict*. Antiracist school leaders help their teams recognize their interdependence, and they send the message that we are all invested in our collective mission. Antiracist school leaders know that they can engage in these arguments about the process or products without making personal attacks. Identities are complex. Each person has a different identity—in fact, multiple identities—and therefore, racial identity development is unlikely to be a linear, one-size-fits-all process (Shim, 2020).

Antiracist leaders must be willing to acknowledge the diverse experiences, temperaments, capacities, and aspects of development for each person they lead. Rather than push people away, use collective pronouns, tell personal stories that signal common virtues, elevate common causes, delineate the lines between in-group and out-group members, and generally use what Van Bavel and Packer (2021) describe as the *tools of identity leadership*. Leverage situations that elevate a shared identity or multiple common identities (like a lot of our staff members, many of our students' caregivers are working mothers, who, in the face of myriad obstacles, are putting forth their best efforts in order to provide their children with the best lives possible). This way, people will be more supportive of each other, and they might even engage in the work outside of school duty hours, away from the watchful gazes of school administrators. When formerly reluctant staff take initiative to coordinate their own antiracist learning, your resisters have changed their orientations, and they are on their ways to becoming antiracist school leaders.

APPLY YOUR LEARNING

Acknowledging the opposition you might encounter could be the scariest part of your transformation into a new antiracist school leader. You might think, "How will I know how to respond?" "What if I do the wrong thing?" "What if I don't know the answers to people's questions?" It's easy to become paralyzed by repeatedly second-guessing your thoughts and actions that could lead to confrontation with those who are put off by antiracism conversations.

You don't need to know everything, you don't have to reply to every complaint, and it's probably not humanly possible to say all the right things all the time. Hold yourself to a different standard. Do your best to formulate opinions based on the information you have. When you get new information, it's appropriate to consider modifying your perspective. There might be a lot of information from this chapter that was new to you, which makes sense. That's why you chose this book. The following items translate some of this chapter's concepts into actionable steps that will help you and your staff embrace the resistance to your collective efforts in ways that don't detour you from the mission. Read through each section, and revisit the chapter if you need help recalling any details.

KNOW

- Emphasize the potential productivity of dissent. "Rebels" can add novelty, curiosity, perspective, diversity, and authenticity that help to engage your staff (Gino, 2018).
- Know possible forms that resistance might take. That allows you to anticipate hurdles and build countermoves into your professional learning progression. (See table 4.1, page 122, for forms of resistance and countermoves.)
- Recognize your impact that triggers resisters, not just your intent.

SAY

- Say, "This is a space for all of us, no matter our views on racism, or bias more broadly. Our collective ideas based on connections to our individual life experiences are stronger or more impactful than any one of our visions or ideas alone."
- Say, "I've had experiences that have shaped me that you won't experience. You've had experiences that shaped you that I won't have. But our dialogue about our experiences has shaped us both."
- Encourage divergent perspectives with statements such as, "I'm good at saying things and making clear decisions. However, I'm not good at saying the best things and making the best decisions. Our ideas are at their best when we all contribute to

the thinking. Alternative viewpoints are often the most helpful to our thinking. Let's make this a safe, encouraging space to share them."
- Acknowledge that bias exists around a multitude of diversity factors and that you choose to focus on or invest in race because the disparities have been so far-reaching and long-existing across data categories.

 **DO**

- Create opportunities for common identities to move to the forefront. That changes the empathetic, identity-based lenses of your staff.
- Cultivate challenge networks.
- Seek out divergent circumstances to counter your bias toward homophily.
- Brainstorm narratives and catchphrases that tell your school's story in ways that highlight your purpose, strategies, or desired practices or outcomes.
- Actively listen to discover the sources of the resistance.
- Assume positive intentions from voices of dissent.

Chapter 5
ELEVATE ANTIRACIST CURRICULUM AND INSTRUCTION

Key Vocabulary

academic empowerment	The provision of intellectual rigor that prepares students to compete in a global marketplace of colleges and careers (Schindel Dimick, 2012).
critical cross-cultural education	A blend of curricula and instructional practices that focus on unequal power relationships, including—but not limited to—race (Rodriguez & Morrison, 2019).
criticality	The ability to recognize societal intersections and influences of "power, anti-oppression, and equity" through historical and contemporary lenses (Muhammad, 2020).

eradicationist pedagogies	Practices that seek to replace the alleged inferior, defective characteristics of historically marginalized groups of people with the supposed characteristics of mainstream society (modified from Baker-Bell, 2020).
political empowerment	Examining historical and contemporary systems of oppression that can be addressed through individual or collective actions (Schindel Dimick, 2012).
racial literacy	Understanding "the complex interactions between the choices of an individual and the institutional and environmental forces that shape these decisions" (Neville, 2020, p. 376).
social empowerment	The promotion of psychologically supportive and anti-oppressive stakeholder relationships, with a particular focus on teacher-student power dynamics (Schindel Dimick, 2012).

The education community has elevated approaches such as diversity, equality, inclusion, and multiculturalism for decades, without much change in our school buildings, other institutions, or society writ large (Rodriguez & Morrison, 2019). Sound bites, slogans, and acronyms haven't prompted significant change, yet many continue to push forward. Perhaps, as professor of education Alberto J. Rodriguez and science education specialist Deb Morrison (2019) assert, the following are some of the reasons why many of us want to address issues of equity, diversity, and social justice.

- We feel a sense of moral righteousness because some elements of unfairness are easy to discern.

- We acknowledge the changing demographics of the United States and the need for our educational institutions to meet the moment.
- We understand that if we don't educate our future workforce, the upcoming leaders of our society, we are doomed.
- We want to grow, and we want to help others grow.

Irrespective of our rationales for continuing the work, change can't be made through talk alone. We must change the infrastructure of our institutions, and, for schools, curricula are significant elements of our infrastructure. Antiracist school leaders consider questions about how we determine which curricula to use, the instructional practices that supplement our curricula, and whose voices carry weight in our decision making.

This chapter emphasizes how educators should present educational opportunities that are connected to their students' lived experiences. It describes how educators should interrogate the roles race plays in their own lives, and it stresses the need for texts and other media that provide authentic connections to all students. Additionally, the chapter considers processes related to curriculum selection, instructional practices, stakeholder relationship building, and other aspects of teaching and learning.

REVIEW AND DESIGN CURRICULA

In contemporary U.S. public schools, Whiteness is centered in most curricular areas, including reading (Muhammad, 2020), mathematics (Feldman, 2018), history (Ranson, 2013), physical education (Dowling & Flintoff, 2018), and art (Farcus, 2021). While it might be tacitly centered, it is centered nonetheless. It could be a selection of "classic literature" that lacks representation of BIPOC authors, an overweighted focus on European painters in art curricula, or an omission of the contributions of early African mathematicians.

Curricula should be multicultural at a minimum, and antiracist if possible. Here's a quick informal way to differentiate between the two. Multicultural curricula emphasize the inclusion of a variety of perspectives and voices across all topics within the scope and sequence of the standards, materials, instructional practices, and assessments. Antiracist curricula take it a step further by underscoring the need for recognition of the differential power dynamics among the various members of our society, both historically and contemporarily. Additionally, antiracist curricula stress the need to take actions that remediate the damage done through the systems of oppression that result from the power inequities.

To audit potential curricular choices, an optimal option would be to convene a panel of experts and stakeholders who would consider research-based criteria regarding antiracism. For instance, Montclair State University professor of teaching and learning Bree Picower (2012) presents several antiracist features that should be included in every elementary school curriculum.

- Encourage all students to have pride in their heritage (self-love and self-knowledge).
- Emphasize that all human beings deserve respect (respect for others).
- Teach students to recognize historical and contemporary injustice, going beyond merely celebrating diversity (issues of social injustice).
- Acknowledge intersectional issues (respect for others).
- Demonstrate the need to stand together for what is right (social movements and social change).
- Encourage students to share what they learn with others (awareness raising).
- Connect students to activities that demonstrate their agency (social action).

Between 2021 and 2023, governors of several states mandated that school curricula avoid any topic that could be discomforting to White students and their families (Flgov.com, 2023; McGee, 2021; Pittman, 2022). The mandates are thinly disguised as a fight against divisiveness in similar ways that White supremacists—and most of the White population of the United States—described Martin Luther King Jr. as divisive in the 1950s. In fact, the avoidance of so-called divisive issues related to race goes back to at least the times of slavery (Mukherjee, 2016). So-called race-neutral curricula might attempt to ignore or play down the structural aspects of racism, but racism manifests nonetheless (Bornstein, 2018).

Antiracist school leaders understand that curricula should not shy away from issues like systemic oppression or cultural competence; in fact, curricula should explicitly target these topics (Najdowski, Gharapetian, & Jewett, 2021). Education development adviser Fiona Ranson (2013) explains how historical events can shed light on present-day topics:

> Key components in an antiracist curriculum include exploring the roots of racism and the development of prejudice from its foundations to violence, and learning about stereotyping and the responses to racism.... However, an antiracist approach recognises that if we are to understand prejudice today, we need to understand historic prejudice. (p. 21)

Educators in every curricular area (including school librarians and art teachers) must educate themselves on the broader work of antiracism to be able to better support their students (Lugo, 2016).

Artist and teacher Adam Farcus (2021) has also found an intersectional focus to be helpful in art instruction. During a discussion in an undergraduate design course, Farcus audited the content in two ways: (1) by asking the students to list the prominent artists with whom they were familiar and (2) by reviewing a textbook that was central to their coursework. In both instances, the lists were dominated by White, male, and cisgender artists. Farcus made it clear that the intention of this audit was not to shame students, the university, or the artists; Farcus wanted to make sure students were aware of the biases and consider why those biases manifest in their classrooms.

Reassess Instruction

Curricula lay out the academic standards that students should master by the end of prescribed development levels, and then it is up to educators to help their students reach those standards. At its core, instruction is based on four essential questions (DuFour, DuFour, Eaker, Many, & Mattos, 2016; Saphier, Haley-Speca, & Gower, 2017).

1. What do you want students to know or be able to do by the end of the lesson (lesson objective)?
2. How will you know if they have achieved the objective (assessment)?
3. How will you help students who have trouble achieving the objective (reteaching)?
4. How will you support students who achieve the objective and are ready for more (enrichment or acceleration)?

This four-question platform serves as the springboard for a number of pedagogical approaches, all of which could be effective with students from various backgrounds. In some cases, writers present strategies that explicitly target all students;

in other cases, they endorse methods that are designed to support specific groups of students. For instance, the Council for Exceptional Children and the University of Florida's Collaboration for Effective Educator Development, Accountability, and Reform (CEEDAR) Center promote twenty-two "high-leverage practices" to support students with special needs (McLeskey et al., 2017). The practices include strategies such as providing time for heterogeneous and homogeneous groups of students to collaborate during lessons based on the principle that knowledge is socially constructed. The social construction of knowledge could be helpful to understand in antiracist school leadership more broadly. We all have different life experiences that develop and solidify our belief systems, whether those experiences occur inside or outside of school settings. The more people—be they students or otherwise—talk with each other about their interpretations of facts and opinions, the greater the likelihood we'll understand that most of the things we think we know are byproducts of beliefs that were handed down from our elders and ancestors, the existence of race being a prime example. If we continue the dialogue in earnest, even when we disagree, there is a chance that we might develop some new truths together.

In another example, mathematics education specialists Sonia Michelle Cintron, Dani Wadlington, and Andre ChenFeng (2021) composed a list of characteristics of antiracist mathematics educators, and they created a workbook full of activities that guide teachers toward examining their mindsets, materials, and practices to check for alignment. According to the team, antiracist mathematics educators exhibit the following behaviors.

- They "design culturally sustaining math spaces" by connecting content and practices to students' home lives and ways of being (Cintron et al., 2021, p. 9).
- They "center ethnomathematics," meaning they draw explicit parallels between mathematics objectives and current and historical forms of oppression as well as methods to combat that oppression (Cintron et al., 2021, p. 9).
- They "make rigor accessible through strong and thoughtful scaffolding" (Cintron et al., 2021, p. 10).
- They "prepare students of color to close the gap in access to STEM fields" through exposing them to careers in the field and people of color who thrive therein (Cintron et al., 2021, p. 10).

- They "embrace and encourage multiple and varying ways of sharing, showing, and communicating knowledge" (Cintron et al., 2021, p. 10).
- They "support students to reclaim their mathematical ancestry" by underscoring the diversity of current and historical mathematicians, including the contributions of people of color to the field (Cintron et al., 2021, p. 10).

Montgomery County Public Schools (2010), a district in the Maryland suburbs of Washington, DC, cultivated a list of twenty-seven "equitable practices" that educators can use to support the learning of diverse classrooms of students. Each practice presented is accompanied by at least one research citation that supports its inclusion on the list. According to the district, the use of these practices demonstrates that teachers believe in their students and they will stick with the students until they master developmentally appropriate standards. The equitable practices are as follows:

1. Welcomes students by name as they enter the classroom
2. Uses eye contact with high- and low-achieving students
3. Uses proximity with high- and low-achieving students equitably
4. Uses body language, gestures, and expressions to convey a message that all students' questions and opinions are important
5. Arranges the classroom to accommodate discussion
6. Ensures bulletin boards, displays, instructional materials, and other visuals in the classroom reflect the racial, ethnic, and cultural backgrounds represented by students
7. Uses a variety of visual aids and props to support student learning
8. Learns, uses, and displays some words in students' heritage language
9. Models use of graphic organizers
10. Uses class-building and team-building activities to promote peer support for academic achievement
11. Uses random response strategies
12. Uses cooperative learning structures
13. Structures heterogeneous and cooperative groups for learning
14. Uses probing and clarifying techniques to assist students to answer
15. Acknowledges all students' comments, responses, questions, and contributions

16. Seeks multiple perspectives
17. Uses multiple approaches to consistently monitor students' understanding of instruction, directions, procedures, processes, questions, and content
18. Identifies students' current knowledge before instruction
19. Uses students' real-life experiences to connect school learning to students' lives
20. Uses wait time
21. Asks students for feedback on the effectiveness of instruction
22. Provides students with the criteria and standards for successful task completion
23. Gives students effective, specific oral and written feedback that prompts improved performance
24. Provides multiple opportunities to use effective feedback to revise and resubmit work for evaluation against the standard
25. Explains and models positive self-talk
26. Asks higher-order questions equitably of high- and low-achieving students
27. Provides individual help to high- and low-achieving students (Montgomery County Public Schools, 2010, p. 1)

One such equitable practice is *wait time*. Wait time occurs when teachers present a prompt and then wait at least three seconds before soliciting responses from students. Wait time allows students to digest the information they just received prior to responding, which can be helpful in several circumstances, including the following.

- An English learner hears the question in English, silently translates the question into their home language, considers a response in their home language, translates the response into English, and then verbally responds to the teacher in English.
- A student with expressive language difficulty just needs a few extra seconds to get their thoughts together.
- A student feels pressured to spit out a quick answer because—in the past—teachers didn't believe the student could answer and typically moved on to a classmate if the student didn't answer right away.

In each instance, students are likely to provide deeper, more complete answers. Just as importantly, students receive the message that the teacher believes that they can provide deeper, more complete answers. Historically, that belief hasn't been conveyed to students of all backgrounds, and it isn't being conveyed to all students today.

Create a System for Assessment and Feedback

In partnership with instruction, assessment represents the other side of the pedagogical coin, and educators should certainly consider antiracist principles as they plan and implement checks for student understanding. After his look into various teachers' grading practices, Joe Feldman (2018) asserts that grading structures should be accurate, bias-resistant, and motivational. It can be easy to overlook the influence our respective cultural prisms might have on assessment traditions. In their book *Building Equity: Policies and Practices to Empower All Learners*, Dominique Smith, Nancy Frey, Ian Pumpian, and Douglas Fisher (2017) express displeasure with one such habit:

> Too often, the grades students receive reflect a mix of compliance and understanding, and the percentage that each contributes to students' grades varies across teachers, schools, districts, and states. . . . When grades are given, they should reflect students' understanding of the content. Grades are abbreviated information about a student's performance in a specific subject and should reflect a level of mastery of the content taught. (p. 134)

The feedback that students receive on their performance is equally critical, and culture plays a significant role in that as well. Teachers should seize opportunities to pull students' backgrounds into the forefront. One way to do this is to provide task feedback in partnership with the students who completed the assignments. Feedback that is co-constructed and public has a better chance of being inclusive of students' values, lived experiences, and cultures, thereby making feedback more applicable and memorable for students (Stanley, 2017).

Sarah Stanley (2017), director of university writing at the University of Alaska Fairbanks, emphasizes this in the following passage:

> The solution is not to replace our [White] impressions of style in favor of teaching conscious rhetorical choices. Rather, the challenge is to recognize how impressions can become a starting point and not the finish line in our discussions with students about stylistic features in their writing. . . . We must not ignore, dismiss, or respond in an isolated manner to aspects of student writing which trigger a racial impression about voice; instead we must create a space for sociocultural style. . . . Feedback about style

> occurs in a power, or assessive, context, initiated by a teacher to students. . . . Our feedback process is often *private* or *interpersonal*, and this choice means we are not able to benefit from the diverse perspectives present in our classrooms. But when teachers share their impression of a particular micro feature, and allow the impression to circulate in a whole classroom environment, we learn to reflect on the limits and possibilities of bringing our impressions of style out into the open, alongside our students. (pp. 8–9)

The teacher's initial impression is the starting point of the feedback. Even if the teacher goes further to consider their potential biases toward a student's performance, feedback can only be complete when it includes the voice of the student. Preferably, the teacher and student will engage in a discussion that results in mutual growth because students flourish in environments where teachers experience professional *development*.

Audit Materials

One year, a school team brainstormed strategies to help accelerate the learning of one of my students during the summer. The school team—which included the student's parents—proposed several activities to support the student, one of which called for the school to provide groups of books throughout the months of June, July, and August.

One of my responsibilities in this effort was to deliver the first set of books to the student's home. So, late one June morning, I walked into the book room of my building, and I grabbed a few books that were at the student's reading level. As I reviewed my collection, I noticed that none of my books featured an Asian or Asian American main character. This should have been critical to my search because, although my student body was composed of 95+ percent Latino and Black students, this particular student was Asian. Now, our book room was small, probably twenty-five feet by fifteen feet, and it contained hundreds of titles across more than a dozen reading levels. I searched high and low. It took me more than forty minutes to locate one of the two books near the student's reading level that featured an Asian main character.

I sent a text to my reading specialist. Later, I recounted the experience to my school leadership team, and I told them, "I like to think of myself as the 'equity guy.' I'm super-confident about my knowledge and skills in this field. How could members of our school family go unrepresented for so long? It's my responsibility to ensure that things like this don't occur. This happened on my watch."

We bought new books, but that was not the point. The primary issue was our nonexistent system for auditing our materials. I shared my concern with administrative peers in my district, and one of them sent me an auditing tool that he used in his school (a similar auditing tool can be found in *Building Equity* [Smith et al., 2017]). This auditing tool presents questions and categories to use during an evaluation of your administration to look for confirmation that antiracist practices are being enacted effectively, while changes to current administrative systems are reviewed for success. I took it back to my leadership team, and we discussed potential modifications. We formed a subcommittee that was charged with auditing our materials, instructional practices, climate, and relationships with parents.

School curricula typically recommend materials that support their optimal implementation. That was the vetting system on which I used to rely. I now know that antiracist school leaders review recommended materials, evaluate the diversity of their representation with a particular lens on the members of the school community, and supplement curricula with materials that elevate the people, places, and stories that are central to their students'—all their students'—lives.

Equity-focused educators agree that "multicultural texts should be naturally integrated into the curriculum where students are exposed to diversity as a regular part of their education and not just 'hauled out' for special holidays" (Holland & Mongillo, 2016, p. 26). They also understand that materials should be available in multiple languages, particularly the prominent languages in the school community (Najdowski et al., 2021).

Antiracist instructional materials help educators present holistic views of our society, affirming the humanity of all its members. Librarian Sujei Lugo (2016) has explained how she considers those kinds of texts for her school library, stressing representation, accuracy, and authenticity. She views material selection as an opportunity to support "counternarratives, vehicles to expose forms of oppression, and mirrors to build a positive self-image" (p. 24).

Antiracist school leaders recognize that superficial representation is necessary but not sufficient.

The selection of materials is crucial, but it should not be a solo endeavor. The optimal strategy is to convene a team of experts and stakeholders to review the current materials and recommend modifications. If a group of experts is unavailable, antiracist school leaders can convene a group of stakeholders—a group that is representative of the community demographics—and perform a similar task. The key is to ask questions about the holistic representation of people, places, and cultures across a variety of diversity factors. Make the request for support; staff and community members will step up.

PRESENT EDUCATIONAL OPPORTUNITIES THAT CONNECT TO STUDENTS' LIVES

The recommendation that educational standards and practices should be connected to students' lived experiences is not a new one. Scholars and policymakers have been debating the role of culture in educational outcomes for a long time (Gay, 2018). Early on, the conversations were about whether the cultures of people of color were assets or deficits with respect to students' academic outcomes. Since the early 1980s, there has been a greater focus on how educators could enhance curricula and instruction by embedding elements of students' lives. For example, in his book *Equity 101*, Curtis Linton (2011) presents a framework for equity that heavily emphasizes "relevancy," which "connects the learner with the instruction and curriculum" (p. 54). Antiracist educational approaches communicate that every person is valued, and creating more homelike schools strongly articulates that message. Relevancy might be a new and challenging concept to some, but caring and skilled educators are more than capable of considering relevancy as they plan.

Cintron and colleagues (2021) use the term *ethnomathematics* to describe how antiracist instructors find ways to blend the cultures and experiences of their students into their classroom approaches. Sometimes, that means exposing how mathematics has always been useful in their everyday lives; other times, that means examining how mathematics has been used to further systems of oppression. Mathematics and other curricular areas have prominent roles in the lives of our students. Making those placements transparent helps educators create prominent roles for our students' lives within our curricula.

Cultural associations are not just beneficial for mathematics instruction; research supports their use across multiple curricular and instructional topics. Rodriguez and Morrison (2019) provide examples of several such studies. For instance, assistant professor of science education Jean R. Aguilar-Valdez and colleagues (2013) showed that science instruction can be more impactful when teachers plan with the multidimensional identities of their Latinx students in mind. The studied teachers' instructional approaches used the students' backgrounds as assets around which teachers organized their classroom structures and lessons. Another study, conducted by researchers Sara Tolbert, Nicole Snook, Corey Knox, and Inyene Udoinwang (2016), reviewed how teachers place science instruction within a social justice context. Teachers provided instruction related to "science-related issues of justice" and not on rote memorization of textbook information (p. 58). When instructional activities combine elements of social empowerment, political empowerment, and academic empowerment (Schindel Dimick, 2012), students read more critically and apply their learning effectively.

Explore Social Justice in STEM

Associate professor of science education Alexandra Schindel Dimick (2012), who composed the Framework for Social Justice Science Education, writes about the importance of science-related social justice, and her study emphasizes social, political, and academic empowerment devices. *Social empowerment* promotes psychologically supportive and anti-oppressive stakeholder relationships, with a particular focus on teacher-student power dynamics. *Political empowerment* exposes the historical and contemporary systems of oppression that can be addressed through individual or collective actions. *Academic empowerment* provides the intellectual rigor that prepares students to compete in a global marketplace of colleges and careers. Combining these three elements, Schindel Dimick (2012) contends, creates engaging, challenging, and transformative educational opportunities for students. Ann Haley Mackenzie (2020), editor of the peer-reviewed journal *The Science Teacher*, provides a few science topics that connect to issues of justice.

- Environmental racism
- Drug epidemics and fallout
- Industrial dumping
- Genetic discrimination
- Population control
- Gender bias and sexism
- Mass incarceration
- Mental health and treatment disparity
- Quality housing and health

Rodriguez and Morrison (2019) highlight the results of three other studies that focus on the inclusion of students' backgrounds in curricula and instruction. When researchers guide preservice teachers to self-reflect on the impact of power relationships in their urban classrooms, it changes teachers' beliefs about how their personal backgrounds will interact with the lived experiences of their students (Mensah, 2012; Rodriguez, 2015). Moreover, when in-service teachers develop the capacity to structure instructional opportunities in ways that are aligned with their students' backgrounds—which are often different from the teachers' backgrounds—teachers are more likely to remain in the field (Morales-Doyle, 2017).

Practice Historical Responsiveness

Antiracist pedagogy disrupts White supremacist ideology in real time, as well as offers students opportunities to understand the concept's historical and current implications (Schultz, 2019). For example, associate professor of language and literacy Gholdy Muhammad (2020) advocates for curricular targets that are not just focused on adequate depths of knowledge and high levels of skills at each grade level; she pushes for pedagogical practices that she calls *historically responsive*. Those are practices that enhance knowledge and skill development through intentional connections to students' multiple identities as well as activities that make demographic power dynamics transparent in ways that encourage students to consider them.

> **If educators are to be able to present educational opportunities that are connected to their students' lived experiences, then educators must be ready to confront issues related to race and language (Inoue, 2019).**

Knowledge, skill, identity, and power have very real contemporary implications for students, staff, caregivers, and community members; and according to Muhammad, it's helpful to orient those aspects within a historical framework. Historical and contemporary understandings activate what she describes as *criticality*, the ability to recognize "how power, anti-oppression, and equity operate throughout society. Criticality enables us to question both the world and texts within it to better understand the truth in history, power, and equity" (Muhammad, 2020, p. 117). Student criticality could bring forth teacher discomfort.

To counter White supremacy ideology, antiracist educators should provide opportunities that make White supremacy visible for staff and students, exposing it even when the perpetrators have good intentions. Staff and students must develop critical lenses that are attuned to racialization and the implications of racial hierarchies (Schultz, 2019).

Sometimes instructors need to lead activities that acknowledge the easily identifiable hierarchies in our society, such as those that stratify dialects (Baker-Bell, 2020). April Baker-Bell (2020), associate professor of language, literacy, and English education at Michigan State University, points out how "anti-Black linguistic racism" problematizes people whom she describes as "Black Language speakers." She asserts that instead of dehumanizing and marginalizing Black Language speakers, educators should recognize Black Language as a grammatically correct dialect of English. Other times, the issues are less transparent. Joshua Bornstein (2018), director of educational leadership programs at Fairleigh Dickinson University, points out how he saw some oppressive school structures hidden in plain sight:

> I noted how the school was implementing positive behavioral interventions and supports by posting a slogan—ROARS, Respectful, Optimistic, Always Responsible, and Safe—around the school. I first reacted to the slogan as an artifact of White hegemony—apparently neutral language that was code for compliance as typically exhibited by Whites. (p. 14)

In her book *Culturally Responsive Teaching: Theory, Research, and Practice*, Geneva Gay (2018) points out that culturally responsive teaching isn't a destination or a repertoire of tactics; it's an ever-evolving state of mind, a posture that reflects an educator's belief that they and their students are whole human beings, and they learn best from each other when they incorporate elements of each other's humanity into their shared experiences. A good teacher includes their students' backgrounds in each lesson. An antiracist teacher helps students understand how their backgrounds have been historically marginalized, how they can recognize marginalization if it reoccurs, and how they can advocate for inclusion. Rodriguez and Morrison (2019) assert the need for that kind of critical multiculturalism: a focus on unequal power relationships, but not limited to race. The authors call its education application *critical cross-cultural education*.

Teachers from backgrounds vastly different from their school communities might not possess the tools to empathize with historically marginalized students and families. They just do not have the proximity to the experiences. Teachers who cocreate a "shared lens with students" can better understand the impact of historical and current marginalization, which will allow them to teach in fellowship with their students (Stanley, 2017). Often, people of color, and therefore students of color, already bring a critical lens toward media elevation and marginalization. So, critical

> **Don't just try to make the school a prominent place in the community; make the community part of who you are.**

literacy and critical media scholars, as well as antiracist educators, should co-construct classroom spaces that include students' perspectives (Baker-Bell, 2020). Therefore, teachers should not prioritize their "pedagogical relationship rather than the experiences of the people in the room" (Stanley, 2017, p. 21).

One can't be culturally responsive unless one knows the culture. Staff, especially antiracist school leaders, must get out into the community on a regular basis. Cultures can be found in communities—in places like homes, parks, stores, community centers, and places of worship—not on lists of students' demographic categories.

HAVE EDUCATORS INTERROGATE THE ROLES RACE PLAYS IN THEIR LIVES

Mary L. Neville (2020), a high school English teacher in Detroit, planned a lesson about the tone of Khaled Hosseini's novel *The Kite Runner*. During the lesson, a student exclaimed, "Miss, I know you don't live in Detroit. Right?" (p. 372). Neville did live in Detroit, but the question wasn't really about a physical location; it was about shared experiences. The student's question made the point that the content of the lesson was disconnected from his life and the lives of his classmates. In addition, Detroit was going through a period of intense gentrification, and Neville, a White teacher from a middle-class background, was leading a classroom full of students of color. At the time, Neville was uncomfortable with discussions of race, class, or culture, so she replied in a superficial manner. She explained that she did live in Detroit, and she moved on. In retrospect, Neville says she should have designed curricular connections and prepared for conversations about racialized spaces, such as schools and communities undergoing gentrification.

Erase the Idea of the Other

Like Neville, many teachers have backgrounds that differ from those of their students, and teachers often form beliefs about their students and school communities based on consumed media and conversations with peers. Sometimes, those media center Whiteness by exoticizing the cultural markers of non-White people as "ethnic," which sets Whiteness as normal and implies that everything else is "the other" (Schultz, 2019). The condescending view of the other also applies to language, especially dialects of English that are often used by people of color in America. Baker-Bell (2020) shares an example:

> Despite there being decades of research on Black Language, despite its survival since enslavement, and despite its linguistic imprint on the nation and globe, many ELA teachers leave their teacher education program without knowing that Black Language is a rule-based linguistic system that includes features of West African languages and has roots as deep and grammatically consistent as Scottish, Irish, and other world Englishes. This lack of awareness, among many things, oftentimes contributes to the anti-Blackness that Black Language–speaking students experience through the curriculum and instruction, and their teachers' attitudes. (pp. 6–7)

Antiracist school leaders consider Whiteness, not just White privilege, without essentializing White people as the unit of measurement by which people of other races or ethnicities are assessed. When we overly center Whiteness, we run the risk of practicing what Baker-Bell (2020) describes as *respectability* or *eradicationist pedagogies*. Baker-Bell uses language as examples. She says that while eradicationist language pedagogies seek to replace so-called inferior, defective Black Language with White Mainstream English, respectability language pedagogies claim to affirm Black Language, but really see it as "a bridge to learn White Mainstream English" (p. 8). Traveling either of those two routes is based on the same racist infrastructure; they uplift the cultures of some groups of people while simultaneously problematizing the cultures of others.

Antiracist school leaders are not baited into the debates about the alleged divisiveness of antiracist pedagogy. For instance, antiracist practices are not just for students and staff of color; White students can benefit as well (Smith & Crowley, 2018). Moreover, this journey cannot be left to staff of color to lead. White school leaders are necessary partners in this work, as there is an extraordinary burden on people of color who carry this work in isolation (Whitaker, 2021).

Develop Racial Literacy

Other times, our socialization leads to a White savior complex that implies that White people, whether operating as individuals or organizations, possess the unique capacity to help the other. University of Tennessee at Chattanooga assistant professor Heath Schultz (2019) points out:

> the figure of the White savior, while well intentioned, maintains a racialized hierarchical relationship by insisting that it is White folks who can help those in need. The White savior is a racialized subject of Whiteness, one that maintains supremacist order in their efforts to purportedly overturn it. (p. 62)

If the media and conversations attempt to be colorblind in efforts to avoid challenging conversations about race, or they reinforce the savior narrative, then it's up to educator preparation programs and school leaders to support the teachers' development as culturally responsive educators. Otherwise, students suffer because they are led by teachers who are what Neville (2020) calls "racially illiterate":

> Racial literacy . . . notes the complex interactions between the choices of an individual and the institutional and environmental forces that shape these decisions. The process of understanding racial inequities as interacting with both the individual and the institutional involves the rejection of an "either/or" binary. The system of schooling within which new teachers learn to teach is the result of continued and state-sanctioned racialized inequities that have dismantled schooling for Black and Brown children, and, simultaneously, this injustice is supported by our individual decisions, particularly as White teachers. (p. 376)

Antiracist school leaders take advantage of opportunities to develop the racial literacy of their colleagues, navigating through—not around—the inevitable discomfort of everyone involved.

Sometimes a personal trainer (antiracist school leader) can facilitate exercises that provide proper amounts of stress and effective techniques that lead to optimal growth without causing injury. Similar to physical fitness, antiracism might have target milestones, but there is no end goal. We just keep working. As Mary Neville (2020) explains, "one can never really 'arrive' at an antiracist state of existence. Instead, one must continually sit in the uncomfortable, indeterminate process of becoming" (p. 379).

> **Racial literacy, cultural responsiveness, and other aspects of antiracism are analogous to muscles; they grow stronger through stress (Singleton & Linton, 2006).**

Racism can be challenging to recognize because it is built into the fabric of the United States. White supremacy is always present in the air we breathe. None of us are immune to this disease. All of us are touched by its influence. All of us are affected by it. *That doesn't mean that we are all bad people—it just means that we need to pay attention to our own thinking and the world around us.* An antiracist orientation requires educators to interrogate the roles that race plays in their own lived experiences, and they intentionally work to counteract the ways their biases impact teaching and learning (Cintron et al., 2021; Inoue, 2019). We must unlearn the "subtle coding of a normalized racial hierarchy and in turn support the reproduction of institutions that uphold White supremacy" (Schultz, 2019, p. 60).

CONCLUSION

Often, incorporating antiracist considerations into instruction leads to vulnerability and discomfort for educators and students alike. Learning through trial and error is a necessary part of the process, as is the likelihood of making mistakes (Inoue, 2019). Teachers mitigate the impacts of some mistakes by doing their proverbial homework about potential outcomes of conversations. They should be ready to engage in race-based conversations, or at least be prepared to respond to students' statements in a supportive manner.

School leaders must be aware of the prominent role that schools play in the wider discussion about the influence of race in our society, as evidenced by volatile board of education meetings across the United States and debates between elected officials. Well-intentioned plans for change can be muted within the context of a resistant or passive political climate. Bornstein (2018) discovered that in real time: "Developing the turnaround plan was the major project of the year. . . . Although the final plan our team submitted authentically responded to deep racialized challenges, the district administration rejected it and substituted one based on neoliberal formulas" (p. 14).

Another argument against antiracism is that it distracts from the core focus of schools, which is to develop critical thinkers who are prepared to thrive in college and careers. The elements of this chapter are parts of high standards and rigorous activities, not substitutes for them. Academic accuracy and critical thinking do not compete with antiracism; they can exist harmoniously (Ranson, 2013; Schindel Dimick, 2012). Fiona Ranson (2013) makes this point when discussing the Holocaust: "Holocaust education can and should have both historical and antiracist aims . . . these aims do not conflict, nor are they mutually exclusive. Rather, they have a role in supporting each other" (p. 20).

APPLY YOUR LEARNING

Now that you have reviewed the many ways to introduce antiracism into your instruction, create a system for assessment and feedback, and audit materials to reflect current antiracist practices, you're ready to take action. Use the following guidelines to know, say, and do what is needed to instill racial literacy in your students and staff and integrate historical responsiveness into your administration's antiracist practices.

KNOW

- Multicultural curricula emphasize the inclusion of a variety of perspectives and voices across all topics within the scope and sequence of the standards, materials, instructional practices, and assessments. Antiracist curricula go a step further, underscoring the need for recognition of the differential power dynamics among the various members of our society, both historically and contemporarily. Additionally, antiracist curricula stress the need to take actions that remediate the damage done through the systems of oppression that result from the power inequities.

- Political arguments against antiracism are often thinly disguised as a fight against divisiveness in similar ways that White supremacists described Martin Luther King Jr. as divisive in the 1950s. In fact, the avoidance of so-called divisive issues related to race goes back to at least the times of slavery.

- Feedback that is co-constructed and public has a better chance of being inclusive of students' values, lived experiences, and cultures, thereby making feedback more applicable and memorable for students.

- When teachers develop the capacity to structure instructional opportunities in ways that are aligned with their students' backgrounds—which are often different from the teachers' backgrounds—teachers are more likely to remain in the field.

- A White savior complex implies that White people, whether operating as individuals or organizations, possess the unique capacity to help "the other."
- The antiracist journey cannot be left to staff of color to lead. White school leaders are necessary partners in the work, as there can be an extraordinary burden on people of color who carry this work in isolation.

SAY

- Say, "A good teacher includes their students' backgrounds in each lesson. An antiracist teacher helps students understand how their backgrounds have been historically marginalized, how they can recognize marginalization if it reoccurs, and how they can advocate for inclusion."
- Ask questions about the holistic representation of people, places, and cultures across a variety of diversity factors.
- Say, "None of us are immune to the disease of racism. That doesn't mean that we are all bad people—it just means that we need to pay attention to our own thinking and the world around us."
- Say, "One can't be culturally responsive unless one knows the culture. To know the cultures of our students and their families, we must ask questions, check our own biases, and engage in authentic community contexts."
- Say, "Antiracist curricular and instructional considerations are components of high standards and rigorous activities, not substitutes for them."
- Say, "Feedback can only be complete when it includes the voice of the student."

✓ DO

- Convene teams to audit curricula, materials, and instructional practices.
- Present educational opportunities that are connected to students' lives by blending their cultures and experiences into classroom approaches.
- Encourage the employment of equitable, high-leverage instructional practices that support all students.
- Establish grading structures that are accurate, bias-resistant, and motivational.
- Take advantage of opportunities to develop the racial literacy of your colleagues, navigating through—not around—the inevitable discomfort of everyone involved.
- Provide opportunities that make White supremacy visible for staff and students, exposing it even when the perpetrators have good intentions.

Chapter 6

MONITOR YOUR IMPACT

Key Vocabulary

attitudes	Implicit or explicit mental associations that stakeholders establish before, during, and after their school days.
behaviors	The observed or reported actions of—and interactions between—every school stakeholder group.
disaggregation	The process of separating data points in ways that focus on particular demographic segments of the student body or other stakeholder groups.
emotions	The internal moods that stakeholders experience before, during, and after their school days.

expectations	The beliefs that stakeholders hold about students' abilities to achieve academic and social standards.
formative data	Short-term, intra-year data that inform decisions (and the possibility of course corrections) in real time.
hard data	Objective, quantifiable data that are culled from official sources recognized by the district.
observational data	Real-time capture of performance by someone other than the performer.
school climate	The amalgamation of emotions, attitudes, expectations, and behaviors of students, staff, and community members (Grazia & Molinari, 2021).
stakeholder voice data	Self-reported information about the application, impacts, and sentiments of various members of the school community, including students, staff, and caregivers.
student well-being	The sense of physical and emotional health, security, knowledge, and skills that support productive participation in the school building as well as the broader community.
summative data	Long-term, year-to-year information that is used to evaluate progress toward big-picture goals.
supplemental supports	The wraparound programming that addresses needs that might not be filled through adherence to curricular and instructional standards.

Antiracist work in schools is more than a series of monthly professional learning activities. It's the process of centering and supporting those in our school communities who have been historically marginalized. It's also an orientation toward the intentional recognition and mitigation of policies and practices that result in disparate outcomes for students, families, and community members.

Schools are complex systems (Roy, 2020). Therefore, snapshots of singular data points such as test scores are insufficient to measure progress. Capturing the essence of a school requires many assessments that incorporate data from a variety of sources, apply several methods, represent perspectives across stakeholder groups, and consider impacts from multiple angles.

In chapter 3 (page 78), I pointed to Guskey's (2016) recommendations for determining the impacts of professional learning, which are summarized as follows.

> **Antiracist school leaders hold themselves accountable for reorienting the entire school's—if not the school system's—way of being, and metrics should always accompany accountability.**

- **Level 1:** Participants' reactions
- **Level 2:** Participants' learning
- **Level 3:** Organizational support and change
- **Level 4:** Participants' use of new knowledge and skills
- **Level 5:** Student learning outcomes

Guskey's framework highlights data that range from participants' self-reported reactions (such as end-of-meeting evaluations) to objective assessments (like student achievement test scores). In this chapter, we'll go beyond stratification and discuss the wide variety of data available to school leaders, whose input is critical, and helpful frameworks for analysis. You'll also hear about ways that some school leaders have collected, analyzed, and shared data about their antiracist efforts in ways that clarified their intentions and motivated their school communities.

COLLECT DATA INTENTIONALLY

With respect to data collection, consider the timelines that relate to the kinds of information you want to collect. Effective school leaders lead the collection of a variety of formative data regularly throughout each school year (National Policy Board for Educational Administration, 2015), which inform decisions about staying with the current plan or making course corrections. Such intra-year milestones, such as activity-to-activity or quarterly data, might be better suited to capture learning, emotions, and student outcomes related to professional learning activities in real time rather than long-term impacts of your practices. The items and benchmarks of these kinds of assessments may change as often as you implement activities, since some items, benchmarks, and other data points could be specific to the activities being evaluated.

Big-picture impacts might be more easily seen through the collection and analysis of data from year to year and the examination of multiyear trends (Raskin, Krull, & Felix, 2021). With these more summative forms of assessment, it is helpful to use the same or very similar items, benchmarks, and data points so that it is easier to recognize any changes over time (Bernhardt, 1998). While summative data might be less helpful than formative data in making quick changes to the plan in real time (Bin Mubayrik, 2020), they help school leadership teams consider refining the mechanisms of school improvement (Lipton & Wellman, 2012). For instance, if a school's referrals to its respective special education, gifted and talented, and discipline programs have been skewed toward particular segments of its student population during the past five years, perhaps there are some prevention, intervention, and referral protocols that could be adjusted, as well as a big-picture emphasis on productive mindsets.

Taken in combination, summative and formative data indicate where the knowledge, skills, beliefs, and impacts of stakeholders lie on the continuum between racist and antiracist. Keep in mind the continuum is a line (which has no end points), not a line segment (which has definitive end points). Short- and long-term milestones might be achieved, but there is not a definitive end to this work. The goal is to orient the school community toward the antiracist end of the continuum and keep moving forward.

A holistic school evaluation requires an evenhanded approach. It's not just about correlating outcomes. Measuring fidelity to the program is important (Babinski, Amendum, Knotek, Sánchez, & Malone, 2018). Gathering and analyzing a wide variety of data allows antiracist school leaders to identify strengths and needs regarding how staff and students internalize and apply new learning, as well as to gauge the capacity of the existing programmatic infrastructure to support the school community's antiracist evolution. The next section outlines some of the sources of data and target areas that might be helpful to consider.

Essential Varieties of Data

School evaluation data sources are plentiful, and antiracist school leaders should focus on at least four varieties: (1) hard data, (2) observational data, (3) stakeholder voice data, and (4) supplemental supports data. They are not categorized as quantitative or qualitative data, because three of the four varieties of data discussed can be collected in qualitative or quantitative fashions. Qualitative and quantitative examples are embedded in the following explanatory paragraphs. Additionally, clear boundaries do not always delineate the categories of data. There is an intersectional feel (or perhaps nature, characteristic, or sense) to data classification that occurs because data sources often blend together. It's possible to think of these groupings less as rigid classifications and more as reminders to be circumspect when setting targets and measuring progress.

HARD DATA

Hard data are objective, quantifiable data that are culled from official sources recognized by the district. Each district should have an internal assessment information system, a data portal, or some other digital platform from which school staff can review, sort, or download information regarding the performance of their students. From the portal, school staff can find test scores, attendance rates, suspension percentages, and other data that provide both snapshots of real-time performance and trends from the past that can indicate a clear trajectory for the future.

In many cases, districts or states provide data platforms that are open to the public. For example, the Florida Department of Education (2022) posts school performance data in a public accountability report, which links to sortable spreadsheets that provide student achievement data for the current year. In my home state of Maryland, the Maryland State Department of Education runs a website that displays disaggregated state test scores for every school and district in the state (https://reportcard.msde.maryland.gov). Chicago Public Schools takes transparency a step further. In addition to student achievement metrics, its website presents a diverse assortment of data for each school, including parent opinions that are embedded in My Voice, My School surveys (www.cps.edu/about/district-data/metrics/surveys).

OBSERVATIONAL DATA

Observational data are unlike self-reported information derived from surveys or interviews. Observations can take place in a variety of settings, and they are completed by someone other than the participants being viewed (as in a teacher observes a student, a student observes a peer, or an administrator observes a paraeducator). Capturing a performance in real time is an effective method of gauging the application of antiracist content covered in previous professional learning activities. Also, since behaviors are typically influenced by beliefs (Kahneman, 2011), viewing practices in authentic contexts gives leaders a sense of how the learning progression is affecting stakeholders' perceptions.

Observations can be conducted using formal protocols, such as an agreement on the date and time, a pre-observation conference, predetermined viewing criteria, a post-observation meeting, and the presentation of an official report. On the other hand, observations might be informal, potentially with impromptu visits and follow-up messages. In the best cases, school leaders find ways to incorporate both forms of observations (Platt, Tripp, Ogden, & Fraser, 2000). That way, the everyday excellence of staff and students can be encouraged, recognized, and celebrated in ways that support everyone's movement toward the collective vision.

Observations can be effective ways to judge competency by application and impact (Copeland & Ross, 2021), and they can simultaneously support the growth of individuals being observed. After all, formative feedback from observations is commonly used by building administrators to judge teacher performance.

Observation protocols would enable evaluators to note more nuanced changes for individual educators as well as the school in aggregate during the year and make more formative changes or course corrections as needed.

> **Observation protocols should assess not only if some things are done but also the degrees to which they are done well, and they should be accompanied by actionable feedback and coaching (Babinski et al., 2017).**

Observations often have instructional foci, and there are plenty of structures available that outline key teaching methods. TeachingWorks (2022), an initiative from the University of Michigan, presents nineteen items that it describes as *high-leverage practices*. *The Skillful Teacher: The Comprehensive Resource for Improving Teaching and Learning* (Saphier et al., 2017) is a book that has served as the foundation for training over ten thousand in-service educators, according to the publisher, Research for Better Teaching. Another widely used set of instructional guidelines is the *Framework for Teaching* by the Danielson Group (2022). Typically, instructional frameworks are determined at the district or state level, but school leaders might have discretion to supplement prescribed frameworks with practices that are customized to their local contexts.

Outstanding educators, especially those with antiracist orientations, excel beyond instructional skills. There are relationship-strengthening skills, restorative practices, and culturally affirming approaches to pedagogy that also deserve attention. Montgomery County Public Schools (2010) in Maryland has a list of twenty-seven "equitable classroom practices" to which educators and observers can refer.

Joshua Bornstein (2018) provides an example of how school leadership teams can compose criteria to guide observations of classroom conversations based on a school-improvement target. His Teacher Evaluation Rubric on Facilitating Questioning and Thinking includes the following ranking categories:

- **Highly Effective:** Teacher provides varied and appropriate opportunities for students to explain their thinking, defend their claims, and build upon their peers' use of evidence.

- **Effective:** Teacher provides varied and appropriate opportunities for students to explain their thinking and defend their claims to their peers.

- **Developing:** Teacher provides opportunities for students to explain their thinking and defend their claims.

- **Ineffective:** Teacher does not provide varied opportunities for students to explain their thinking or defend their claims. (Bornstein, 2018, p. 17)

This section intentionally refrains from using *classroom* in connection with *observations*. That's because observations do not have to involve administrators walking into rooms to observe teachers leading lessons. Treat observations as opportunities to be creative. They can comprise peers conducting instructional audits in the form of peer walkthroughs (also called *instructional rounds*, *peer observations*, or *focused classroom visits*). Some schools and districts conduct environmental audits, materials audits, curricular audits, and policy audits. School leaders can observe students, their caregivers, and other community members. For example, record the frequency and content of comments in settings like class discussions, PTA meetings, and school town halls. If helpful, figure 6.1 (page 158) demonstrates how Bornstein's criteria can be modified in ways that place students as the primary performers.

Ranking	Description
Highly Effective (A)	Student explains their thinking, defends their claims, and builds on their peers' use of evidence.
Effective (B)	Student explains their thinking and defends their claims to their peers.
Developing (C)	Student explains their thinking.
Ineffective (D)	Student does not explain their thinking.

Source: Adapted from Bornstein, 2018.

FIGURE 6.1: Student evaluation rubric on responding to questions.

STAKEHOLDER VOICE DATA

Stakeholder voice data are self-reported information about the application, impacts, and sentiments of various members of the school community, including students, staff, and caregivers. These data allow antiracist school leaders to view the work through the lens of the people who do the heavy lifting each day (Safir & Dugan, 2021).

Some of the data will be quantitative, such as Likert scales and frequency estimates. Dominique Smith and colleagues (2017) list upwards of sixty items that they recommend leaders ask when auditing equity among students and staff. Items ask stakeholders to express their level of agreement with statements such as, "Students are being prepared to function as members of a diverse society" (Smith et al., 2017, p. 192) and "Teachers have high expectations for me. They believe in me and my abilities" (Smith et al., 2017, p. 198).

Other forms of voice data will be qualitative, such as narrative descriptions and anecdotal comments. Associate professors of special education Amy J. Olson and Carly A. Roberts (2018) evaluated how preservice teachers' beliefs and practices were affected by coursework and support from current teacher educators. The preservice teachers were interviewed and submitted documents (like lesson plans, curriculum notes, assignments, syllabi, and presentation examples) to discuss with evaluators. Several of those document-based discussions demonstrated that preservice teachers' philosophies, knowledge, and practices were shaped by their veteran colleagues. The researchers found it helpful for preservice teachers to point to artifacts as concrete evidence of their evolving pedagogical mindsets. Perhaps antiracist school leaders can include such artifact-supported conversations as they determine how to collect and analyze data related to stakeholder voice. Those discussions could take place via one-on-one conversations, grade-level or content-alike groups, or context-mixed formats.

SUPPLEMENTAL SUPPORTS DATA

Whereas the hard and observational data give school leaders clarity about the content being learned, applied, and achieved, voice data elevate the humanity represented in the data. Collecting statements from those closest to—and most impacted by—the work adds flesh to the bones of quantitative results.

Like observations, formats for stakeholder voice collection are limited only by the school leadership team's imagination and motivation. There should be protocols for individual self-reports, like digital or paper surveys (with questions phrased at a reading level that is accessible to a wide variety of participants), end-of-meeting evaluations, and end-of-lesson (or end-of-activity, end-of-marking-period, and more) student surveys. Schools should also provide opportunities to collect group self-reports in focus groups, town hall conversations, or group consensus surveys. In addition to traditional survey topics like perceptions of school safety and academic rigor, voice data could also explore topics such as school inclusiveness, staff-student relationships, cultural representation, and caregiver educational aspirations. When their perspectives are solicited, stakeholders might express opinions on issues that stretch beyond the boundaries of direct instruction and assessment toward needs that traditional schools haven't always supported. Antiracist schools provide supplemental supports in attempts to address such concerns, and those efforts should also be evaluated.

USE SUPPLEMENTAL SUPPORTS TO IDENTIFY ANTIRACIST TARGET AREAS

Supplemental supports refer to the wraparound programming that addresses needs that might not be filled through adherence to curricular and instructional standards. They are the academic enrichment, reteaching, and early intervention programs; the physical, emotional, and social well-being activities; the stakeholder involvement and empowerment actions; and the community support efforts. Supplemental programs are responses to the question, "What do our students need in addition to good first instruction by their homeroom teachers?"

School-day academic interventions, after-school sports, student clubs, emotional support groups, and parent workshops are the kinds of programs that would fit the supplemental supports category. They're the types of data that might not be easily picked up by instructional observations or viewed on district data platforms. Schools can track the availability of programs, the frequency of occurrence, and the fidelity of implementation. Measuring the demographics of the groups who are targeted by the programs as well as those who participate is also valuable. Here are a few sample data points to track over time.

- The number (or variety) of academic support and enrichment programs, and student performances therein
- The number of students served by social, physical, and emotional well-being programs, and the application of skills learned
- The number (or variety) of caregiver and community connection, support, or empowerment programs

Whether the supplemental supports directly target students, caregivers, staff, or the community more broadly, the ultimate aims are in support of students. Therefore, antiracist school leaders regularly search for evidence that indicates whether all student groups are being supported by these programs. If they are not, leaders determine which student groups are not meeting with success in these programs, and they lead conversations about how to resolve breakdowns in care.

> Because antiracist schools always keep an eye on inequities, particularly racial disparities, collecting a variety of sources of data helps them to decide which areas to target.

Target Areas for Observation

Each source of data has the potential to shed light on multiple target areas that indicate the vitality of a school community and the impact of particular initiatives. Such target areas can include the following: student achievement, school climate, student well-being, staff knowledge and application, and staff well-being. A broad spectrum of data monitoring makes school staff more likely to engage in circumspect considerations that evaluate movement toward an antiracist vision. The following are target areas to observe.

STUDENT ACHIEVEMENT

School leaders are regularly held accountable for student achievement, and that often takes the form of hard data, summative objective measures such as standardized test scores and graduation rates. Objective metrics claim to compare student outcomes to academic standards established by influential organizations such as the local school district or state department of education. Some states align themselves with national standards like the Common Core State Standards (National Governors Association Center for Best Practices & Council of Chief State School Officers, 2010) or the Next Generation Science Standards (NGSS Lead States, 2013). Other states create their own standards to which their districts adhere. By whichever standards, student achievement, in the form of test scores, remains among the most utilized metrics of teacher and school evaluation.

Report card grades, which also ostensibly compare students' performance to grade-level standards, are less objective because they include teachers' perceptions of students' knowledge, skills, and behavior.

In addition to relating student proficiency to rigid academic standards, there are other options to benchmark student performance. For instance, students' growth could be related to their previous levels of performance. Since some students begin school years already with multiyear academic deficits, they could potentially make more than a year's worth of growth and still not reach target standards.

Student growth could also be factored in other ways. Some organizations pay attention to how students perform relative to their expected rates of growth. For instance, NWEA (2020), formerly known as the Northwest Evaluation Association, provides the Measures of Academic Progress, a series of mathematics, science, and English language arts tests that give scores in comparison to standards, expected growth, and growth from previous levels of performance. Also, students' growth could be compared to students' growth in peer institutions with similar demographic data and local contexts. If staff are using packaged academic interventions, intervention systems often present expected outcomes as well.

SCHOOL CLIMATE

School climate is the amalgamation of emotions, attitudes, expectations, and behaviors of students, staff, and community members (Grazia & Molinari, 2021). These ingredients combine to create an environment that is either supportive of—or toxic toward—student achievement and well-being (Aldridge & McChesney, 2018; Daily, Mann, Kristjansson, Smith, & Zullig, 2019). Climate affects the readiness for teaching and learning among both staff and students, and it indicates the fertility of the soil in which school leaders sow seeds of antiracism.

Behaviors are the observed or reported actions of—and interactions between—every school stakeholder group. Those behaviors could be staff interactions with one another, staff interactions with students, staff interactions with families and community members, and student interactions with one another. Sometimes those interactions are observed, such as student-to-student conversations during a mathematics lesson or staff conversations during meetings with peers. Other times, the interactions can be reported, such as a student voice survey that asks students if their teachers speak to them in ways that make the students feel supported. It is also possible that examining behaviors that occur in isolation would shed light on a school's climate. For example, the amounts of time teachers spend planning lessons or the amounts of time students spend studying outside of school could influence the view of a school's academic climate.

Other aspects of school climate can be more challenging to inspect. Attitudes, emotions, and expectations, for example, relate to states of mind. *Attitudes* are implicit or explicit mental associations that stakeholders establish before, during, and after their school days; *emotions* are the internal moods that stakeholders experience before, during, and after their school days; and *expectations* are the beliefs that stakeholders hold about students' abilities to achieve academic and social standards.

Each of these elements can manifest in observed behaviors. Listening to staff comments during planning meetings about students' potentials to reach grade-level standards and asking teachers pointed questions during pre- and post-observation conferences are ways attitudes and expectations can surface.

School leaders can also tease out these state-of-mind elements by juxtaposing quantitative data. Comparisons of the demographics of special education referrals to the referrals for giftedness designations, for example, are not just barometers of belief; they can generate discussions that could unearth latent emotions, attitudes, and expectations held by any stakeholder group.

Bornstein's (2018) exploration of school culture suggests that school stakeholders' actual behaviors might lag behind their stated expectations. When the school he studied transitioned from an in-school suspension room to a restorative practices reflection room, the staff and students "took several months to reset . . . [and] by the end of the year, it still did not function well . . . [and staff and students inconsistently] adopted new ways to handle difficult situations" (Bornstein, 2018, p. 17). With that said, school leaders were still able to share a 45 percent decrease in out-of-school suspensions and an 80 percent decrease in in-school suspensions. Celebrating accomplishments like these can kick-start a virtuous cycle in which outcomes influence beliefs, beliefs affect behaviors, and behaviors improve outcomes.

One question that I always asked during prospective educator interviews went something like the following: "Our Hispanic students who are eligible for free and reduced-price meals are often the students who achieve at lower levels. Why do you think that is the case?" I asked this question irrespective of whether it held true for every year. I wanted to hear if candidates' responses placed the blame solely on the deficits of students and their families (such as lack of language proficiency, uneducated parents, and parents who work multiple jobs and can't help with school), or if the responses reflected an emphasis on school practices or structural issues that reduced our capacity to reach and teach all our students (like culturally unresponsive instruction, concentration of poverty in certain areas without appropriate wraparound supports, and unexamined stakeholder expectations and beliefs).

Following interviews, I offered feedback sessions to every candidate. For those applicants who accepted feedback meetings, I made it a point to dwell on the question about Hispanic students. We would discuss what I looked for in responses to the question, and if their individual replies aligned with my criteria. Sometimes, candidates asked why questions like this were important to me. I would explain that our students needed teachers who were predisposed to seeing their strengths, because such teachers are more likely to have growth mindsets and high expectations for themselves and their students.

Also, I typically added I needed team members with revolutionary mindsets. Our staff was not filled with saviors who joined our school to offset the deficits of our students and their families. As revolutionaries, we understood our collective ability to recognize and counteract the systemic inequities that resulted in disparate outcomes for our students.

> As a school community, we need to grow with each other; but we also need to grow from each other.

In order to learn from each other, we have to see strengths within each other. That asset-based perspective is critical for staff, and helpful for students, caregivers, and community members.

STUDENT WELL-BEING

Student well-being is the sense of physical and emotional health, security, knowledge, and skills that support productive participation in the school building as well as the broader community. In my opinion, when it is viewed at a school- or districtwide level, there can be high rates of student well-being without high rates of student achievement. However, there cannot be high rates of student achievement without high rates of student well-being.

Sometimes, student well-being data can be relatively straightforward to quantify. For instance, schools often track information such as office referrals, suspensions, and attendance rates. Other measurable indicators of student well-being could include visits to the school health room (for example, the nurse's office), mental health referrals (for example, to the school counselor, outside therapists, or crisis interventionists), social-emotional learning lessons implemented by staff, class meetings facilitated, and restorative conversations completed.

In other cases, student well-being information might not be as measurable, but still equally important to collect. Anecdotal comments during one-on-one or small-group conversations with students, caregivers, and staff, when considered in aggregate or aligned with some of the quantitative data, also illustrate the mental and physical condition of the student body. Interviews, surveys that include open-ended items, and observations present opportunities to capture intangible information that school leaders who overly rely on hard data might overlook.

STAFF KNOWLEDGE AND APPLICATION

Gauging staff members' acquisition of antiracist concepts is intuitive because school leaders assess their knowledge of vital information across a variety of content, whether it be recognition of signs of potential child abuse, the most recent district initiative covered during preservice activities, or some other valuable news. In some cases, schools and districts employ tactics such as end-of-module quizzes for online trainings or exit tickets at the conclusion of professional learning activities. School leaders use observations to judge staff members' application of recently conveyed or essential concepts and skills. In addition, school leaders solicit voice data from staff to gain self-reported data about staff members' retention and use of significant material.

The same processes can apply to professional learning regarding antiracism. Voice surveys, such as end-of-meeting evaluations, can include items that require participants to share their levels of understanding of antiracist concepts and their perspectives on practices that they use with their students; observers can set criteria related to antiracist information covered during professional development activities; and exit tickets can include items that are central to understanding antiracism. For instance, people often conflate four foundational terms in antiracism: (1) *race*, (2) *nationality*, (3) *culture*, and (4) *ethnicity*. Asking staff to define these through an exit ticket—and then participate in small-group discussions about the words—is an effective way to measure and support retention simultaneously. Figure 6.2 is an example of a two-question exit ticket that is related to a hypothetical professional development activity about foundational terms.

Monitor Your Impact 165

Foundational Terms Exit Ticket

Date _____

Name _____

1. What is the difference (or differences) between culture and race?

2. How have race, culture, and ethnicity affected teaching and learning in your classroom (or your role)?

FIGURE 6.2: Foundational terms exit ticket.

You can refer to the definitions presented in chapter 1 (page 15) when interpreting responses to question 1. Responses to question 2 should indicate that race, culture, and ethnicity affect interactions among adults and children, and therefore exercise significant influences on teaching and learning. Be on the lookout for answers that minimize the biases that we all harbor, perhaps emphasizing concepts such as colorblindness, equality, or racism as individual overt acts.

Figure 6.3 is another example of a two-item exit ticket. This exit ticket revisits content on language objectives, which are supports for English learners, that was covered in a previous meeting.

School leaders could also review notetaking documents that staff complete during meetings as a way to check for understanding. Figure 6.4 (page 166) displays a sample blank active notetaking sheet that can be used to fit any topic. I recommend using this sheet with "implicit bias" at the center, as a first step.

Language Objective Exit Ticket

Date _____

Name _____

1. List two language objectives that you used during recent lessons.

2. How did the use of those language objectives affect your lessons?

FIGURE 6.3: Language objective exit ticket.

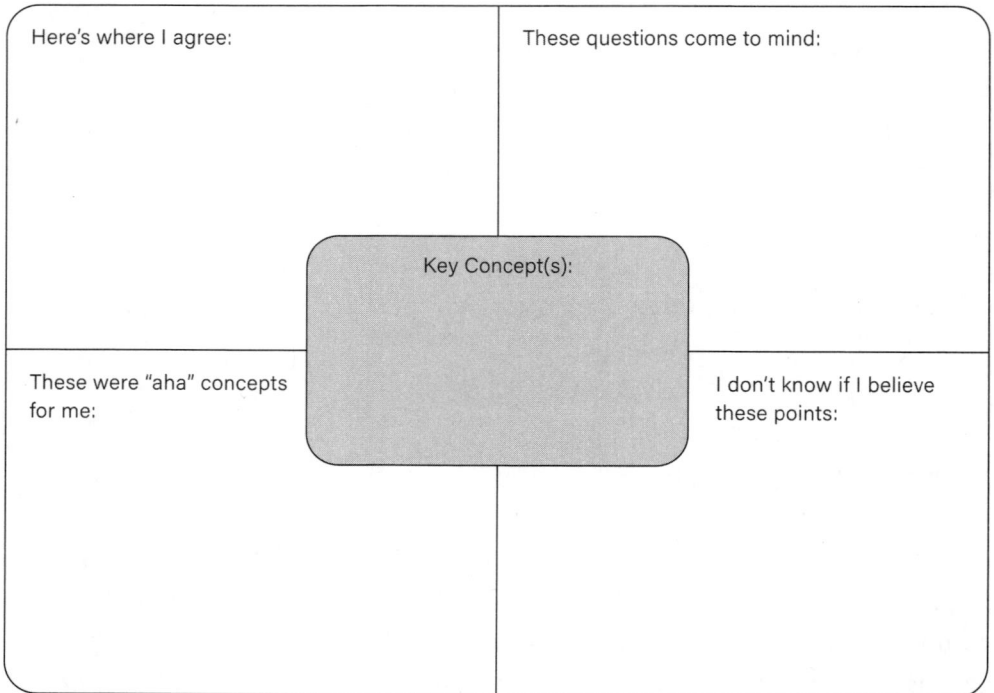

FIGURE 6.4: Sample notetaking sheet.

STAFF WELL-BEING

I've often heard people seem to take pride in using some variation of the sentence, "I'm all about the kids." Sometimes, I think some people use that as an excuse for practices that are detrimental to the well-being of school staff. When it comes to schools, if the adults aren't doing well, then the students probably aren't doing well (Causton & MacLeod, 2020). It's like a traditional family; if the caregivers aren't doing well, then it will be really hard for their children to do well. Therefore, if you are all about the students, then you must also be all about the staff. The well-beings of all individuals are inextricably linked.

In my career, I've been a teacher or administrator of Title I schools (schools with a high percentage of students who are eligible for free or reduced-price meals) since the early 2010s. Teachers and support professionals have told me that they enjoy working with the students, but sometimes they don't feel supported, or they're asked to do tasks that are not required of staff in non–Title I schools. By and large, these have been good teachers. So, I grew to understand it as my responsibility to help them feel supported and to reduce extraneous procedural or paperwork burdens.

Measuring staff well-being can be more challenging than measuring student well-being because there are additional layers of privacy for adults, and districts require schools to report fewer hard data points. However, opportunities to gain insight into staff well-being exist. Staff voice surveys are a fairly direct measure of staff well-being. School leaders can also refer to teacher retention data as an indicator of staff well-being. Perhaps they can find numbers or percentages on a district platform, or they can manually compute their own findings based on the staff who have left over the years.

Organizational Charts for Data Sources

Figure 6.5 (page 168) models an organizational chart using data sources that apply across target areas. A single kind of activity can generate data across multiple target areas. For instance, someone who observes a teacher during an instructional activity can collect data that show the teacher's application of professional development concepts, the students' mastery of new objectives, and a snapshot of the school culture. In another example, a series of student focus group conversations could yield information about why the students' everyday practices lead to achievement results, their view of the school's climate, and self-care strategies that they implement.

It is completely understandable to have ten or more sources in several boxes. On the other hand, an empty box is unacceptable. If no items come to mind for a particular box, that means your team requires a greater variety of backgrounds and diversity of thought.

REVIEW AND INTERPRET DATA

There are a number of protocols for data analysis that vary in vernacular and differ around the edges, but they all follow a similar routine of many effective forms of school data analysis: review data, interpret data, draw conclusions, and target change (Coburn & Turner, 2011).

Root Cause Analysis and Fishbone Diagrams

Root cause analysis, on the other hand, is designed to drill down specifically to what schools can control (Lipton & Wellman, 2012). A root cause analysis begins with a layout of pertinent data followed by a discussion of the current state of the school as indicated by the data. Next, analysts brainstorm any potential factors that influence the story told by the data. Then, the team sets aside all the factors that

Target Area	Hard Data	Stakeholder Voice Data	Observational Data	Supplemental Supports Data
Student achievement	• State or district standardized mathematics assessment • State or district standardized reading assessment • State or district standardized science assessment • Standardized English learner (EL) assessment (for example, WIDA) • Graduation rates • Grade point averages • Report card grades	• Targeted student survey or interview items • Targeted caregiver survey or interview items	• Students' attainment of lesson objectives	• Increase or decrease in the number of out-of-school-time academic support or enrichment programs • Disaggregation of standardized tests by intervention or enrichment program participation • Performance assessments within academic intervention or enrichment programs (for example, relative growth, relative to standards) • Student artifacts, portfolios, or performances for academic intervention programs
Student well-being	• District-directed student surveys, disaggregated by school • District-directed caregiver surveys, disaggregated by school • Attendance rates • Student bullying reports • Student self-harm attempts	• Student evaluations of social, physical, and emotional well-being programs • Caregiver evaluations of social, physical, and emotional well-being programs • Student surveys conducted by school staff • Caregiver surveys conducted by school staff • Individual student conversations or interviews • Student focus groups • Parent focus groups • Staff focus groups • Parent-teacher conferences • Student-staff conferences • Discipline conferences (for example, suspension reinstatement and office referral conversations)	• Environmental observations (for example, in classrooms, on the playground, and at the bus stop) • Student-to-student statements • Student-to-staff statements • Student-to-self statements	• Number of psychological counselors employed • Number of students served by counselors • Number of social, physical, and emotional well-being programs • Number of students served by social, physical, and emotional well-being programs • Knowledge or skill application growth among students served as measured by social, physical, and emotional well-being programs

Monitor Your Impact 169

School climate	• State- or district-directed student survey • State- or district-directed staff survey • State- or district-directed caregiver survey	• PTA member meetings • PTA executive meetings with school administrators • Student government association meetings • Employee union representative meetings with school administrators	• School staff meetings • Educator collaborative planning meetings • Individualized education program (IEP) meetings • Content of staff-to-community newsletters • Environmental observations (for example, in the cafeteria, on the playground, at the bus stop, in IEP meetings, and in parent-teacher conferences)	• Variety of academic intervention or enrichment programs (Are all student groups supported?) • Variety of social, physical, and emotional well-being programs for students (Are all student groups supported?) • Variety of caregiver and community connection, support, or empowerment programs
Staff knowledge and application	• Staff attendance in professional learning activities • Consistency of strategy use as indicated by compilations or averages of focused observations	• Pre- and post-observation conferences • Staff evaluations of professional learning activities • Staff self-reported consistency of application (for example, "I use both content and language objectives to let students know what they will learn during each lesson") • Student-reported consistency of staff application (for example, "My teacher uses content and language objectives to let me know what I will learn during each lesson") • Staff meeting exit ticket items (for example, "List two language objectives that you recently used to support your EL students. How did they affect the lesson?")	• Content of lesson plans • Peer visits or walkthroughs • Formal observations • Informal observations (for example, content lessons, community circles, or restorative conversations) • Feedback on student assignments and assessments	• Staff access to or use of strategies aligned with academic intervention programs • Action research on strategy use, including impact on students
Staff well-being	• Staff attendance rates • Staff retention data • State- or district-directed staff survey	• Staff evaluations of social, physical, and emotional well-being activities for staff • Staff focus groups • School leadership team meetings with school administrators • Individual teacher interviews or conversations • Staff exit surveys	• Environmental observations (for example, at planning meetings, in the faculty lounge, or in well-being programs)	• Number of social, physical, and emotional well-being activities for staff • Number of staff served by social, physical, and emotional well-being activities

FIGURE 6.5: Data sources across target areas.

Visit go.SolutionTree.com/diversityandequity for a free reproducible version of this figure.

are beyond the school's sphere of influence. The factors that are left become the foundation of strategies and targets for the upcoming school year. Some school-improvement teams use fishbone diagrams to visually represent their deduction of school-based influences on student outcomes (Bernhardt, 1998). Figure 6.6 is a sample fishbone diagram related to the achievement of Hispanic students who are English learners and eligible to receive free or reduced-price meals at a school.

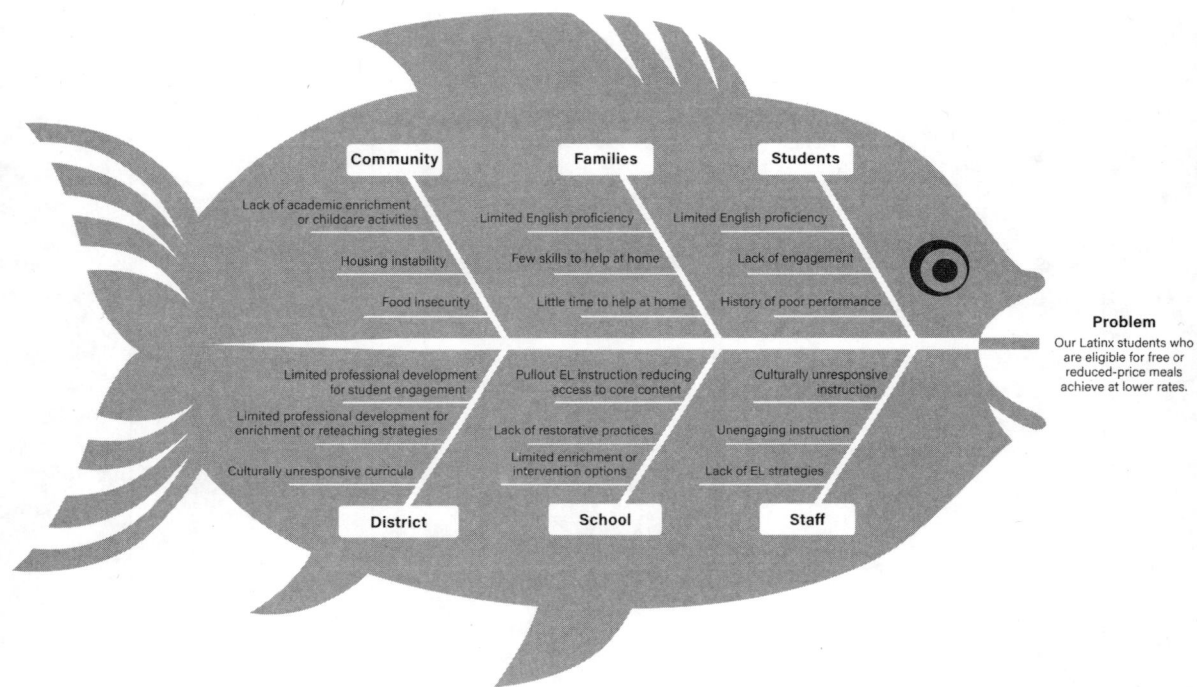

FIGURE 6.6: Fishbone (cause-and-effect) diagram example.

The Focused Conversation Method

The *focused conversation method*, as explained by curriculum consultant R. Brian Stanfield (2000), is another protocol that moves teams through the process of capturing data, interpreting data, and determining next steps. According to this protocol, sometimes called the *ORID* protocol due to the first letters of each stage, there are four stages: (1) objective, (2) reflective, (3) interpretive, and (4) decisional. In the objective stage, the team reviews the facts as presented in available formats. Next, the team reflects on how they emotionally connect to the information. Then, the team considers what the data indicate about their school context. Last, the team determines what new steps they will take to improve the current state of affairs. Montgomery County Public Schools (n.d.) in Maryland shared a system called ORID to guide staff in the use of the focused conversation method. The focused conversation data analysis system is tiered as follows (see figure 6.7).

Data + Collaboration = Results		
What? What do the data say factually?	**So What?** What conclusions or inferences might you draw from the facts?	**Now What?** What action steps will you take?

a. What do the data tell us?

b. What are the patterns? What stands out?

c. What questions do you have?

Source: Robinson Sammons & Smith, 2017, p. 127.

FIGURE 6.7: What, So What, Now What? template.

- **Objective level:** The purpose of this level is to examine the data and identify factual information. Sample questions at this level include:
    » What do you see?
    » What factual statements can you make based on the data?
- **Reflective level:** At this level, the team encourages participants to make connections and encourages the free flow of ideas and imagination. Sample questions to ask at this level include:
    » What surprised you?
    » What encouraged you?
    » What discouraged you?

» How does this make you feel?

- **Interpretive level:** At this level, focused conversation identifies patterns and determines their significance or meaning. This level is for articulating underlying insights. Sample questions to ask at this level include:
    » What is the "big idea"?
    » What do the data tell us? What new insights do you have?
    » What good news is there for us to celebrate?
    » What don't the data tell us and what else might we need to know?

- **Decisional level:** Those who reach this level are ready to propose the next steps, develop an action plan, and make decisions.
    » What are our proposed next steps?
    » What decisions can we make?
    » What is our action plan for moving forward?

Data Interpretation

As stated earlier, antiracist school staff maintain vigilance regarding inequities among student outcomes. If the data are only compiled and presented in ways that display the entire student body, real problems could be obscured. It's equivalent to using your temperature as the sole indicator of health. If you notice a fever, you might be alerted to a new issue or a long-standing disease. Only by looking at multiple body systems will you—or your physician—feel confident about diagnosing the disorder and prescribing an intervention.

Therefore, disaggregation is critical. *Disaggregation* is the process of separating data points in ways that focus on particular demographic segments of the student body or other stakeholder groups. When disaggregation occurs, disparities between groups can surface (Raskin et al., 2021). Antiracist school leaders ensure that their staffs consider historically marginalized groups of students, such as students of color, students who are eligible for free or reduced-price meals, students with special needs, and students with limited English proficiency.

As a reminder, data should be reviewed through the use of trends over time rather than singular moments in time. Reviewing outcomes across several years avoids reliance on snapshots from a given year. It also undercuts arguments about the effect of exceptional events such as new curricula, a "tough class," a catastrophic weather event, or a pandemic. Trends help analysts see the impact of a system rather than an individual.

CONCLUSION

Antiracism isn't a pop-up activity. It can't be evaluated with a single summative assessment. It requires that you build a system of ongoing assessment that gauges the clarity of your plan and effectiveness of your strategies. It is important to keep in mind that none of these data analysis protocols force school leaders to view their processes through an antiracist lens; school leaders must intentionally supplement any framework with intentional discussions around the impact of race and other intersectional characteristics. It's equally important to remember to reflect on the team members' personal biases, because their beliefs color their interpretation of the data, and therefore the desire and targets for change (Coburn & Turner, 2011). This is partly why it's so important that the school leadership team is composed of members with various backgrounds. A greater number of diverse perspectives present in a psychologically safe setting results in greater ideas.

APPLY YOUR LEARNING

Data are complicated to gather and understand, but the benefits of integrating hard data, observational data, and stakeholder data to observe target areas in your administration will yield a wealth of insight that will assist you to implement lasting change. Review the following know, say, and do guidelines to ensure successful data collection in student achievement, school climate, staff and student well-being, and staff knowledge.

KNOW

- School leaders must know how to collect and present different forms of data, trends, and snapshots.
- There are multiple sources of data to collect across a variety of target areas.

- The analyst's beliefs color their interpretation of the data, and therefore the desire and targets for change (Coburn & Turner, 2011).
- Reviewing outcomes across several years avoids reliance on snapshots from a given year. It undercuts arguments of events such as new curricula, a "tough class," a catastrophic weather event, or a pandemic.
- Disaggregation is critical. When data points are separated in ways that focus on particular demographic segments of the student body or other stakeholder groups, disparities between groups can surface (Raskin et al., 2021).

SAY

- Say, "Student achievement might be the primary metric used by outsiders to evaluate our effectiveness, but we know that student well-being, staff well-being, and application of our learning—both students' and staff's—are all important aspects of our school culture. So, we're going to make sure that we make a holistic determination of our success."
- Say, "We can understand that last year, our students were negatively impacted by being forced to engage in virtual instruction. When we review disaggregated data [from the same category] for the years leading up, we find similar results."
- Say, "Monitoring data in this way helps us keep the focus on the systems we have in place. It doesn't point the finger at individuals."

✓ DO

- Gather and analyze small samples of data individually to prepare for leading the analysis of the large samples of data for the school.
- Determine appropriate frameworks for data collection and analysis.
- Solicit representatives from every stakeholder group to join the evaluation team.

EPILOGUE

Imagine that you're absent-mindedly driving down the road when another driver cuts you off. Just as some profane thoughts enter your mind and approach your tongue, you notice that the aggressive driver is driving the same make and model of car as you—or the rear windshield holds a sticker representing your favorite sports team, political organization, branch of the military, or hobby. Does your mood change a bit? Do you give the driver the benefit of the doubt? Do you think something akin to, "Maybe the driver is having a bad day, is late for an important appointment, or is rushing to a family emergency."

As we established in chapter 4 (page 124), *homophily* is defined as a tendency to gravitate toward the familiar, and is part of the human condition. As human beings, we are hardwired to notice similarities and differences (Nordell, 2021). We feel good when our group wins; we feel better when our rival groups lose (Van Bavel & Packer, 2021). Since the advent of slavery, we have been socialized to view race as our primary group (Kendi, 2016). What if we viewed our primary characteristic as something else, like our school community?

Perhaps you're a fan of a sports team. Imagine that it's near the end of a game, and your team is about to make a play that could win or lose it. Does your pulse increase just a bit? Does your breathing become a little shallower? Does your focus sharpen a little more on what is being done to and by your team?

If your team wins, endorphins and dopamine wash over you, and you feel terrific in that moment. And if your team loses? Well, you know . . . let's not think about that. Those emotions could extend even longer, depending on how attached you are to your team and the relative importance of the game.

And those feelings are not just related to whether our team succeeds or fails; our feelings can be even more intense when our rival succeeds or fails (Van Bavel & Packer, 2021). To some extent, many of us live vicariously through our teams.

Fandom is a choice. Sometimes, it might not feel like a choice, especially when everyone in your community is a fan—your family, teachers, local media, business owners, politicians, and even your religious leaders. Fandom could seem more like a cultural birthright. Though our environment might blur the lines between choice and ordained characteristics, fandom is a choice nonetheless.

Being viewed as a member of a particular race might not be a choice. However, choosing to view a race as your primary team is a choice. Due to the emphasis you've seen placed on race by your family, media, schools, and society writ large, it might seem like a cultural necessity. It's a choice nonetheless.

I didn't write this book to tell you that you're wrong for choosing race as your primary team. I wrote it because I want you to own your choice, be aware of a similar mentality in others, and—most importantly—consider the impact those adult choices have on the teaching, learning, and development of children.

What if we moved "being a member of my school community" higher on our primary-teams hierarchy than race, gender, or political affiliation? How would we view the diverse strengths and needs of our students and their families? How intensely would we advocate for policies and practices that benefit our team?

For half a millennium, we've been socialized to view race as one of our primary teams. Although it might seem like a cultural necessity, it's a choice that most of us make, one that has very tangible outcomes for the children in our care. The data are stark but very clear.

That bias is in all of us, and it manifests in our thoughts and actions in ways that affect teaching, learning, and community building. However, we can take steps to address the bias and help our colleagues do the same. Sometimes, it's not the students who need the intervention; it's us. That's the essence of antiracist school leadership, which is also a trait that we all possess. Now that we understand the basics about what to know, say, and do, let's get started.

GLOSSARY

academic empowerment	The provision of intellectual rigor that prepares students to compete in a global marketplace of colleges and careers (Schindel Dimick, 2012).
allies	People who work "toward something that is mutually beneficial and supportive to all parties involved" (Love, 2019, p. 117). They are advocates for friends of color and racial equality (Fingerhut & Hardy, 2020).
antiracism	The practice of seeking, deconstructing, or reconstructing systems of oppression that benefit one or more racial groups at the expense of other racial groups.
attitudes	Implicit or explicit mental associations that stakeholders establish before, during, and after their school days.
backward design	Deconstruction of learning objectives at each level of a learning progression to determine the prerequisite knowledge and skills necessary to engage in the learning. Those prerequisite elements become the objectives of the prior level of the progression, and the planners repeat the protocol until the prerequisite knowledge and skills reflect the current school context (Bowen, 2017).

behaviors	The observed or reported actions of—and interactions between—every school stakeholder group.
builders	People who commit to examining themselves and systems that surround them, as well as modifying problematic aspects of themselves and social systems (Chugh, 2018).
caste	"A fixed and embedded ranking of human value that sets the presumed supremacy of one group against the presumed inferiority of other groups on the basis of ancestry and often immutable traits, traits that would be neutral in the abstract but are ascribed life-and-death meaning in a hierarchy favoring the dominant caste whose forebears designed it" (Wilkerson, 2020, p. 17).
coconspirators	People who collaborate in ways that reconstruct the current status quo, even if it means giving up their own privilege (Love, 2019).
cognitive diversity	A collection of team members from various backgrounds who are more likely to view the world differently, approach challenges differently, and build community differently.
constructive dissent	A push to interpret visions, purposes, strategies, or metrics from alternative viewpoints.

Glossary

critical consciousness	One's understanding that systems of oppression are effectively resisted when marginalized populations recognize inequities, can reconstruct the systems, and are motivated to make use of their knowledge and skills to force change.
critical cross-cultural education	A blend of curricula and instructional practices that focus on unequal power relationships, including—but not limited to—race (Rodriguez & Morrison, 2019).
criticality	The ability to recognize societal intersections and influences of "power, anti-oppression, and equity" through historical and contemporary lenses (Muhammad, 2020).
critical Whiteness	A thoughtful interrogation of Whiteness's impact on social contexts.
cultural proficiency	An understanding of one's own identity, others' identities, and the ways cultural lenses impact teaching and learning.
disaggregation	The process of separating data points in ways that focus on particular demographic segments of the student body or other stakeholder groups.
emotions	The internal moods that stakeholders experience before, during, and after their school days.
equity	All students have what they need to reach and exceed common goals (Linton, 2011).

eradicationist pedagogies	Practices that seek to replace the alleged inferior, defective characteristics of historically marginalized groups of people with the supposed characteristics of mainstream society (modified from Baker-Bell, 2020).
expectations	The beliefs that stakeholders hold about students' abilities to achieve academic and social standards.
fear zone	An emotional and intellectual state of being in which one ignores, avoids, or disbelieves the existence of systemic racism.
formative data	Short-term, intra-year data that inform decisions (and the possibility of course corrections) in real time.
growth zone	An emotional and intellectual state of being in which one recognizes one's place (advantages and disadvantages) within systemic racism, as well as a commitment to promoting antiracism with a strong sense of self-efficacy.
hard data	Objective, quantifiable data that are culled from official sources recognized by the district.
heterophily	Interest in connecting with activities or individuals that elevate perspectives that are counter to our demographic characteristics or current beliefs.
homophily	Interest in connecting with activities or individuals that elevate perspectives that are similar to our demographic characteristics or current beliefs.

intersectionality	The recognition and support of the multiple identities of each person, with a specific focus on historically marginalized identities (Mims & Williams, 2020).
learning zone	An emotional and intellectual state of being in which one accepts the existence of systemic racism, as well as a commitment to learning more about the topic.
observational data	Real-time capture of performance by someone other than the performer.
political empowerment	Examining historical and contemporary systems of oppression that can be addressed through individual or collective actions (Schindel Dimick, 2012).
professional learning progression	A step-by-step set of learning targets that build on each other to move staff from their current levels of knowledge and skills to desired levels of knowledge and skills (Jin et al., 2019).
race	A social categorization of human beings by immutable physical characteristics such as skin color, nose width, eye shape, lip fullness, and hair texture, with a heavy emphasis on skin color.
racial identity	A social perspective about group patterns, physical characteristics, sociocultural patterns, racialized group interactions, and one's place in a racialized society (Mims & Williams, 2020; Syed et al., 2018).
racial literacy	Understanding "the complex interactions between the choices of an individual and the institutional and environmental forces that shape these decisions" (Neville, 2020, p. 376).

racism	The belief that the social construct of race is associated with inherent physical, intellectual, temperamental, or moral characteristics that position some racial groups as naturally superior or inferior to other racial groups.
racist	Someone who supports racist policies or practices through their actions or inactions (Kendi, 2019).
school climate	The amalgamation of emotions, attitudes, expectations, and behaviors of students, staff, and community members (Grazia & Molinari, 2021).
social empowerment	The promotion of psychologically supportive and anti-oppressive stakeholder relationships, with a particular focus on teacher-student power dynamics (Schindel Dimick, 2012).
sociopolitical development	Understanding of the forces that affect society, with a particular focus on groups that exist toward the low end of the power spectrum, those who occupy lower castes (Zion et al., 2015).
stakeholder voice data	Self-reported information about the application, impacts, and sentiments of various members of the school community, including students, staff, and caregivers.
student well-being	The sense of physical and emotional health, security, knowledge, and skills that support productive participation in the school building as well as the broader community.

summative data	Long-term, year-to-year information that is used to evaluate progress toward big-picture goals.
supplemental supports	The wraparound programming that addresses needs that might not be filled through adherence to curricular and instructional standards.
systemic oppression	A system of advantages and disadvantages based on race. In the United States, oppressive frameworks operate within systems of education, justice, economics, entertainment, and housing, among others.
volunteers	People who sustain their efforts to organize in ways that benefit people who might be strangers (Fingerhut & Hardy, 2020); people who support causes when those causes are convenient and nonthreatening to their personal identities or social status.
Whiteness	Privileged ways of thinking, doing, and being that are attributed to a generic White racial identity.
White supremacy	The belief that the White race possesses inherent physical, intellectual, temperamental, or moral characteristics that naturally position White people as the superior racial group.
White supremacy culture	A set of cultural principles that promotes the superiority of a supposed White racial way of thinking and being.

REFERENCES AND RESOURCES

Acuff, J. B. (2019). Editorial: Whiteness and art education. *Journal of Cultural Research in Art Education*, *36*(1), 8–12.

Aguilar-Valdez, J. R., LópezLeiva, C. A., Roberts-Harris, D., Torres-Velásquez, D., Lobo, G., & Westby, C. (2013). Ciencia en nepantla: The journey of nepantler@s in science learning and teaching. *Cultural Studies of Science Education*, *8*(4), 821–858.

Alaca, B., & Pyle, A. (2018). Kindergarten teachers' perspectives on culturally responsive education. *Canadian Journal of Education*, *41*(3), 753–782.

Aldridge, J. M., & McChesney, K. (2018). The relationships between school climate and adolescent mental health and wellbeing: A systematic literature review. *International Journal of Educational Research*, *88*(1), 121–145.

Allison, M. (n.d.). *How White people can talk to each other about disrupting racism.* DoSomething.org. Accessed at www.dosomething.org/us/articles/how-white-people-can-talk-to-each-other-about-disrupting-racism on February 20, 2023.

The Atlantic. (2018, October 16). *How to talk to kids about race* [Video file]. Accessed at www.youtube.com/watch?v=QNEKbVq_ou4 on June 16, 2023.

Babinski, L. M., Amendum, S. J., Knotek, S. E., Sánchez, M., & Malone, P. (2018). Improving young English learners' language and literacy skills through teacher professional development: A randomized controlled trial. *American Educational Research Journal*, *55*(1), 117–143.

Baker-Bell, A. (2020). *We been knowin*: Toward an antiracist language and literacy education. *Journal of Language and Literacy Education*, *16*(1), 1–12.

Berchini, C. (2019). Reconceptualizing Whiteness in English education: Failure, fraughtness, and accounting for context. *English Education*, *51*(2), 151–181.

Bernhardt, V. L. (1998). *Data analysis for comprehensive schoolwide improvement*. Larchmont, NY: Eye on Education.

Biewen, J. (2020, September). *The lie that invented racism* [Video file]. TED Conferences. Accessed at www.ted.com/talks/john_biewen_the_lie_that_invented_racism/transcript on June 16, 2023.

Bin Mubayrik, H. F. (2020). New trends in formative-summative evaluations for adult education. *SAGE Open, 10*(3), 1–13.

Bornstein, J. (2018). Transformative leadership to confront White supremacist discipline practices during turnaround school reform. *The SoJo Journal: Educational Foundations and Social Justice Education, 4*(2), 5–24.

Bowen, R. S. (2017). *Understanding by design* [Teaching guide]. Nashville, TN: Vanderbilt University Center for Teaching. Accessed at https://cft.vanderbilt.edu/guides-sub-pages/understanding-by-design on May 19, 2023.

Brown, B. (2018). *Dare to lead: Brave work. Tough conversations. Whole hearts.* New York: Random House.

Brown, B. (Host). (2020, June 3). How to be an antiracist [Audio podcast episode]. In *Unlocking us*. Accessed at https://brenebrown.com/podcast/brene-with-ibram-x-kendi-on-how-to-be-an-antiracist on May 19, 2023.

Brown University. (2017, June 27). *How structural racism works* [Video file]. Accessed at www.youtube.com/watch?v=bC3TWx9IOUE on June 16, 2023.

Butler, S. (Director). (2006). *Mirrors of privilege: Making Whiteness visible* [Film]. Oakland, CA: World Trust Educational Services.

Capio, C. M., Uiga, L., Lee, M. H., & Masters, R. S. W. (2020). Application of analogy learning in softball batting: Comparing novice and intermediate players. *Sport, Exercise, and Performance Psychology, 9*(3), 357–370.

Carbado, D. W., & Harris, C. I. (2019). Intersectionality at 30: Mapping the margins of anti-essentialism, intersectionality, and dominance theory. *Harvard Law Review, 132*(8), 2193–2239.

Catalyst Project. (n.d.). *15 ways to strengthen anti-racist practice.* Accessed at www.collectiveliberation.org/15-ways-to-strengthen-anti-racist-practice on February 20, 2023.

Causton, J., & MacLeod, K. (2020). *From behaving to belonging: The inclusive art of supporting students who challenge us.* Alexandria, VA: ASCD.

CBS News. (2012, November 18). *Born good? Babies help unlock the origins of morality* [Video file]. Accessed at www.youtube.com/watch?v=FRvVFW85IcU on June 16, 2023.

Center for Racial Justice in Education. (n.d.). *Resources for talking about race, racism and racialized violence with kids.* Accessed at www.centerracialjustice.org/resources/resources-for-talking-about-race-racism-and-racialized-violence-with-kids on May 19, 2023.

Chaudhary, V. B., & Berhe, A. A. (2020). Ten simple rules for building an antiracist lab. *PLoS Computational Biology, 16*(10), e1008210.

Chin, M. J., Quinn, D. M., Dhaliwal, T. K., & Lovison, V. S. (2020). Bias in the air: A nationwide exploration of teachers' implicit racial attitudes, aggregate bias, and student outcomes. *Educational Researcher, 49*(8), 566–578.

Chugh, D. (2018). *The person you mean to be: How good people fight bias.* New York: Harper Business.

Cintron, S. M., Wadlington, D., & ChenFeng, A. (2021). *Dismantling racism in mathematics instruction: Exercises for educators to reflect on their own biases to transform their instructional practice.* A Pathway to Equitable Math Instruction. Accessed at https://equitablemath.org/wp-content/uploads/sites/2/2020/11/1_STRIDE1.pdf on October 1, 2021.

Clarke, J. A. (2019). They, them, and theirs. *Harvard Law Review, 132*(3), 894–991.

Coburn, C. E., & Turner, E. O. (2011). Research on data use: A framework and analysis. *Measurement: Interdisciplinary Research and Perspectives, 9*(4), 173–206.

Copeland, P., & Ross, A. (2021). Assessing antiracism as a learning outcome in social work education: A systematic review. *Advances in Social Work, 21*(2).

Corenblum, B., & Meissner, C. A. (2006). Recognition of faces of ingroup and outgroup children and adults. *Journal of Experimental Child Psychology, 93*(3), 187–206.

Corwin. (n.d.). *Cultural proficiency.* Accessed at https://us.corwin.com/books/cult-prof-for-leaders-4e-257901?id=325036 on September 5, 2023.

Covey, S. R. (2020). *The seven habits of highly effective people* (Rev. ed.). New York: Simon & Schuster.

Coyle, D. (2018). *The culture code: The secrets of highly successful groups.* New York: Bantam Books.

Crowley, R. (2019). White teachers, racial privilege, and the sociological imagination. *Urban Education, 54*(10), 1462–1488. https://doi.org/10.1177/0042085916656901

Daily, S. M., Mann, M. J., Kristjansson, A. L., Smith, M. L., & Zullig, K. J. (2019). School climate and academic achievement in middle and high school students. *Journal of School Health, 89*(3), 173–180.

The Danielson Group. (2022). *The framework for teaching.* Accessed at https://danielsongroup.org/the-framework-for-teaching on February 20, 2023.

DiAngelo, R. (2018). *White fragility: Why it's so hard for White people to talk about racism.* Boston: Beacon Press.

Diem, S., & Welton, A. D. (2021). *Anti-racist educational leadership and policy: Addressing racism in public education.* New York: Routledge.

Dorrell, T., Herndon, M., & Dorrell, J. (n.d.). *Antiracist allyship starter pack.* Accessed at https://docs.google.com/spreadsheets/u/2/d/e/2PACX-1vTkmrhfhYUfCcTbp3NoDmxKZUAN7xMiVuhqIlNBizKz-Ih7yPPqTPFgYzmd5NgKtEdpVugB6GoZwPWR/pubhtml on May 19, 2023.

Dowling, F., & Flintoff, A. (2018). A whitewashed curriculum? The construction of race in contemporary PE curriculum policy. *Sport, Education and Society, 23*(1), 1–13.

DuFour, R., DuFour, R., Eaker, R., Many, T. W., & Mattos, M. (2016). *Learning by doing: A handbook for Professional Learning Communities at Work* (3rd ed.). Bloomington, IN: Solution Tree Press.

Dunbar, M., Mirpuri, S., & Yip, T. (2017). Ethnic/racial discrimination moderates the effect of sleep quality on school engagement across high school. *Cultural Diversity and Ethnic Minority Psychology, 23*(4), 527–540.

EAB. (2020, October 14). *Want to talk about racism with other education leaders? These are important terms you need to know.* Accessed at https://eab.com/insights/expert-insight/academic-affairs/important-racism-terms on May 19, 2023.

Echelon Insights. (2021). *Views on race-related issues in K–12 education.* Minneapolis, MN: PIE Network. Accessed at https://pie-network.org/wp-content/uploads/2021/10/Updated_Views-on-Race-Related-Issues-in-K-12-education_Echelon-Insights.pdf on February 20, 2023.

El-Amin, A., Seider, S., Graves, D., Tamerat, J., Clark, S., Soutter, M., et al. (2017). Critical consciousness: A key to student achievement. *Phi Delta Kappan, 98*(5), 18–23.

Emdin, C. (2016). *For White folks who teach in the hood . . . and the rest of y'all too: Reality pedagogy and urban education.* Boston: Beacon Press.

Farcus, A. R. (2021). Seeing and reading color: Resisting hegemonic power from within a foundations art classroom. *Art Education, 74*(5), 49–54.

Feldman, J. (2018). *Grading for equity: What it is, why it matters, and how it can transform schools and classrooms.* Thousand Oaks, CA: Corwin.

Ferlazzo, L. (2020, January 9). Ways to implement restorative practices in the classroom. *Education Week.* Accessed at www.edweek.org/teaching-learning/opinion-ways-to-implement-restorative-practices-in-the-classroom/2020/01 on June 14, 2023.

Fingerhut, A. W., & Hardy, E. R. (2020). Applying a model of volunteerism to better understand the experiences of White ally activists. *Group Processes & Intergroup Relations, 23*(3), 344–360.

Flgov.com. (2023, May 15). *Governor Ron DeSantis signs legislation to strengthen Florida's position as national leader in higher education*. Accessed at www.flgov.com/2023/05/15/governor-ron-desantis-signs-legislation-to-strengthen-floridas-position-as-national-leader-in-higher-education on June 14, 2023.

Florida Department of Education. (2022). *Florida school accountability reports*. Accessed at www.fldoe.org/accountability/accountability-reporting/school-grades/index.stml on February 20, 2023.

Freire, P. (1986). *Pedagogy of the oppressed* (M. B. Ramos, Trans.). New York: Continuum. (Original work published 1970)

Froehle, C. (2016, April 14). *The evolution of an accidental meme*. Accessed at https://medium.com/@CRA1G/the-evolution-of-an-accidental-meme-ddc4e139e0e4#.pqiclk8pl on February 20, 2023.

Gay, G. (2018). *Culturally responsive teaching: Theory, research, and practice* (3rd ed.). New York: Teachers College Press.

Gershenson, S., & Papageorge, N. (2018). The power of teacher expectations: How racial bias hinders student attainment. *Education Next, 18*(1), 64–70.

Gino, F. (2018). *Rebel talent: Why it pays to break the rules at work and in life*. New York: Dey Street Books.

Gorski, P. C. (2019). Avoiding racial equity detours. *Educational Leadership, 76*(7), 56–61.

Gorski, P. C., & Dalton, K. (2020). Striving for critical reflection in multicultural and social justice teacher education: Introducing a typology of reflection approaches. *Journal of Teacher Education, 71*(3), 357–368.

Grant, A. (2021). *Think again: The power of knowing what you don't know*. New York: Viking.

Grazia, V., & Molinari, L. (2021). School climate multidimensionality and measurement: A systematic literature review. *Research Papers in Education, 36*(5), 561–587.

Greater Good Science Center. (2020, June 3). *Antiracist resources from Greater Good*. Accessed at https://greatergood.berkeley.edu/article/item/antiracist_resources_from_greater_good on June 16, 2023.

Grinage, J. (2019). Reopening racial wounds: Whiteness, melancholia, and affect in the English classroom. *English Education, 51*(2), 126–150.

Gurel, E., & Tat, M. (2017). SWOT analysis: A theoretical review. *The Journal of International Social Research, 10*(51), 994–1006.

Guskey, T. R. (2016). Gauge impact with 5 levels of data. *Journal of Staff Development, 37*(1), 32–37.

Hagerman, M. A. (2019). Conversations with kids about race. *Phi Delta Kappan, 100*(7), 17–21.

Hall, R. E. (2018). Anti-racist racism as millennial pattern of prejudice: The stealth perpetuation of White supremacy. *Race, Gender & Class, 25*(1/2), 64–76.

Hammond, Z. (2015). *Culturally responsive teaching and the brain: Promoting authentic engagement and rigor among culturally and linguistically diverse students.* Thousand Oaks, CA: Corwin.

Harris, D. (n.d.). *It's time to take action.* Bethesda, MD: MAEC. Accessed at https://cee-maec.org/its-time-to-take-action on May 19, 2023.

Harvard Kennedy School. (n.d.). *Racial justice, racial equity, and anti-racism reading list.* Accessed at https://hks.harvard.edu/faculty-research/library-knowledge-services/collections/diversity-inclusion-belonging/anti-racist on June 23, 2023.

Heberle, A. E., Rapa, L. J., & Farago, F. (2020). Critical consciousness in children and adolescents: A systematic review, critical assessment, and recommendations for future research. *Psychological Bulletin, 146*(6), 525–551.

Helms, J. E. (2017). The challenge of making Whiteness visible: Reactions to four Whiteness articles. *The Counseling Psychologist, 45*(5), 717–726.

Holland, K. F., & Mongillo, G. (2016). Elementary teachers' perspectives on the use of multicultural literature in their classrooms. *Language and Literacy, 18*(3), 16–32.

Howard, D. C. (2015). *Complex people: Insights at the intersection of Black culture and American social life.* Laurel, MD: HUE Initiatives.

Hung, M., Smith, W. A., Voss, M. W., Franklin, J. D., Gu, Y., & Bounsanga, J. (2020). Exploring student achievement gaps in school districts across the United States. *Education and Urban Society, 52*(2), 175–193.

Ibrahim, A. (n.d.). *From Black Lives Matter: Antiracist resources.* Accessed at www.library.fandm.edu/blacklivesmatter on July 2, 2021.

Ibrahim, A. M. [@AndrewMIbrahim]. (2020, June 6). *Learning a lot and striving to be better. Created this visual mental model as a way to help keep myself accountable (Adapted from one I had seen for #COVID a couple months ago.) Becoming Anti-Racist: Fear, Learning, Growth. #BlackLivesMatter* [Image attached] [Post]. X. Accessed at https://twitter.com/andrewmibrahim/status/1269423199273525250?lang=en on July 7, 2023.

Inoue, A. B. (2019). Classroom writing assessment as an antiracist practice confronting White supremacy in the judgments of language. *Pedagogy: Critical Approaches to Teaching Literature, Language, Composition, and Culture, 19*(3), 373–404.

Interaction Institute for Social Change. (2016, January 13). *Illustrating equality vs equity*. Accessed at https://interactioninstitute.org/illustrating-equality-vs-equity on May 19, 2023.

Isola, R. R., & Cummins, J. (2019). *Transforming Sanchez School: Shared leadership, equity, and evidence*. Philadelphia: Caslon.

Jewell, T. (2020). *This book is anti-racist: 20 lessons on how to wake up, take action, and do the work*. Minneapolis, MN: Frances Lincoln Children's Books.

Jin, H., Mikeska, J. N., Hokayem, H., & Mavronikolas, E. (2019). Toward coherence in curriculum, instruction, and assessment: A review of learning progression literature. *Science Education, 103*(5), 1206–1234.

Jones, F. H., Jones, P., Talbott, J. J. L., & Jones, B. T. (2014). *Tools for teaching: Discipline, instruction, motivation: Primary prevention of classroom discipline problems*. Santa Cruz, CA: Fredric H. Jones & Associates.

Jones, T. M., Diaz, A., Bruick, S., McCowan, K., Wong, D. W., Chatterji, A., et al. (2021). Experiences and perceptions of school staff regarding the COVID-19 pandemic and racial equity: The role of colorblindness. *School Psychology, 36*(6), 546–554.

Kahneman, D. (2011). *Thinking, fast and slow*. New York: Farrar, Straus and Giroux.

Kao, C.-Y. (2020). How figurativity of analogy affects creativity: The application of four-term analogies to teaching for creativity. *Thinking Skills and Creativity, 36*.

Kemple, K. M., Lee, I. R., & Harris, M. (2016). Young children's curiosity about physical differences associated with race: Shared reading to encourage conversation. *Early Childhood Education Journal, 44*(2), 97–105.

Kendi, I. X. (2016). *Stamped from the beginning: The definitive history of racist ideas in America*. New York: Nation Books.

Kendi, I. X. (2019). *How to be an antiracist*. New York: One World.

Kendi, I. X. (2020, June). *The difference between being "not racist" and antiracist* [Video file]. TED Conferences. Accessed at www.ted.com/talks/ibram_x_kendi_the_difference_between_being_not_racist_and_antiracist?language=en on June 16, 2023.

Kerby, H. W., Brittland, K. D., Cantor, J., Weiland, M. J., & Babiarz, C. L. (2016). Demonstration show that promotes and assesses conceptual understanding using the structure of drama. *Journal of Chemical Education, 93*(4), 613–618.

KQED. (2020, July 7). *Above the noise: Understanding anti-racism* [Video file]. PBS Digital Studios. Accessed at www.pbs.org/video/understanding-anti-racism-xmzrzb on June 16, 2023.

Ladson-Billings, G. (2017). "Makes me wanna holler": Refuting the "culture of poverty" discourse in urban schooling. *The Annals of the American Academy of Political and Social Science, 673*(1), 80–90.

Leong, R. (2020, May 26). *The problem with that new equity vs. equality cartoon you're sharing.* Accessed at https://medium.com/@leong.richard212/the-problem-with-that-new-equity-vs-equality-cartoon-youre-sharing-f1ebdfc793e8 on February 20, 2023.

Lindblom, K. (2017). Book review: *Raising race questions: Whiteness and inquiry in education. English Journal, 106*(4), 74–75.

Lindsey, D. B., Martinez, R. S., Lindsey, R. B., & Myatt, K. T. (2020). *Culturally proficient coaching: Supporting educators to create equitable schools* (2nd ed.). Thousand Oaks, CA: Corwin.

Lindsey, R. B., Nuri-Robins, K., Terrell, R. D., & Lindsey, D. B. (2019). *Cultural proficiency: A manual for school leaders* (4th ed.). Thousand Oaks, CA: Corwin.

Linton, C. (2011). *Equity 101: The equity framework.* Thousand Oaks, CA: Corwin.

Lipton, L., & Wellman, B. (2012). *Got data? Now what? Creating and leading cultures of inquiry.* Bloomington, IN: Solution Tree Press.

Love, B. L. (2019). *We want to do more than survive: Abolitionist teaching and the pursuit of educational freedom.* Boston: Beacon Press.

Love, B. P., & Hayes-Greene, D. (2018). *The groundwater approach: Building a practical understanding of structural racism.* Greensboro, NC: Racial Equity Institute.

Lozenski, B. D. (2017). Beyond mediocrity: The dialectics of crisis in the continuing miseducation of Black youth. *Harvard Educational Review, 87*(2), 161–185.

Lugo, S. (2016). A Latino anti-racist approach to children's librarianship. *Teacher Librarian, 44*(1), 24–27.

Mackenzie, A. H. (2020). Social justice in the science classroom. *The Science Teacher, 87*(7), 6–9.

Maeda, J. (2019). *Design in tech report 2019.* Accessed at https://designintech.report/wp-content/uploads/2019/03/dit2019_v00.pdf on May 3, 2023.

Malott, K. M., Schaefle, S., Paone, T. R., Cates, J., & Haizlip, B. (2019). Challenges and coping mechanisms of Whites committed to antiracism. *Journal of Counseling and Development, 97*(1), 86–97.

Matias, C. E., Henry, A., & Darland, C. (2017). The twin tales of Whiteness: Exploring the emotional roller coaster of teaching and learning about Whiteness. *Taboo: The Journal of Culture and Education, 16*(1), 7–29.

Matias, C. E., & Mackey, J. (2016). Breakin' down Whiteness in antiracist teaching: Introducing critical Whiteness pedagogy. *Urban Review, 48*(1), 32–50.

Matias, C. E., Montoya, R., & Nishi, N. W. M. (2016). Blocking CRT: How the emotionality of Whiteness blocks CRT in urban teacher education. *Educational Studies, 52*(1), 1–19.

Mayfield, V. (2020). *Cultural competence now: 56 exercises to help educators understand and challenge bias, racism, and privilege.* Alexandria, VA: ASCD.

McGee, K. (2021, June 15). Texas "critical race theory" bill limiting teaching of current events signed into law. *The Texas Tribune.* Accessed at www.texastribune.org/2021/06/15/abbott-critical-race-theory-law on June 15, 2023.

McGhee, H. (2020, April). *Racism has a cost for everyone* [Video file]. TED Conferences. Accessed at www.ted.com/talks/heather_c_mcghee_racism_has_a_cost_for_everyone on June 16, 2023.

McGhee, H. (2021). *The sum of us: What racism costs everyone and how we can prosper together.* New York: One World.

McLeskey, J., Barringer, M.-D., Billingsley, B., Brownell, M., Jackson, D., Kennedy, M., et al. (2017). *High-leverage practices in special education.* Arlington, VA: Council for Exceptional Children & CEEDAR Center.

Menkart, D., Murray, A. D., & View, J. L. (Eds.). (2004). *Putting the movement back into civil rights teaching: A resource guide for K–12 classrooms.* Washington, DC: Teaching for Change and the Poverty & Race Research Action Council.

Mensah, F. M. (2012). Positional identity as a lens for connecting elementary preservice teachers to teaching in urban classrooms. In M. Varelas (Ed.), *Identity construction and science education research* (pp. 105–121). Boston: Sense.

Merolla, D. M., & Jackson, O. (2019). Structural racism as the fundamental cause of the academic achievement gap. *Sociology Compass, 13*(6), 1–13.

Miller, E. T. (2019). New possibilities for antiracist pedagogy in secondary English language arts classrooms [Book review]. *English Journal, 108*(4), 97–99.

Mims, L. C., & Williams, J. L. (2020). "They told me what I was before I could tell them what I was": Black girls' ethnic-racial identity development within multiple worlds. *Journal of Adolescent Research, 35*(6), 754–779.

Mislán, C., & Dache-Gerbino, A. (2018). Not a Twitter revolution: Anti-neoliberal and antiracist resistance in the Ferguson movement. *International Journal of Communication, 12,* 2622–2640.

Modan, N. (2022, September 2). 7 charts highlighting the pandemic's impact on 2022 NAEP scores. *K–12 Dive.* Accessed at www.k12dive.com/news/7-charts-highlighting-the-pandemics-impact-on-2022-naep-scores/631098 on June 15, 2023.

Montgomery County Public Schools. (n.d.). *ORID: Focused conversation data analysis*. Accessed at www.montgomeryschoolsmd.org/info/baldrige/staff/qualitytools/ORID focusedconversationdataanalysis.pdf on August 19, 2022.

Montgomery County Public Schools. (2010). *A resource for equitable classroom practices*. Rockville, MD: Author. Accessed at https://www2.montgomeryschoolsmd.org /siteassets/district/departments/clusteradmin/equity/ECP.pdf on June 15, 2023.

Morales-Doyle, D. (2017). Justice-centered science pedagogy: A catalyst for academic achievement and social transformation. *Science Education, 101*(6), 1034–1060.

Morris, M. W. (2018). *Pushout: The criminalization of Black girls in schools*. New York: The New Press.

Mosley, D. V., Hargons, C. N., Meiller, C., Angyal, B., Wheeler, P., Davis, C., et al. (2021). Critical consciousness of anti-Black racism: A practical model to prevent and resist racial trauma. *Journal of Counseling Psychology, 68*(1), 1–16.

Muhammad, G. (2020). *Cultivating genius: An equity framework for culturally and historically responsive literacy*. New York: Scholastic.

Mukherjee, R. (2016). Antiracism limited: A pre-history of post-race. *Cultural Studies, 30*(1), 47–77.

Murray, A. D. (2018). *The development of the alternative Black curriculum, 1890–1940: Countering the master narrative*. New York: Palgrave Macmillan.

Najdowski, A. C., Gharapetian, L., & Jewett, V. (2021). Toward the development of antiracist and multicultural graduate training programs in behavior analysis. *Behavior Analysis in Practice, 14*(2), 462–477.

Namugenyi, C., Nimmagadda, S. L., & Reiners, T. (2019). Design of a SWOT analysis model and its evaluation in diverse digital business ecosystem contexts. *Procedia Computer Science, 159*, 1145–1154.

National Center for Education Statistics. (2018). *Percentage of students suspended and expelled from public elementary and secondary schools, by sex, race/ethnicity, and state: 2017–18*. Washington, DC: Author. Accessed at https://nces.ed.gov/programs /digest/d21/tables/dt21_233.40.asp on May 19, 2023.

National Center for Education Statistics. (2019a). *2019 NAEP mathematics assessment*. Washington, DC: U.S. Department of Education.

National Center for Education Statistics. (2019b). *2019 NAEP reading assessment*. Washington, DC: U.S. Department of Education.

National Center for Education Statistics. (2019c). *2019 NAEP science assessment*. Washington, DC: U.S. Department of Education.

National Center for Education Statistics. (2021a). *Children 3 to 21 years old served under Individuals With Disabilities Education Act (IDEA), part B, by race/ethnicity and age group: 2000–01 through 2020–21.* Washington, DC: Author. Accessed at https://nces.ed.gov/programs/digest/d21/tables/dt21_204.40.asp on May 19, 2023.

National Center for Education Statistics. (2021b). *Public high school graduation rates.* Washington, DC: Author. Accessed at https://nces.ed.gov/programs/coe/indicator/coi/high-school-graduation-rates on May 19, 2023.

National Center for Education Statistics. (2021c). *Public school students eligible for free or reduced-price lunch.* Washington, DC: Author. Accessed at https://nces.ed.gov/fastfacts/display.asp?id=898 on May 19, 2023.

National Governors Association Center for Best Practices & Council of Chief State School Officers. (2010). *Common Core State Standards.* Washington, DC: Authors.

National Museum of African American History and Culture. (n.d.). *Talking about race.* Accessed at www.nmaahc.si.edu/learn/talking-about-race on February 20, 2023.

National Policy Board for Educational Administration. (2015). *Professional standards for educational leaders 2015.* Reston, VA: Author.

Nelson, S., Syed, M., Tran, A., Hu, A., & Lee, R. (2018). Pathways to ethnic-racial identity development and psychological adjustment: The differential associations of cultural socialization by parents and peers. Developmental Psychology, 54(11). 10.1037/dev0000597

Neville, M. L. (2020). "I know you don't live in Detroit, right?" An attempt at racial literacy in English education. *English Education, 52*(4), 372–381.

NGSS Lead States. (2013). *Next Generation Science Standards: For states, by states.* Washington, DC: The National Academies Press.

Nieto, S. (2008). Nice is not enough: Defining caring for students of color. In M. Pollock (Ed.), *Everyday antiracism: Getting real about race in school* (pp. 28–31). New York: The New Press.

Nordell, J. (2021). *The end of bias: A beginning—The science and practice of overcoming unconscious bias.* New York: Metropolitan Books.

NWEA. (2020). *Linking study report: Predicting performance on the Colorado Measures of Academic Success (CMAS) based on NWEA MAP growth scores.* Portland, OR: Author.

Ohito, E. O. (2019). "I just love Black people!" Love, pleasure, and critical pedagogy in urban teacher education. *Urban Review, 51*(1), 123–145.

Okun, T. (2021). *White supremacy culture—Still here.* Accessed at https://dismantlingracism.org/uploads/4/3/5/7/43579015/white_supremacy_culture_-_still_here.pdf on June 8, 2021.

Olson, A. J., & Roberts, C. A. (2018). Teacher educators' perspectives: Preparing preservice teachers to provide access to the general curriculum. *Remedial and Special Education*, *39*(6), 365–376.

Olsson, J. (2011). *Detour-spotting for White anti-racists*. Accessed at https://culturalbridges tojustice.org/detour-spotting on May 19, 2023.

Ondish, P., Cohen, D., Lucas, K. W., & Vandello, J. (2019). The resonance of metaphor: Evidence for Latino preferences for metaphor and analogy. *Personality and Social Psychology Bulletin*, *45*(11), 1531–1548.

The Opportunity Agenda. (2020, July). *Ten lessons for talking about race, racism, and racial justice*. Accessed at https://opportunityagenda.org/messaging_reports/talking -about-racism on June 15, 2023.

Patel, L. (2016). The irrationality of antiracist empathy. *English Journal*, *106*(2), 81–84.

PBS Kids for Parents. (n.d.). *Talking to young children about race and racism*. Accessed at www.pbs.org/parents/talking-about-racism on May 19, 2023.

Pender, K. N., Hope, E. C., & Riddick, K. N. (2019). Queering Black activism: Exploring the relationship between racial identity and Black activist orientation among Black LGBTQ youth. *Journal of Community Psychology*, *47*(3), 529–543.

Picower, B. (2012). Using their words: Six elements of social justice curriculum design for the elementary classroom. *International Journal of Multicultural Education*, *14*(1), 1–17.

Pinder, S. O. (2011). *Whiteness and racialized ethnic groups in the United States: The politics of remembering*. Lanham, MD: Lexington Books.

Piper, R. E. (2019). Navigating Black identity development: The power of interactive multicultural read alouds with elementary-aged children. *Education Sciences*, *9*(2).

Pittman, A. (2022, March 14). Gov. Reeves claims critical race theory "humiliates" White people at bill signing. *Mississippi Free Press*. Accessed at www.mississippi freepress.org/21960/gov-reeves-claims-critical-race-theory-humiliates-white-people -at-bill-signing on June 15, 2023.

Platt, A. D., Tripp, C. E., Ogden, W. R., & Fraser, R. G. (2000). *The skillful leader: Confronting mediocre teaching*. Acton, MA: Ready About Press.

POV. (2016, December 16). *Implicit bias: Peanut butter, jelly and racism* [Video file]. Accessed at www.pbs.org/video/pov-implicit-bias-peanut-butter-jelly-and-racism on June 16, 2023.

Practical Psychology. (2020, December 17). *Ingroup bias (definition & examples)* [Video file]. Accessed at www.youtube.com/watch?v=A_MqKZxQjMI on June 16, 2023.

Project Zero. (2019). *The 4 C's: A routine for structuring a text-based discussion.* Accessed at https://pz.harvard.edu/sites/default/files/The%204%20Cs_1.pdf on February 20, 2023.

Ranson, F. (2013). Holocaust education: The history curriculum and the antiracist curriculum. *Race Equality Teaching, 31*(2), 20–24.

Rashid, Q. [@QasimRashid]. (2021, October 26). *If you want to ban fiction novels about slavery because they're traumatic to white kids but praise Confederate statues despite their trauma on Black kids, then it isn't children you're protecting its white supremacy. #Beloved* [Post]. X. Accessed at https://twitter.com/QasimRashid/status/1452982449600872456 on June 16, 2023.

Raskin, C., Krull, M., & Felix, A. (2021). *Principal leadership for racial equity: A field guide for developing race consciousness.* Thousand Oaks, CA: Corwin.

Reynolds, A., & Lewis, D. (2017, March 30). Teams solve problems faster when they're more cognitively diverse. *Harvard Business Review.* Accessed at https://hbr.org/2017/03/teams-solve-problems-faster-when-theyre-more-cognitively-diverse on May 4, 2023.

Robinson Sammons, L., & Smith, N. N. (2017). *A handbook for unstoppable learning.* Bloomington, IN: Solution Tree Press.

Rodriguez, A. J. (2015). Managing sociocultural and institutional challenges through sociotransformative constructivism: A longitudinal case study of a high school science teacher. *Journal of Research in Science Teaching, 52*(4), 448–460.

Rodriguez, A. J., & Morrison, D. (2019). Expanding and enacting transformative meanings of equity, diversity and social justice in science education. *Cultural Studies of Science Education, 14,* 265–281.

Roegman, R., Allen, D., Leverett, L., Thompson, S., & Hatch, T. (2019). *Equity visits: A new approach to supporting equity-focused school and district leadership.* Thousand Oaks, CA: Corwin.

Roy, D. (2020). *Skinned knees and ABCs: The complex world of schools.* New York: Routledge.

Ryan-Bryant, J. D. (2018). Anti-racist pedagogy in and against lynching culture. *Radical Teacher, 110*(1), 46–54.

Safir, S., & Dugan, J. (2021). *Street data: A next-generation model for equity, pedagogy, and school transformation.* Thousand Oaks, CA: Corwin.

Saphier, J., Haley-Speca, M. A., & Gower, R. (2017). *The skillful teacher: The comprehensive resource for improving teaching and learning* (7th ed.). Acton, MA: Research for Better Teaching.

Schindel Dimick, A. (2012). Student empowerment in an environmental science classroom: Toward a framework for social justice science education. *Science Education*, *96*(6), 990–1012.

Schultz, H. (2019). Disrupting White vision: Pedagogical strategies against White supremacy. *Journal of Cultural Research in Art Education*, *36*(3), 59–74.

Seale, E. (2020). Strategies for conducting post-culture-of-poverty research on poverty, meaning, and behavior. *The American Sociologist*, *51*(8), 402–424.

Shelton, S. A., & Barnes, M. E. (2016). "Racism just isn't an issue anymore": Preservice teachers' resistances to the intersections of sexuality and race. *Teaching and Teacher Education*, *55*, 165–174.

Shim, J. M. (2020). Meaningful ambivalence, incommensurability, and vulnerability in an antiracist project: Answers to unasked questions. *Journal of Teacher Education*, *71*(3), 345–356.

Shutack, C. (2022, February 5). *106 things White people can do for racial justice.* Accessed at https://medium.com/equality-includes-you/what-white-people-can-do-for-racial-justice-f2d18b0e0234 on February 20, 2023.

Sidney, P. G., & Thompson, C. A. (2019). Implicit analogies in learning: Supporting transfer by warming up. *Current Directions in Psychological Science*, *28*(6), 619–625.

Singleton, G. E. (2015). *Courageous conversations about race: A field guide for achieving equity in schools* (2nd ed.). Thousand Oaks, CA: Corwin.

Singleton, G. E., & Linton, C. (2006). *Courageous conversations about race: A field guide for achieving equity in schools.* Thousand Oaks, CA: Corwin.

Smith, D., Frey, N., Pumpian, I., & Fisher, D. (2017). *Building equity: Policies and practices to empower all learners.* Alexandria, VA: ASCD.

Smith, W. L., & Crowley, R. M. (2018). Social studies needs (new) White people: The case for including allies in the curriculum. *The Social Studies*, *109*(4), 202–214.

Stanfield, R. B. (Ed.). (2000). *The art of focused conversation: 100 ways to access group wisdom in the workplace.* Gabriola Island, British Columbia, Canada: New Society.

Stanford University. (2020, July). *Anti-racism toolkit: How to talk about anti-racism.* Accessed at https://drive.google.com/file/d/1QjMw-5GE95PiyRIjSqVdKp-KlcyyBfmj/view on June 15, 2023.

Stanley, S. (2017). From a whisper to a voice: Sociocultural style and anti-racist pedagogy. *Journal of Basic Writing*, *36*(2), 5–25.

Stuart Wells, A., & Cordova-Cobo, D. (2021, May 24). *The post-pandemic pathway to anti-racist education: Building a coalition across progressive, multicultural, culturally responsive, and ethnic studies advocates*. New York: The Century Foundation. Accessed at www.tcf.org/content/report/post-pandemic-pathway-anti-racist-education-building-coalition-across-progressive-multicultural-culturally-responsive-ethnic-studies-advocates/?session=1 on May 19, 2023.

Sullivan, S. (2014). *Good White people: The problem with middle-class White anti-racism*. Albany: State University of New York Press.

Suyemoto, K. L., Curley, M., & Mukkamala, S. (2020). What do we mean by "ethnicity" and "race"? A consensual qualitative research investigation of colloquial understandings. *Genealogy*, *4*(3), 1–24.

Syed, M., Juang, L. P., & Svensson, Y. (2018). Toward a new understanding of ethnic-racial settings for ethnic-racial identity development. *Journal of Research on Adolescence*, *28*(2), 262–276.

Talks at Google. (2018, February 6). *Ijeoma Oluo: So you want to talk about race* [Video file]. Accessed at www.youtube.com/watch?v=TnybJZRWipg on June 16, 2023.

Tanner, S. J., & Berchini, C. (2017). Seeking rhythm in white noise: Working with Whiteness in English education. *English Teaching: Practice and Critique*, *16*(1), 40–54.

TeachingWorks. (2022). *High-leverage practices*. Accessed at https://tle.soe.umich.edu/HLP on February 20, 2023.

Terrell, R. D., Terrell, E. K., Lindsey, R. B., & Lindsey, D. B. (2018). *Culturally proficient leadership: The personal journey begins within* (2nd ed.). Thousand Oaks, CA: Corwin.

Theoharis, G., & Scanlan, M. (Eds.). (2020). *Leadership for increasingly diverse schools* (2nd ed.). New York: Routledge.

Thurston, B. (2019, May). *How to deconstruct racism, one headline at a time* [Video file]. TED Conferences. Accessed at www.ted.com/talks/baratunde_thurston_how_to_deconstruct_racism_one_headline_at_a_time on June 16, 2023.

Tolbert, S., Snook, N., Knox, C., & Udoinwang, I. (2016). Promoting youth empowerment and social change in/through school science. *Journal for Activist Science and Technology Education*, *7*(1), 52–62.

Trying Together. (n.d.). *Anti-racism tools*. Accessed at https://tryingtogether.org/community-resources/anti-racism-tools on June 16, 2023.

Tuff, G., & Goldbach, S. (2021). *Provoke: How leaders shape the future by overcoming fatal human flaws*. Hoboken, NJ: Wiley.

University of Chicago Harris School of Public Policy & the Associated Press-NORC Center for Public Affairs Research. (2022). *UChicago Harris/AP-NORC poll*. Chicago: Authors. Accessed at https://apnorc.org/wp-content/uploads/2022/04/Harris-March-2022-topline-final.pdf on May 19, 2023.

U.S. Department of Education Office of Civil Rights. (2014). *Civil rights data collection data snapshot: Teacher equity* (Issue Brief No. 4). Washington, DC: Author. Accessed at https://cdn.uncf.org/wp-content/uploads/PDFs/CRDC-Teacher-Equity-Snapshot.pdf?_ga=2.50664169.1716348519.1680457088-1240625112.1680457087 on April 2, 2023.

Utt, J., & Tochluk, S. (2020). White teacher, know thyself: Improving anti-racist praxis through racial identity development. *Urban Education, 55*(1), 125–152.

Van Bavel, J. J., & Packer, D. J. (2021). *The power of us: Harnessing our shared identities to improve performance, increase cooperation, and promote social harmony*. New York: Little, Brown Spark.

Vulchi, P., & Guo, W. (2018, May 7). *What it takes to be racially literate* [Video file]. TED Conferences. Accessed at www.ted.com/talks/priya_vulchi_and_winona_guo_what_it_takes_to_be_racially_literate on June 16, 2023.

Waters, M. (2018). *Black citizenship in the age of Jim Crow: Classroom materials*. New York: New York Historical Society.

Watts Smith, C. (2021, July). *3 myths about racism that keep the US from progress* [Video file]. TED Conferences. Accessed at www.ted.com/talks/candis_watts_smith_3_myths_about_racism_that_keep_the_us_from_progress on June 16, 2023.

Welton, A., Diem, S., & Carpenter, B. W. (2019). Negotiating the politics of antiracist leadership: The challenges of leading under the predominance of Whiteness. *Urban Education, 54*(5), 627–630.

Wernick, L. J., Espinoza-Kulick, A., Inglehart, M., Bolgatz, J., & Dessel, A. B. (2021). Influence of multicultural curriculum and role models on high school students' willingness to intervene in anti-LGBTQ harassment. *Children and Youth Services Review, 129*.

Whitaker, M. C. (2021). When the teacher is the token: Moving from antiblackness to antiracism. *Northwest Journal of Teacher Education, 16*(2), 1–15.

White, A. (2021, February 24). *You have an anti-racist book list—now what?* [Blog post]. PBS Education. Accessed at www.pbs.org/education/blog/you-have-an-anti-racist-book-list-now-what on May 19, 2023.

Whitenack, D. A., Golloher, A. N., & Burciaga, R. (2019). Intersectional reculturing for all students: Preparation and practices for educational leaders. *Educational Leadership and Administration: Teaching and Program Development, 31*, 33–53.

Wiggins, G., & McTighe, J. (2005). *Understanding by design* (Expanded 2nd ed.). Alexandria, VA: ASCD.

Wilkerson, I. (2020). *Caste: The origins of our discontents*. New York: Random House.

Young, J. L. (2019). To heal our world, we must first heal our girls: Examining Black girl achievement. *Multicultural Learning and Teaching, 15*(2), 1–12.

Zion, S., Allen, C. D., & Jean, C. (2015). Enacting a critical pedagogy, influencing teachers' sociopolitical development. *Urban Review, 47*(5), 914–933.

INDEX

A

"Above the Noise" (KQED), 32
About Race With Reni Edd-Lodge podcast, 32
academic empowerment, 74–75, 141
    defined, 129, 179
accessing the current literature, 33
acknowledging intersectionality, 114–118
Aguilar-Valdez, J. A., 140
Alaca, B., 86, 96
Allen, C. D., 83
Allen, D., 101
allies, 45–47, 53, 96
    defined, 41, 62, 179
Allison, M., 31
anecdotal comments, 158
anti-dark oppression, 12
The Anti-Racism Daily Podcast, 32
Anti-Racism Toolkit (Stanford University), 31
"Anti-Racism Tools" (Trying Together), 31
antiracism, 1
    administrative focus on, 9–11
    author's definition, 51
    critics of, 107–109
    defined, 15, 179
    definitions related to, 19
    gender and, 115
    Kendi definition, 33
    opposition to, 93–94
    power of education, 4
    questions about, 2
    vs. assimilationism, 52
    what it means, 9
Antiracist Allyship Starter Pack (Dorrell et al.), 31
antiracist curriculum and instruction, 12–13, 130–131
    applying your learning, 148
    having teachers look at the roles race plays in their lives, 144–147
    know, say, do, 148–150
    opportunities that connect to students' lives, 140–144
    reviewing and designing curricula, 131–140
    vocabulary, 129–130
Anti-Racist Educational Leadership and Policy (Diem & Welton), 100–101
Anti-Racist Educator Reads podcast, 32
The Anti-Racist Educator podcast, 32
antiracist pedagogy
    resistance to learning about, 106
"Antiracist Resources from Greater Good" (Greater Good Science Center), 31
antiracists
    distinguishing from racists and nonracists, 107–113
    must be willing to listen, 124
appealing to ignorance, 109–110
applying your learning, 13
    casting an antiracist vision, 65
    educating yourself and committing, 38–40
    elevating antiracist curriculum and instruction, 148–150
    encouraging and embracing resistance, 126–127
    monitoring your impact, 173
    planning professional learning experiences, 103
Arab Spring, 57
Arbery, A., 48–49
ask, reflect, adjust, 36–37
assessment. *See* creating a system for assessment and feedback
asset focus, 57
assimilation, 108
    vs. antiracism, 52

The Atlantic, 32
attitudes, 162–163
    defined, 151, 179
auditing
    materials, 138–140
    processes, 13
authentic application, 57, 111, 139, 156
"Avoiding Racial Equity Detours" (Gorski), 31
awareness raising, 132

B

backward design, 12, 51
    defined, 67, 179
    implementing, 71
Baker-Bell, A., 143, 145
balancing who gets centered, 113–114
    acknowledging intersectionality, 114–118
    recognizing and counteracting resistance in real time, 118–123
    sample forms of resistance and countermoves, 122–123
Be Antiracist With Ibram X. Kendi podcast, 32
behaviors, 161–162
    defined, 151, 180
Beloved (Morrison), 118
Berhe, A. A., 59–61
bias, 115–116
    implicit, 124
Biewen, J., 32
Black Lives Matter, 57
Black, Indigenous, and People of Color (BIPOC), 7
    amplifying their voices, 60
    centering their experiences, 113–123
    White supremacy culture and, 7–8
    working with, 60
Bland, S., 49
blog posts, 20
BONDCast, 3
Born Good? (CBS News), 32
Bornstein, J., 143, 147, 157–158, 162
Brown University, 32
Brown v. Board of Education, 5
Brown, B., 120–121
builders, 62–64
    cultivating, 64
    defined, 41, 62, 180

Building Equity (Smith et al.), 99, 137, 139
building in structured and spontaneous opportunities for learning and applications, 84–87
building Our Network of Diversity (BOND) Project, 3

C

call to action, 14
Cappio, C. M., 58
caregivers. *See* families
caste
    defined, 15, 180
    maintaining the system, 36–37
Caste (Wilkerson), 9, 31
casting an antiracist vision, 42–43, 64–66
    anticipatory talking points, 46
    applying your learning, 65
    creating criteria for leadership decision making, 59–62
    cultivating a community of builders, 62–64
    declaring public intent, 43–50
    drafting your own definitions, 51
    evaluating leaders and systems, 43–44
    know, say, do, 66
    using accurate vocabulary, 50–51
    using storytelling and visuals, 52–59
    vocabulary, 41–42
Catalyst Project, 31
CBS News, 32
Center for Racial Justice in Education, 31
center learning progressions, 69–70
    creating psychological safety, 73
    example, 72
    following the steps of the professional learning progression, 70–73
centering, 113–123
challenge, 27–28
change is the goal, 75
changes, 27–28
charting a path toward sociopolitical development, 74–75
Chaudhary, V. B., 59–61
ChenFeng, A., 134–135
Chicago Public Schools, 155
Chugh, D., 34–35, 62
Cintron, S. M., 134–135
Civil War, 1, 118–119

coconspirators, 62
    defined, 42, 180
Code Switch podcast, 32
cognitive diversity, 111
    defined, 105, 180
collecting data intentionally, 153–154
    essential varieties of data, 155–159
colorblindness, 96, 146
    resistance to antiracism, 109–110
committing, 11–12, 15–18, 37–38, 117
    applying your learning, 38
    ask, reflect, adjust, 36–38
    causes of disproportionate racial
        outcomes, 18–22
    essential elements, 31
    examples of how to identify
        problematic policies, 20
    fear, learn, grow, 22–29
    know, say, do, 39–40
    recommended resources, 29–36
    vocabulary, 15–18
Common Core State Standards, 161
community connections, 80–87
Complex People (Howard), 31
concepts, 27–28
conceptual diagrams, 56–57, 59, 64
    professional learning progression
        diagram, 57
    racial inequities logic model, 56
conducting a literature review, 21–22
Confederate icons, 118–119
connections, 27–28
    cultural, 57
    facilitating in your community, 80–86
    to students' lives, 118, 140–144
constructive dissent, 111
    defined, 105, 180
content
    developing for learning progressions,
        73–75
    optional vs. essential, 71
Cordova-Cobo, D., 31
Council for Exceptional Children, 134
Courageous Conversations About Race
    (Singleton), 73
Courageous Conversations training
    (Singleton), 98
Covey, S., 70
COVID-19 pandemic, 88
Coyle, D., 111–112

creating a system for assessment and
    feedback, 137–138
creating criteria for leadership decision
    making, 59–62
creating psychological safety, 73
critical civic inquiry (CCI), 83
critical consciousness, 12, 57
    aiming for, 103
    antiracist education builds, 69
    defined, 68, 181
    for students and staff, 69
    goals and actions, 76
    targeting, 75
critical cross-cultural education, 143–144
    defined, 129, 181
critical literacy, 143–144
critical Whiteness, 96
    defined, 68, 181
criticality, 142–143
    defined, 129, 181
Crohn's disease, 125
cultivating a community of builders, 62–64
cultivating challenge networks, 128
Cultural Competence Now (Mayfield), 26,
    31, 99
cultural connections, 57
cultural proficiency
    defined, 68, 181
Cultural Proficiency (Lindsey et al.), 35–36,
    99
cultural responsiveness, 146
Culturally Proficient Coaching (Lindsey
    et al.), 100
Culturally Proficient Leadership (Terrell
    et al.), 99
Culturally Responsive Leadership website, 99
culturally responsive pedagogy, 57
    training is not enough, 115–116
Culturally Responsive Teaching (Gay), 143
Culturally Responsive Teaching and the Brain
    (Hammond), 31
The Culture Code (Coyle), 111
culture, 1
    conflated with race, nationality, and
        ethnicity, 164
    role in educational outcomes, 140–141
Cummins, J., 101
curiosity, 111
curriculum selection, 12

D

Danielson Group, 157
Dare to Lead (Brown), 121
data interpretation, 172–173
de facto oppression, 18
declaring public intent, 43–47, 64, 66
    anticipatory talking points, 46
    drafting an open letter, 48–50
    have a follow-up plan, 47–48
deficit-based theories, 117
"Detour-Spotting for White Activists" (Olsson), 31
developing a vision, 12
developing content for learning progressions, 73–74
    charting a path toward sociopolitical development, 74–75
    targeting critical consciousness, 75–76
developing intersectional identity, 93
developing racial literacy, 145–147
Development of the Alternative Black Curriculum, 1890–1940 (Murray), 76
DiAngelo, R., 17, 31
Diem, S., 101
"The Difference Between Being 'Not Racist' and Antiracist" (Kendi), 32
digital media, 57–58, 123
Dimmick, A. S., 141
disadvantaged identities, 93–95
disaggregated data, 51
disaggregation, 172–174
    defined, 151, 181
disbelief in systematic or structural racism, 119–120
Dismantling Racism Works website, 31, 99
disproportional racial outcomes, 118
    conducting a literature review, 21–22
    finding what's been missing, 19–21
    rooted in history, 18
    understanding the causes, 18–19
dissent
    constructive, 105, 111, 180
    emphasizing the potential, 111–113
distinguishing between racists, nonracists, and anitracists, 106–108
    emphasizing the potential productivity of dissent, 111–113
    investigating the rationale for resistance, 109–110
diversity, 1, 111
    affirming views of, 117
    questions about, 2
Dorrell, J., 31
Dorrell, T., 31
drafting an open letter, 48–50, 64
    example, 49
du jure oppression, 18

E

EAB, 31
Edd-Lodge, R., 32
educating yourself, 11–12, 15–18, 37–38
    applying your learning, 38
    ask, reflect, adjust, 36–38
    causes of disproportionate racial outcomes, 18–22
    essential elements, 31
    examples of how to identify problematic policies, 20
    fear, learn, grow, 22–29
    know, say, do, 39–40
    recommended resources, 29–36
    vocabulary, 15–18
Ellis, M., 49
Emdin, C., 17, 31
emotional deflection, 121
emotions, 154, 162
    defined, 151, 181
    triggers, 81, 127
emphasizing the potential productivity of dissent, 111–113
empowerment. *See* academic empowerment; political empowerment; social empowerment
encouraging and embracing resistance, 12, 106–107, 125–126
    applying your learning, 126–127
    balancing who gets centered, 113–123
    distinguishing between perspectives, 106–113
    know, say, do, 127–128
    reckoning with homophily, 124–125
    vocabulary, 105–106
encouraging divergent perspectives, 127–128
The End of Bias (Nordell), 124
English Journal, 109
English learners, 118
Equity and Excellence in Education (EEE).

See McDaniel College
Equity 101 (Linton), 99, 140
equality vs. equity box storyboard, 54
equity, 1
    defined, 42, 181
    invisible issue, 97
    leaders prefer the term, 50
    questions about, 2
    using the word to make us less uncomfortable, 8–9
equity detours, 25
Equity Literacy Institute, 9
Equity Visits (Roegman et al.), 100
eradicationist pedagogies, 145
    defined, 130, 182
erasing the idea of "the other," 144–145
essential varieties of data, 155
    hard data, 155
    observational data, 155–157
    stakeholder voice data, 155, 158
    supplemental supports data, 155, 159
ethnic studies, 1
ehnicity
    conflated with race, nationality, and culture, 164
ethnomathematics, 134, 140
evaluating antiracism across aspects of school, 86–87
    including personal connections to students and families, 88–91
    using restorative practices, 87–88
evaluating leaders and systems, 43–44
evaluating your practices, 75–77
expectation, 162
    defined, 152, 182
exploring the roles race plays in our lives, 144
    developing racial literacy, 145–147
    erasing the idea of the other, 144–145

F

facilitating connections in your community, 80–81
    building in structured and spontaneous opportunities for learning and application, 84–68
    making opportunities for group conversations and personal reflections, 82–84
    strengthening the facilitator's toolbox, 81–82
families
    communicating with, 66
    connecting with, 88–91
    history as a trigger, 120–121, 123
fandom, 177–178
Farcus, A. R., 133
fear zone, 12, 18, 22–24, 39–40
    defined, 16, 182
    moving to the learning zone, 24–26
feedback. *See* creating a system for assessment and feedback
Feldman, J., 101, 137
"15 Ways to Strengthen Anti-Racist Practice" (Catalyst Project), 31
finding what's been missing from your education, 19–21
fishbone diagrams, 167–170
    example, 170
Fisher, D., 99, 137
Florida Department of Education, 155
Floyd, G., 48–49, 87
focus classroom visits. *See* peer walkthroughs
focused conversation method, 170–172
    what, so what, now what? template, 171
For White Folks Who Teach in the Hood … and the Rest of Y'all Too (Emdin), 17, 31
formative data, 154
    defined, 152, 182
formative feedback, 156
foundational terms, 164–165
    exit tickets, 165
    sample notetaking sheet, 166
Four Cs, 26–28
    defined, 27
Framework for Social Justice Education, 141
Framework for Teaching (Danielson Group), 157
"freedom dreaming," 27
Freire, P., 75
Frey, N., 99, 137
Froehle, C., 54

G

Gay, G., 143
Gay-Straight Alliance, 116
gender racism, 115

Gino, F., 111
The Giving Tree (Silverstein & Ruth)
    picture, 55
glossary, 14, 179–185
Gorski, P. C., 9, 31
Grading for Equity (Feldman), 100
Grant, A., 124–125, 126
Greater Good Science Center, University of California, Berkeley, 21, 31
grit, 11
groundwater approach, 53
group conversations, 82–84
growth zone, 12, 18, 39–40
    defined, 16, 182
    enriching, 28–29
    moving from learning zone to, 23, 26–28
guilt
    resistance to antiracism, 107, 109–110
Guo, W., 32
Guskey, T. R., 78–80, 103, 153

H

Hammond, M. A., 31
hard data, 155, 160, 168, 173
    defined, 152, 182
Hart, M., 95
Hatch, T., 101
have a follow-up plan, 47–48
Hayes-Greene, D., 53
Herndon, M., 31
heterophily, 105, 182
high-leverage practices, 156
hijack or paralyzed zone, 25
historical responsiveness, 142–144
Holocaust education, 147
homophily, 177
    defined, 106, 182
    reckoning with, 124–125
homophobia, 115
Hosseini, K., 144
"How Structural Racism Works" (Brown University), 32
How to Be an Antiracist (Kendi), 9–10, 17–18, 31, 33, 121
"How to Deconstruct Racism, One Headline at a Time" (Thurston), 32
"How to Talk to Kids About Race" (*The Atlantic*), 32
"How White People Can Talk to Each Other About Disrupting Racism" (Allison), 31
Howard, D. C., 31
Howard High School (Wilmington, Del.), 5
Huhaniak, H., 77
humor, 82

I

Ibrahim, A. M., 22, 24–25, 39–40
identification of inequities, 57
identity, 1
ignorance, 110
    appealing to, 109–110
"Ijeoma Oluo" (Talks at Google), 32
"Implicit Bias" (POV), 32
including personal connections to students and families, 88–91
    examples, 89–90
inclusion, 1
    questions about, 2
Indigenous people. *See* Black, Indigenous, and People of Color
"Ingroup Bias (Definition & Example)" (McGhee), 32
instructional practice, 12
instructional rounds. *See* peer walkthroughs
intersectional antiracism, 117–118
intersectional focus, 133
intersectional identity
    developing, 93
intersectionality
    acknowledging, 114–118
    defined, 106, 183
    elevating, 109–110
Intersectionality Matters! podcast, 32
investigating the rationale for resistance, 109–110
Isola, R. R., 101

J

Jean, C., 83
Jewell, T., 31
journaling, 32, 83

K

Kao, C.-Y., 58
Kendi, I. X, 9–10, 17–18, 31, 32–35, 108, 115, 120–121, 125
King, M. L. Jr., 132, 147

The Kite Runner (Nosseini), 144
know, say, do, 13–14
    casting an antiracist vision, 66
    educating yourself and committing, 39–40
    elevating antiracist curriculum and instruction, 148–150
    encouraging and embracing resistance, 127–128
    monitoring your impact, 173–175
    planning professional learning experiences, 104
Knox, C., 141
KQED, 32

L

Leadership for Increasingly Diverse Schools (Theoharis & Scanlan), 101
Leadervation Learning, 82
Leading Equity podcast, 32
leading student activities, 21
leaning into uncomfortable topics, 95, 101–102
learning zone, 12, 18, 39–40
    defined, 16, 183
    moving from fear zone to, 23–26
    moving to the growth zone, 26–28
Leong, R., 55–56
Leverett, L., 101
LGBTQ+ students, 116
"The Lie That Invented Racism" (Biewen), 32
Likert scales, 158
Lindblom, K., 109
Lindsey, D. B., 31, 35–36, 99, 101
Lindsey, R. B., 31, 35–16, 81, 99, 101
linguistic racism, 143
Linton, C., 99, 140
literature
    lack of diversity, 131, 138–140
Love, B., 27, 53, 62
Lozenski, B. D., 29–30
Lugo, S., 139

M

Mackenzie, A. H., 141
Mackey, J., 96
Make America Great Again, 57

Martinez, R. S., 101
Maryland State Department of Education, 155
Matias, C. E., 96, 121
Mayfield, V., 26, 31, 82–83, 99
McDaniel College, 3, 77, 95–96
    Equity and Excellence in Education (EEE) program, 76, 95
McGhee, H., 31–32, 34–35
McTighe, J., 71
measuring the impact of professional learning progressions, 77–80
Menkart, D., 77
metaphoric speech, 58
microaggressions, 93, 115
Minorities Scholars Program, 64
Mirrors of Privilege (Butler), 114
Momentum podcast, 32
monitoring your impact, 13, 153
    applying your learning, 173
    collecting data intentionally, 153–159
    know, say, do, 173–175
    reviewing an interpreting data, 167–173
    using supplemental supports, 159–167
    vocabulary, 151–152
Montgomery County Public Schools (Md.), 116, 135, 157, 170
Morrison, D., 130–131, 140–143
Morrison, T., 118
Muhammad, G., 142
Mukherjee, R., 50
multicultural curricula, 131
multiyear trends, 154
Murray, A. D., 75–77, 97
My Voice, My School surveys, 155
Myatt, K. T., 101

N

narrative descriptions, 158
National Museum of African History and Culture, 31
nationality
    conflated with race, culture, and ethnicity, 164
Nevile, M. L., 144, 146
Next Generation Science Standards, 161
non-racial diversity
    technique to avoid race, 116

nonracists
    connecting with, 120
    defined, 106
    distinguishing from racists and antiracists, 107–113
    strategies used to avoid working on antiracism, 106–107
Nordell, J., 124
novelty, 111
Nuri-Robins, K., 31
NWEA, 161

O

observational data, 155–157, 168, 173
    defined, 152, 183
    student evaluation rubric, 158
occupy movement, 57
Okun, T., 7–8
Olson, A. J., 158
Olsson, J., 31
Ondish, P., 58
"106 Things White People Can Do for Racial Justice" (Shutack), 31
open-mindedness, 124–125
The Opportunity Agenda, 31
opportunity
    leaders prefer the term, 50
optional vs. essential content, 71
organizational charts, 167
ORID protocol, 170–172

P

Pacific Educational Group, 98
Packer, D. J., 126
passive aggression, 121–123
PBS Kids for Parents, 31
peer observations. *See* peer walkthroughs
peer walkthroughs, 157
The Person You Mean to Be (Chugh), 34–35
personal reflections, 82–84, 96–97
perspective, 111
Picower, B., 132
pictorial metaphors, 53–54, 59, 64
    equality vs. equity box storyboard, 54
    The Giving Tree picture, 55–56
planning professional learning experiences, 12, 68–69, 102–103
    applying your learning, 103
    center learning progressions, 69–73
    developing content for learning progressions, 73–75
    evaluating antiracism across aspects of school, 86–91
    evaluating your practices, 75–77
    facilitating connections in your community, 80–86
    know, say, do, 104
    leaning into uncomfortable topics, 101–102
    measuring the impact of professional learning progressions, 77–80
    supporting racial identity development, 91–101
    vocabulary, 67–68
Pod for the Cause podcast, 32
podcasts, 29, 32
policies and practices
    contribute to disproportional racial outcomes, 18–19
political empowerment, 141
    defined, 130, 183
The Post-Pandemic Pathway to Anti-Racist Education (Stuart Wells, Cordova-Cobo), 31
POV, 32
The Power of Us (Van Bavel & Packer), 34–35
practicing historical responsiveness, 142–144
presenting opportunities that connect to students' lives, 140–141
    exploring social justice in STEM, 141–142
    practicing historical responsiveness, 142–144
prioritizing opportunities for group conversations and personal reflections, 82–84
privilege
    examining, 93–94
    reluctance to examining, 109–110
problematic practices
    dismantling, 19–20
productive conflict, 11, 126–127
professional development, 138
professional learning progression
    centering, 69–70
    creating psychological safety, 73
    defined, 68, 183

example, 72
following the steps, 70–72
making Whiteness visible, 114
Project Zero (Harvard University), 27
projection, 121
Pumpian, I., 99, 137
Putting the Movement Back Into Civil Rights Teaching (Menkart et al.), 77
Pyle, A., 86, 96

Q

QAnon, 57

R

race, 1
asking people to describe, 91
conflated with nationality, culture and ethnicity, 164
defined, 16, 183
is a social construct, 16
not a biological construct, 107–108
race theory, 1
"race-neutral" curricula, 132
racial identity
defined, 68, 183
racial identity development
defined, 19, 91
how Whiteness manifests in schools, 96–98
supporting, 91–96
"The Racial Justice, Racial Equity, and Antiracism Reading List" (Harvard Kennedy School), 21–22
racial literacy
defined, 130, 183
developing, 145–148
racially diverse leadership, 60
racism, 1
author's definition, 51
defined, 16, 184
disbelief in, 122
history of the word, 7
influence on school communities, 21
justifying a focus on, 56
Kendi definition, 33
leaders reluctant to use the term, 50
racists
defined, 16, 106, 184
distinguishing their perspective from nonracists and antiracists, 107–113
Ranson, F., 132–133
Rashid, Q., 118–119
reassessing instruction, 133–137
Rebels, 111–113, 127
reckoning with homophily, 124–125
recognizing and counteracting resistance, 118–121
sample forms and countermoves, 122–123
recommended resources
accessing, 30–36
articles and reports, 31
books, 31
educating yourself and committing, 29–36
planning professional learning experiences, 98–101
podcasts, 32
speaking, 31
videos, 32
websites, 31
writing, 32
redirection, 82
relevancy, 140
Research for Better Teaching, 156
resistance
applying your learning, 126–127
balancing who gets centered, 113–123
distinguishing between perspectives, 106–113
encouraging and embracing, 12, 106–107, 125–126
know, say, do, 127–128
knowing possible forms, 127
reckoning with homophily, 124–125
recognizing and counteracting in real time, 118–121
sample forms and countermoves, 122–123
vocabulary, 105–106
"Resources for Talking About Race, Racism, and Racialized Violence With Kids" (Center for Racial Justice in Education), 31
respect, 132
respectability pedagogies, 145
restorative practices

defined, 87
using, 87–88
reviewing and designing curricula, 131–133
    assessment and feedback, 137–138
    auditing materials, 138–140
    reassessing instruction, 133–137
reviewing and interpreting data
    data interpretation, 172–173
    data sources across target areas, 168–169
    focused conversation method, 170–172
    root cause analysis and fishbone diagrams, 167–170
Rice, T., 49
Roberts, C. A., 158
Rodriguez, A. J., 130–131, 140–143
Roegman, R., 101
root cause analysis, 167–170
Ruth, T., 55–56
Ryan-Bryant, J., 84

S

Saphier, J., 156
savior mentality, 96, 149
Scanlan, M., 101
school administrators
    most significant influence on teachers' use of materials, 114
school climate, 161–163, 169
    defined, 152, 184
Schultz, H., 145–146
The Science Teacher, 141
segregation, 108
segregationists
    connecting with, 120
self-compassion, 92
self-love, 132
sexism, 115
Shady Grove Middle School (Gaithersburg, Md.), 76
shame, 107, 146–147
Shutack, C., 31
Silverstein, S., 55
Singleton, G. E., 73, 98
The Skillful Teacher (Saphier et al.), 156
slavery, 1
Smith, C. W., 32
Smith, D., 99, 137, 158
Snook, N., 141

social action, 132
social construction of knowledge, 134
social empowerment, 141
    defined, 140, 184
social group identity development, 19
social justice, 132
    in STEM, 141–142
social media. *See* digital media
social norms, 109–110, 113–114
sociocultural consciousness, 117
sociopolitical development, 74–76
    defined, 68, 184
staff evaluation, 12–13
staff knowledge and application, 164–166, 169
staff well-being, 166–167, 169
stakeholder voice data, 155, 158, 168, 173
    defined, 152, 184
stakeholders
    encouraging buy-in, 43, 45–48
    collaborating with, 64, 66
relationship building, 12
Stamped From the Beginning (Kendi), 17, 31
Stanfield, R. B., 170
Stanford University, 31
Stanley, S., 137–138
STEM
    social justice in, 141–142
Stephens, J., 97–98
storytelling. *See* using storytelling and visuals
stratifying dialects, 143, 145
strengthening the facilitator's toolbox, 81
    awareness of emotional triggers, 81
    humor, 82
    validation or redirection, 82
Stuart Wells, A., 31
student achievement, 160–161, 168
student well-being, 163–164, 168
    defined, 152, 184
students with special needs, 118
The Sum of Us (McGhee), 31, 34–35
summative data, 154
    defined, 152, 185
superficial representation, 139
supplemental supports, 159–160, 168
    defined, 152, 185
    organizational charts for data sources, 167
    targeting areas for observation, 160–167

supporting family deficits, 43–44
supporting racial identity development, 91–96
    examining how Whiteness manifests in schools, 96–98
    using supportive resources, 98–101
supporting staff deficits, 42–43
supportive resources. *See* using supportive resources
systemic biases, 64
systemic oppression
    defined, 16, 185
    overt disbelief, 119–120

T

"Talking About Race" (National Museum of African History and Culture), 31
"Talking to Young Children About Race and Racism" (PBS Kids for Parents), 31
Talks at Google, 32
targeting areas for observation, 160
    school climate, 161–163
    staff knowledge and application, 164–166
    staff well-being, 166–167
    student achievement, 160–161
    student well-being, 163–164
targeting critical consciousness, 75
    goals and actions, 76
Taylor, B., 48–49
Teacher Evaluation Rubric on Facilitating Questioning and Thinking (Bornstein), 157
Teaching While White podcast, 32
Teaching Works (University of Michigan), 156
TED Talks, 29
"Ten Lessons for Talking About Race, Racism, and Racial Justice" (The Opportunity Agenda), 31
"Ten Simple Rules for Building an Antiracist Lab" (Chaudhary & Berhe), 59–61
Terrell, E. K., 99
Terrell, R. D., 99
Theoharis, G., 101
Think Again (Grant), 124
This Book Is Antiracist (Jewell), 31
Thompson, S., 101
"3 Myths About Racism That Keep the US From Progress" (Smith), 32
Thurston, B., 32
Time to Act podcast, 32
Tochluk, S., 93–94
Tolbert, S., 141
tools of identity leadership, 126
Transforming Sanchez Schools (Isola & Cummins), 101
Trying Together, 31

U

Udoinwang, I., 141
unchanging demographic hierarchies, 25
understanding how learners construct knowledge, 118
University of Florida
    Collaboration for Effective Educator Development, Accountability, and Reform (CEEDAR) Center, 134
University of Maryland, 3
University of Michigan
    Teaching Works, 156
unproductive talking, 118–119, 121
using accurate vocabulary, 50–51, 64
    crafting your own definitions, 51
using storytelling and visuals
    conceptual diagrams, 56–57
    digital media, 57–58
    pictorial metaphors, 53–56
    professional learning progression diagram, 57
    racial inequities logic model, 56
    verbal analogies, 52–53, 64
    your own visual framework, 58–59
using supplemental supports, 159–160
    organizational charts for data sources, 167
    targeting areas for observation, 160–167
using supporting resources, 98–101
Utt, J., 93–94

V

validation, 82
Van Bavel, J. J., 126
verbal analogies, 52, 59, 64, 66
    groundwater approach, 53
    White supremacy as an operating system, 53–53

View, J. L., 77
visuals. *See* storytelling and visuals
vocabulary, 14
    antiracist curriculum and instruction, 129–130
    casting an antiracist vision, 41–42
    educating yourself and committing, 15–18
    encouraging and embracing resistance, 105–106
    monitoring your impact, 151–152
    planning professional learning experiences, 67–68
volunteers, 62
    defined, 42, 185
Vulchi, P., 32

W

Wadlington, D., 134–135
wait time, 136–137
"Want to Talk About Racism With Other Education Leaders?" (EAB), 31
We Want to Do More Than Survive (Love), 27
Welton, A. D., 101
"What It Takes to Be Racially Literate" (Vulchi & Guo), 32
whataboutism, 116
White fragility, 132
White Fragility (DiAngelo), 17, 31
White supremacy
    antiracist education exposes, 69
    as an operating system, 52–53
    author's definition, 51
    defined, 16, 185
    dominates US culture, 92
    in schools, 68–69
    justifying a focus on, 56
    leaders reluctant to use the term, 50
    making visible, 142–143
    our collective and individual investments, 114
    remains, 106
    resistance to learning about, 106
    uncomfortable topic, 92
White supremacy culture, 12, 21, 57
    author's definition, 51
    defined, 16, 185
    questions about, 2
    what it means to combat it, 6–7
    what it means, 7–9
"White Teacher, Know Thyself" (Utt & Tochluk), 93
White, A., 31
Whitenack, D. A., 117–118
Whiteness, 7, 12, 57
    analyzing, 102–103
    as a primary lens, 107–108
    centered in most curriculum areas, 131
    defined, 106, 185
    how it manifests in schools, 96–98
    not the same as "White people," 113
    over-centering, 145
    resistance to learning about, 106
    staff members invested in, 109–110
    teachers must recognize their own, 113–114
    uncomfortable topic, 92
Wiggins, G., 71
Wilkerson, I., 9, 31
women of color
    often left out of the discussion, 117

Y

"You Have an Anti-Racist Book List—Now What?" (White), 31
your own visual framework, 58–59
    example, 59

Z

Zion, S., 83, 86
zones of understanding, 18

Leading Through an Equity Lens
Kim Wallace
Learn how to transform your organizational culture and improve student outcomes through advancing equity-centered initiatives. This book includes practical action steps to help school and district leaders integrate implementations that amplify opportunities and diminish systemic barriers for historically marginalized students.
BKG120

Beyond Conversations About Race
Washington Collado, Sharroky Hollie, Rosa Isiah, Yvette Jackson, Anthony Muhammad, Douglas Reeves, and Kenneth C. Williams
Written by a collective of brilliant authors, this essential work provokes respectful dialogue about race that catalyzes school-changing action. The book masterfully weaves together an array of scenarios, discussions, and challenging topics to help prepare all of us to do better in our schools and communities.
BKG035

Evident Equity
Lauryn Mascareñaz
Make equity the norm in your school or district. *Evident Equity* provides a comprehensive method that leaders can use to integrate equitable practices into every facet of their school communities and offers real-life examples at the elementary, middle, and high school levels.
BKG032

Supporting Underserved Students
Sharroky Hollie and Daniel Russell, Jr.
Discover a clear two-step roadmap for aligning PBIS with culturally and linguistically responsive teaching. First, you'll dive deep into why there is an urgent need for this alignment. Then, you'll learn how to move forward to better serve all learners, especially those from historically underserved populations.
BKG010

Visit SolutionTree.com or call 800.733.6786 to order.

Wait! Your professional development journey doesn't have to end with the last pages of this book.

We realize improving student learning doesn't happen overnight. And your school or district shouldn't be left to puzzle out all the details of this process alone.

No matter where you are on the journey, we're committed to helping you get to the next stage.

Take advantage of everything from **custom workshops** to **keynote presentations** and **interactive web and video conferencing**. We can even help you develop an action plan tailored to fit your specific needs.

Let's get the conversation started.

Call 888.763.9045 today.

SolutionTree.com